Report from Xunwu

Mao Zedong in 1931 at age 38 (from the Nym Wales Collection, Envelope G, Hoover Institution Archives, Stanford University)

Mao Zedong

REPORT FROM XUNWU

Translated, and with an Introduction and Notes, by

ROGER R. THOMPSON

Stanford University Press 1990

STANFORD, CALIFORNIA

Stanford University Press
Stanford, California
©1990 by the Board of Trustees
of the Leland Stanford Junior University
Printed in the United States of America

Original printing 1990

Last figure below indicates year of this printing:
02 01 00 99 98 97 96 95 94 93 92

CIP data appear at the end of the book

Acknowledgments

This translation of Mao Zedong's *Report from Xunwu* would not have been possible without the contributions of a number of people. Two people both shared and helped to shape my vision of this project from the very beginning. The excitement of discovery was first conveyed to Melissa Walt Thompson, who helped me see the possibilities for the *Report from Xunwu*. Shortly thereafter, my editor at Stanford University Press, Muriel Bell, began to nurture this effort. Her enthusiasm, advice, and advocacy were constants that sustained this project.

Like Mao, who had his informants in Xunwu, I have been fortunate in being able to draw on the knowledge and help of many people. Parker Po-fei Huang has fielded numerous queries with the patience and wisdom of the gentleman and scholar that he is. So too has Kate Hsun-mei Guan, whose contributions grace much of the text. Her help came with equal parts of energy, encouragement, and intelligence. The Chinese writer Ye Junjian helped in unraveling some of the more obscure references to local names and terms. Others who provided assistance are Wei Li, Song Haoshi, and Yue Zumou. The maps were developed in collaboration with Leslie Voit, who based the regional map on Japanese maps published in 1917–20 by the Tōa Dōbunkai. The map of Xunwu County is based on Japanese Army topographical maps, at a scale of 50,000:1, that were compiled in 1928 and revised in

1938. The maps in this book were produced on an Apple Macintosh Plus Personal Computer using the Adobe Illustrator '88 software program. My interest in maps was well served by Ms. Voit's perceptive and committed work. To Neal Bousfield I express my gratitude for allowing me to publish some of the pictures taken by his father, Cyril Bousfield, who lived in Xunwu County, except during furloughs, from 1912 to 1928. I also thank Nancy Hearst, Helen Foster Snow, and Christopher Lee for their help with photographs, and Marilyn Young for suggesting the poster used on the dust jacket. A microfilm of the correspondence of Cyril Bousfield and his wife, Lillian ("Lillie"), with the American Baptist Foreign Mission Society was kindly provided by the American Baptist Historical Society. I greatly appreciate the efforts of Beverly Carlson and James Lynch, of the Historical Society, and Priscilla Shaw, of the American Baptist Foreign Mission Library.

It gives me great pleasure to bring attention to the indefatigable efforts of Antony Marr, Associate Curator of the East Asian Collection in the Sterling Memorial Library at Yale University. He has kept abreast of the flood of books and journals coming out of the People's Republic of China in the past decade, and several of his acquisitions were of significant importance in the writing of the Introduction. Thanks also are due Hideo Kaneko, Curator of the East Asian Collection, who obtained for the collection a microfilm copy of the 1901 edition of the gazetteer for Xunwu County. I also thank Richard Price, chair of the Department of History at the University of Maryland, College Park, who provided support at a crucial moment, thus making it possible to prepare maps, photographs, and a character list for publication.

A number of scholars helped me while I was writing the Introduction. Foremost among them is Stephen Averill, who generously shared his deep knowledge of the Communist movement in Jiangxi during the 1920's and 1930's and also sent me useful citations and information on Xunwu County. Professor Averill has been an exemplar of collegiality. Helen Siu,

Angus McDonald, Hong-Yung Lee, Nicholas Lardy, Harry Harding, and Timothy Cheek were kind enough to read and respond to a draft of the Introduction.

There is one person who has contributed to the entire work with a commendable degree of professional and scholarly commitment. It has been my good fortune to have my manuscript placed in the skillful hands of John R. Ziemer, of Stanford University Press.

This project was also influenced by a group of people who, early in my studies, shared their knowledge of Chinese history, language, and culture with me: my teachers at Stanford University, the late Kao Kung Yi, Chuang Yin, H. L. Kahn, and Lyman Van Slyke. During graduate training at Yale University, I was privileged to study Chinese history with Jonathan Spence. I hope this book displays the sense of adventure that Professor Spence brings to the study of history.

Finally, to return to the person I mentioned at the beginning, I thank Melissa, who served as a knowledgeable and sensitive consultant and confidante throughout this project. She was also a wonderful companion during our exploration of an obscure, but not unimportant, place in China.

R.R.T.

Contents

Twelve pages of photographs follow p. 134.
For maps of southeast China and Xunwu County, see pp. 50–51.

Introduction

Introduction

Mao Zedong made a key decision in May 1930. Rejecting urgent requests by the leaders of the Chinese Communist Party (CCP) that he come to Shanghai for a major conference, Mao instead went to Xunwu County, in the southeastern corner of Jiangxi Province. At the place where Jiangxi, Fujian, and Guangdong meet, Mao found himself at a crossroads. The young Marxist was besieged with party directives (both Chinese and Russian) that he could not reconcile with the reality of the Chinese countryside he had been studying or fighting in since 1925. During the month or so that Mao spent in Xunwu County, he produced two compositions that would become key documents in CCP history. Together these documents represent Mao Zedong's effort to reconcile Marxist theory with Chinese reality. Mao began "The Work of Investigation" with a sentence that still echoes in China: "If you face some problems but have not made any investigations, then stop before you make any pronouncements on those problems." This essay, published for the first time in 1964 under the better-known title "Oppose Bookism" (Mao's original title for a shorter draft version), shared space on Mao's writing desk with the other key document he wrote in May 1930, the *Report from Xunwu*. Seeking to ground his own theoretical pronouncements in observable reality, Mao conducted a series of investigation meetings over a period of two weeks that allowed him to describe in fine detail the rhythms of both everyday life and revolutionary struggle in this border county. Originally scheduled for publication in 1937 and reported lost by 1941, Mao Zedong's *Report from Xunwu* was published for the first time at the end of 1982.

We meet hundreds of people in this report, from Uncle Shitcrock, the most powerful man in the county, to peasants so poor that they sold their children to buy food. In between these extremes Mao sketched, among others, salt merchants, rich peasants, landlords, tailors, blacksmiths, butchers, firecracker makers, prostitutes, government officials, recipients of degrees granted by the now-distant Qing dynasty (1644–1912), young students, and women struggling to make a new life.

We are told how much to pay for rice, wine, pork, and bean curd and how to borrow money, write a contract to rent land, and pay taxes. Local schools, temples, and ancestral halls are named and discussed, as are hair and clothing styles past and present, and lists of goods bought and sold at the periodic markets. Few details seem to have escaped Mao Zedong.

Students of history, society, and culture, as well as students of revolution, Communism, Mao Zedong, and contemporary Chinese politics should find the *Report from Xunwu* illuminating. It opens a window on the process by which, at the local level, Mao and the CCP were able to transform the disasters of 1927, especially the split with the Nationalists (Kuomintang; KMT) and the failure of the Autumn Harvest Uprisings, into the triumphal establishment of a relatively secure revolutionary base in Jiangxi in 1931.

The *Report from Xunwu* also sheds light on one aspect of the CCP's early history that has not received sufficient attention: the relationship between the national revolution implied in the "rise of the CCP" and the local struggles that were part of this broad picture. Too often these "local revolutions" have been reduced to footnotes in the history of the CCP. In order to understand one such local revolution, that in Xunwu

County, some knowledge of the events in the bitter struggle for power that had split the ruling elite in Xunwu since at least 1916 is necessary. A key event in this particular narrative, the failed uprising that began on 25 March 1928, is described in some detail below, since the *Report from Xunwu*, written about two years later, is in part a record of vengeance. But the report is also a snapshot of local Chinese society at a critical point in the transition from late imperial times to the establishment of a new and viable regime. The *Report from Xunwu* can be mined for data on the society, economy, politics, and history of one county and region in China at this important juncture in Chinese history.

Furthermore, the *Report from Xunwu* reveals an important stage in Mao's personal intellectual development. We can also place it in the context of the international attention paid to rural China by a wide range of observers in the 1920's and 1930's. This document was produced at an important moment in Mao Zedong's attempt to adapt Marxism to Chinese reality. The investigation meeting, and the insights that resulted, would become an important part of this ongoing effort. Mao's technique not only served his revolutionary purpose but directly challenged the methodology and perspectives of Western social scientists and their Chinese associates. We can trace the development of this aspect of Mao's thought and practice back to at least 1916.

Finally, the 1982 publication of the *Report from Xunwu* is significant politically and adds to our understanding of the succession crisis following Mao's death in 1976. Deng Xiaoping used the *Report from Xunwu* to justify his assessment of the essence of this early period in the history of Chinese Communism. Deng knew the people and places of this period well, for he had been responsible for the administration of Xunwu from at least the spring of 1932 until April 1933. Armed with this intimate knowledge, Deng was determined to write an unwritten chapter in Mao's life and highlight a time when Mao's adversaries in the CCP criticized him indirectly by lashing out at men like Deng and Mao's personal secretary, the Xunwu native Gu Bo. Deng proclaimed that visionaries like Mao, and himself, were "seeking truth from facts" and had been developing, from the earliest years, a specifically Chinese form of socialism. Given the contemporary significance of this document and the tortuous path, stretching over half a century, from composition to publication, the nature of the text itself, its compilation, and its authenticity and accuracy are important concerns.

When Mao paused for about a month in Xunwu County, he had several goals clearly in mind. He wanted to survive, he wanted to protect the Fourth Army led by his comrade-in-arms Zhu De, and he wanted the CCP, with a firm base in rural China, to lead a national revolution that would rid China of the twin scourges of warlords and imperialists. No one, not even Mao, could be absolutely certain what should be done, especially after the calamitous events of the previous three years.

A lack of resolution was tearing the CCP apart in 1930. Founded some nine years earlier, the CCP had been allied with the KMT from 1923 to 1927. Their agreement allowed CCP members to join the KMT but retain their membership in the CCP. Although in retrospect a strange collaboration, at the time both the CCP and the KMT had rallied to the banner raised by the revolutionary hero Sun Yatsen. Adherents of both parties saw themselves as revolutionaries seeking to vanquish the warlords who had carved up China and to expel the foreign imperialists who wielded so much power.

This fervor intensified after the May Thirtieth Incident in 1925. A student demonstration in Shanghai in support of a workers' strike ended in violence, with the death of eleven Chinese at the hands of the foreign-controlled police. This sparked protests, strikes, and boycotts by a broad segment of the Chinese population in Shanghai and elsewhere. A month later, on 1 July 1925, a Nationalist government was established in Canton, directly challenging the legitimacy of the warlord regime in Beijing that was the putative national government.

The Canton government began consolidating its hold on the southern provinces of Guangdong and Guangxi in early 1926 and then, in July, turned its attention to nearby Hunan, sending troops to aid one of the claimants to power in that province. As the tide of battle turned in favor of the Canton government led by Chiang Kai-shek, and its new Hunan allies, Chiang declared, on 9 July, that the Northern Expedition had begun. With the goal of unifying China, Chiang left Canton for the north on 27 July. By the end of the year, political and military authorities allied with Canton had been established in the provincial capitals of Hunan (Changsha), Jiangxi (Nanchang), and Fujian (Fuzhou). But just as the armies making this possible traveled along three roads on their way north, so, too, the coalition fashioned under Sun Yatsen's leadership unraveled in three directions. The power of Sun's legacy—he had died in March 1925—was insufficient to bind these contentious revolutionary forces together. The more progressive wing of the KMT—the left wing—cooperated with the Communists, to the dismay of the KMT's right wing, led by Chiang Kai-shek. Relationships deteriorated. Throughout 1926 more and more Communists were pushed to the sidelines or deprived of their KMT membership. But not all—Mao Zedong was principal of the sixth class of the KMT's Peasant Movement Training Institute in Canton from May to October 1926.[1]

Chiang Kai-shek's tolerance of Communists in the KMT camp decreased as his power increased. Nevertheless, the Nationalist government moved the capital from Canton to the city of Wuhan in Hubei, the center of power of the KMT's left wing, on 1 January 1927. But this arrangement did not last long. On 22 March Shanghai fell to Chiang's troops. Nanjing fell a day later. Then the front collapsed. On 12 April Chiang turned on workers in Shanghai, cutting down hundreds of them in cold blood. The specters of death or imprisonment stalked the CCP and its working-class allies in other places, and on 17 April the tension could no longer be tolerated. The Nationalist government in Wuhan dismissed Chiang as commander-in-chief. But Chiang had an army and could well afford to ignore the order; he established a new Nationalist government in Nanjing on 18 April.[2]

Blood continued to flow. The Wuhan government, still under the control of the left wing of the KMT and its CCP allies, witnessed a further turn to the left in areas under its control. These leaders, impotent in the face of Chiang's might, were equally unable to influence the peasant movements under way in the countryside, especially to the south in nearby Hunan Province. Episodes of scattered violence became more numerous, and over one hundred landlords, duly tried and sentenced by Special Courts to Try Local Bullies and Evil Gentry, were executed in Hunan. But this was the beginning of the end. By 22 May 1927 Changsha had fallen to forces opposing the disintegrating Wuhan government, and in the ensuing White terror peasants were butchered in the tens of thousands.[3]

The CCP became more isolated. Purged from the ranks of even the KMT left in June and July,[4] the CCP, in defiance of reality, cloaked its action under the mantle of the KMT's left wing one more time. The failed Nanchang Uprising of 1 August 1927 marked the end of this alliance. The CCP was in shock. One final effort, this time in Hubei and Hunan, was the series of insurrections known as the Autumn Harvest Uprisings, which occurred from September to October 1927 and were led in part by Mao Zedong. These, too, were disasters, so much so that Mao called off a planned attack on Changsha. Instead, he gathered a thousand men and in October 1927 headed for Jinggangshan, a remote, mountainous area on the Hunan-Jiangxi border. There, in April 1928, Mao combined his forces with those of Zhu De, a Northern Expedition commander who had recently led his troops into the CCP fold.

Meanwhile, in Shanghai, Party Central was insisting, even

after the tragedies of 1927, that a successful revolution still required gaining control of big cities, although it was now admitted that peasants and the Red Army could aid the urban proletariat and that radical redistribution of land—seizing the fields of landlords but protecting the fields of rich peasants—was the most effective means of mobilizing the peasants, especially poor peasants. At times Mao seemed sympathetic to these ideas, which are associated with Li Lisan, the dominant figure in the upper echelons of the CCP from June 1928 to October 1930. However, the degree of Mao's support for Li Lisan's policies is a hotly debated topic in China today.[5] At the beginning of the mountain retreat of 1927–28, Mao advocated radical policies, but he was unable to maintain a secure base there and perhaps began thinking that prudence on the land question might be more advisable.

Mao was still searching for answers when he and Zhu De left their mountain hideout on 14 January 1929. Leaving behind Peng Dehuai, like Zhu De a veteran of the Northern Expedition, to guard Jinggangshan, Mao and Zhu decided to skirt the enemy-controlled Gan River valley and moved south from Jinggangshan toward the Jiangxi-Guangdong border before turning their force of some 3,600 men east toward Fujian. By 31 January they had reached Changpu, a market town in the southern part of Xunwu County. Mao and the Fourth Army paused to meet with local revolutionaries and to discuss how to overthrow the people who ran Xunwu County and establish a revolutionary base.[6] Mao was speaking to a band of revolutionaries who were regrouping after a disastrous attempt in March 1928 to seize power in Xunwu. One of the survivors of that debacle, a young Xunwu revolutionary named Gu Bo, listened intently to Mao's comments.[7] The two men would meet again.

After leaving Changpu, the main force of the Fourth Army turned north, skirting Xunwu City to the east at Jitan. There, on the morning of 2 February, Mao led this force against Jiangxi provincial troops in a desperate battle near the Xunwu

Gu Bo, circa 1930 (from Xia Daohan, "Gu Bo," in *Zhonggong dangshi renwu zhuan*, 1983, 12)

River. The survivors of this battle left Xunwu County the following day.[8] For the rest of 1929, Zhu and Mao would attempt to gain control of southern Jiangxi and parts of nearby Fujian. At the same time, Mao returned to some of the questions he had been asking on Jinggangshan. As he crisscrossed southern Jiangxi and western Fujian, Mao had numerous opportunities, like the one in Xunwu in January 1929, to test his theories against the experiences of local revolutionaries like Gu Bo. And by late 1929 and early 1930, there would be many successes to analyze in southern Jiangxi.[9]

But the record becomes sketchy at this point. In many of the standard histories of this period, which focus on leaders like Mao, Zhu De, and Peng Dehuai—all of whom were in the area—there is little information on the period December 1929 through May 1930. Only recently could scholars say for certain, for example, where Mao was in May 1930.[10] We now know that he was in Xunwu making what was probably the most detailed investigation of local society he would ever make. Mao had many goals in mind. He did want to learn about social, economic, and political conditions in places like Xunwu, but he also wanted to gather data that would be useful to him as he sought to gain an advantage in the power struggle he was waging with Party Central in Shanghai. This explains, perhaps, the silences in the histories of this period for the first five months in 1930.

What was to be done? Mao, like his Party Central colleagues in Shanghai, was still asking that question. Historians have pointed out the lack of significant policy differences between Mao and Li Lisan at this time. What seems more significant is Mao's opposition to Li Lisan's attempt to centralize party decisionmaking and ensure the responsiveness of lower-level cadres like Mao to the instructions of Party Central. This struggle over questions of power and responsibilities is symbolized, in fact, by the very existence of the *Report from Xunwu*, for Mao was in Xunwu at the precise moment when his presence was repeatedly requested by Li Lisan and Party Central at the National Congress of Delegates from Soviet Areas, held near Shanghai.[11] Mao refused to go, deciding instead to remain in southern Jiangxi, where he could study the cases of local revolution that were taking place under the leadership of local activists, and with the occasional assistance of the Fourth Army. Mao wanted to understand both how a revolution could be won through the efforts of peasants and how a mass-based party composed primarily of peasants could be built. This vision differed from the much smaller party organization advocated by men like Li Lisan and Wang Ming who were influenced by Moscow's plan for a party composed of intellectuals in alliance with an urban proletariat.[12]

Xunwu County, in Jiangxi hill country, seemed to offer some answers to Mao's questions. The red flag hoisted over Xunwu City on 2 May 1930 had been raised in southern Xunwu by local Communists who had triumphed six months before Mao

Zedong and Zhu De returned from the north. Mao would want to know everything about that victory. And in Comrade Gu Bo, a Xunwu native who at 24 years of age was thirteen years younger than Mao, he had a key to the history, the people, the economy, and the politics of the area. Gu Bo was the current leader of the revolution in Xunwu County that had consolidated the Communist grasp on the southern half of Xunwu. This contributed to the successful advance of the Fourth Army troops, which swept down from the north in late April. With the fall of Xunwu City on 2 May 1930, Gu Bo could survey once again the scene of the terrible defeat he and his comrades had suffered two years earlier, when the uprising begun on 25 March 1928 collapsed. This central event in the local history of the Communist movement in Xunwu defined the character of men and women; its shadow is cast throughout the *Report from Xunwu*.[13] It was part of a bitter factional struggle whose origins can be traced to the early 1920's. Glimpses of the struggle are captured in the *Report from Xunwu*, but it may be useful here to narrate salient events in the local history of Xunwu County from the early 1920's until the arrival of Mao in May 1930.

In 1921 a group of young Xunwu students studying in nearby Mei County in Guangdong organized the Society of Fellow Students Studying in Guangdong. One founder of this group was He Zizhen, a teacher in Xunwu. Indeed he had taught Gu Bo, who also helped establish this society. As the political situation in China intensified, the tensions within the Society of Fellow Students became unbearable, and in 1925 radical students like Gu Bo left and organized a new society, the Xunwu Poor Peasant Cooperative Society. There were few poor peasants in this society, but its members felt they were fighting for the welfare of this segment of society. Gu Bo returned to Xunwu for summer vacation in 1925, and in June of that year the Cooperative Society held a large meeting in Xunwu City. According to information in the *Report from Xunwu*, this society attracted supporters from small-landlord families. The battle lines were forming, and the first blows came in 1927 in the national context of the KMT's purge of Communists in April, when the Cooperative Society faction clashed with He Zizhen's new organization, the New Xunwu Society. In the analysis of Mao and his informants, the New Xunwu Society represented the interests of middle and large landlords. Whatever its actual composition, the relationship between the factions identified with He Zizhen and his one-time student Gu Bo deteriorated further.

This factionalism among the elite can be glimpsed in the societies just mentioned and the schools with which they were associated. The Cooperative Society faction sponsored the Sun Yatsen School (soon renamed the Sun Yatsen Middle School) in Xunwu City, with branches in five other places in Xunwu County. These schools appear to have been established in early 1928.[14] Opposing this movement was a school associated with the New Xunwu Society led by men like He Zizhen. This was not a competition simply for students; there was a close correlation between educational ties, social connections, and political power. In early 1928, the balance of power tilted toward He Zizhen and his associates, who controlled the police and militia and some tax monies. Nevertheless, Gu Bo and his comrades tried to counter with armed forces gained by allying with a local secret society, the Three Point Society (Sandian Hui). This society, with adherents throughout Xunwu County, was apparently used as a cover for efforts at organizing peasant associations.[15]

Gu Bo had also secretly established a committee of the Xunwu branch of the Chinese Communist Party early in 1928.[16] Although we have no evidence of the responsiveness of Gu and his associates to the leadership of either regional or national Communist organs, at this time, in one of the darkest hours of the CCP, official policy called for establishing revolutionary organizations called soviets that would seize administrative and political power wherever possible.[17] Whether or not people like Gu Bo were carrying out party directives, it is clear that southern Jiangxi was in the midst of troubled times in early 1928. A report dated 20 March in the *North China Herald* mentioned violence and unrest in areas north of Xunwu.[18]

This was the background for the 25 March 1928 uprising. Although the *Report from Xunwu* often refers to the uprising, it reveals little about the event itself. Nor was it covered in newspapers like the *North China Herald*, even though its correspondents discussed Communist activities in several other areas of Jiangxi.[19] Fortunately, Dr. Cyril E. Bousfield, a medical missionary stationed in Xunwu since 1912, wrote detailed reports just after the uprising. Bousfield began his report of 29 March 1928: "The experiences of the past six days have been almost too terrible to write."[20] Bousfield's ideas on the lines of division in Xunwu differed from those of Mao. For Bousfield, attitudes toward Christianity and the West were the decisive criteria. The Sun Yatsen Middle School faction, anti-Christian and anti-imperialist, was opposed to the New Xunwu faction, whose supporters were favorable toward Christianity.

Bousfield began with an account of the events of 23 March, when some one hundred "robbers," calling themselves "Communists," attacked the "Hsin-Sun [New Xunwu] school" and "destroyed everything in it." On the second day, according to Bousfield, the Sun Yatsen faction called up support from all quarters, and the following day a "new lot of robbers began to pour in." This third day in Bousfield's narrative—Sunday, 25 March—marks the beginning of the uprising in CCP historiography.[21]

Two days later one of Bousfield's Chinese associates made contact with a central committee, headed by Gu Bo, which declared that a soviet government had been established. One of the first orders of this new Xunwu soviet was that land deeds were to be handed over for burning, on pain of death. The goal of these men, or "boys" as Bousfield called them, was to destroy all government, family ties, and religion.[22] To emphasize this rhetorical attack on local government, the Xunwu County yamen was torched during the widespread destruction, looting, and killings in Xunwu City and the countryside that reportedly took place on 28 March.

But the uprising ended as quickly as it began when word came during the night that government troops were on their way to Xunwu City. The insurgents fled, and quiet returned to Xunwu on 29 March 1928, followed by a White terror, with numerous executions of the insurgents and looting of their homes. Bousfield reported on 1 April that ten summary executions had been performed by afternoon. After a brief interrogation of a suspect, "there is a five minutes' walk to the river bank, and the crack of a rifle or two, and they walk back without him." Bousfield reprised the events of 2 April: "More were shot to-day. It was raining, so the river bank was considered too far. They took them to the South Gate, which is about 2 minutes' walk nearer, for execution."[23]

Men like He Zizhen, who had fled the county, returned and re-established control, backed by provincial troops. Their counterrevolutionary attacks could be devastating. The *Report from Xunwu* tells us that in Datian, where Gu Bo had grown up, "nearly a hundred able-bodied men and dozens of elderly people and children were killed. In some cases, entire families were slaughtered. Some thirty people became Red Guards or went to other counties to participate in revolutionary work. The population of the township was reduced from 800 to 600, and much land was left uncultivated."

Gu Bo survived the immediate suppression and fled to Guangdong. But he returned a few months later, in the summer of 1928, to continue the fight for control of Xunwu County. Forsaking Xunwu City, Gu Bo and his associates concentrated their attention on the countryside in southern Xunwu. Gu persuaded a comrade, Kuang Caicheng, to return from Singapore to help him organize the peasants to engage in rent resistance and to help build an armed force of guerrillas.[24] It was this force that, in November 1929, established a Xunwu Military Committee on Yangtian Peak and changed the name of the Xunwu Chinese Communist Party Branch to the

Xunwu Chinese Communist Party County Committee.[25] Revolutionary activities intensified in the Datian area, where Gu Bo was able to supervise the redistribution of the land of one of Xunwu's eight great landlords, Mei Hongxing, Gu Bo's maternal grandfather and the man in whose home Gu had been raised. Mei Hongxing, who had reportedly just died, and the more affluent members of the Mei family, who had fled to Guangdong, were spared the humiliation of personally witnessing these events. With this triumph, the organs of revolutionary power—the Xunwu Military Committee, renamed the Xunwu County Revolutionary Committee, and the CCP County Committee—left their mountain stronghold and established their revolutionary headquarters in Datian.[26]

This land revolution in the southern part of Xunwu, discussed in great detail in Chapter 5 of the *Report from Xunwu*, was a prelude to the final assault that united the local Communist forces in the southern half of the county, referred to as the Second Battalion of the Fiftieth Regiment of the Red Army, and the Fourth Army. According to a recently published chronology of these events, on 11 April 1930 Mao convened a meeting in Xinfeng (Jiangxi) of leaders of the Fourth Army that decided to march on the county seats of Huichang (Jiangxi) and Xunwu. Reaching Huichang first, on 17 April, Mao paused to receive a group of soldiers from the Xunwu battalion. The march on Xunwu continued, and by the end of April a major victory had been won in Chengjiang District, north of Xunwu City, by the Xunwu Red Army battalion and troops of the Fourth Army. At that time Communist forces reportedly captured over a thousand armed combatants, along with a large quantity of ammunition. But Mao himself did not witness this, having remained behind in Huichang. From afar Mao could hear of the Red Army's capture of Xunwu City on 2 May and the establishment of the Xunwu County Soviet on 6 May 1930. Shortly thereafter Mao arrived in the county.[27] As occupying troops had done in the past, Mao commandeered the compound of the American Baptist Tremont Temple Hospital, not far from South Gate of Xunwu City, for his headquarters. It was here that he conducted the investigations that resulted in the *Report from Xunwu*.[28]

With the Red Army largely in control of the county—Mao mentions pockets of resistance in strongholds in Shuangqiao and Huangxiang districts—he could turn his attention to other projects. One was an investigation of Xunwu County; the other a theoretical essay whose central argument was the importance of informing theoretical speculations with careful empirical investigations. Desiring to investigate conditions in Xunwu County, Mao drew on the efforts to survey landholdings launched the previous November by Gu Bo and his comrades. This first investigation failed, however, because it asked for too much information, including population, class status, cultural level, ethnicity, age, landownership, land boundaries, land area, and yearly harvest. In January 1930 the procedure had been simplified: only the name of the household head and information on the number of family members, how many could farm, how many made a living in commerce or industry, the amount of land they owned, and the quantity of land they should receive in the land redistribution were required. According to the *Report from Xunwu*, this information was collected by "conferences on the redistribution of land" made up of one delegate from each household. A table was set up for each village, and a representative took down the required information. This information was then turned over to the township government, which would check the figures and then announce the redistribution. Subsequently, investigators dispatched by the township governments went to all the villages to check the validity of the peasants' reports. When we consider that Gu Bo had essentially set up a county government in exile in Datian at the end of 1929, a government he moved to Xunwu City in May 1930, we can get a better sense of the origin of much of the detailed information contained in the *Report from Xunwu*.[29]

When the Xunwu investigation began, then, in May 1930,

many data had already been collected. But Mao sought additional information from a group of native informants. Relying on the connections of Gu Bo and introductions provided by him, Mao gathered together a recipient of a Qing civil service examination degree, a former president of the local chamber of commerce, an ex-bureaucrat who had been responsible for county government finances, some peasants and merchants, and several cadres. Mao encouraged the participation of these eleven people, who ranged in age from 22 to 61, in a series of investigation meetings held over a two-week period. These informants provided personal knowledge on a variety of topics and also contributed documents to the investigation effort. With the help of these people, Mao produced a report of approximately 80,000 characters that covered diverse subjects: administration, commerce, transportation, communication, education, land tenure, taxation, religion, and social practices.

Much depended, of course, on the life experiences represented by Mao's informants, who brought their particular expertise to the investigations. Especially detailed information probably derives from close quizzing by Mao of the firsthand experiences of his informants. For example, the information on the structure and operation of general stores was gained, most probably, from Guo Youmei, a store owner and a former president of the chamber of commerce. Guo was also the probable source of the intriguing discussion of the United Welfare Society, which had characteristics of a secret society, a religious sect, and a social club, for Guo had been a member of the by-then defunct society. The detailed information on taxation in Xunwu County may well have been provided by Liu Liangfan, who had been involved in county tax collection in the past. The extended discussion of foundries and blacksmithing could have been based on Zhao Jingqing's experiences, which included ironworking. Each of these men attended all the investigation meetings. Further examples include Mao's riveting discussion of the practice of selling children, drawn entirely from the testimony of three peasants who had firsthand knowledge of this practice, or Chen Zhuoyun, whose experience in a tailor's shop is probably evidenced in the detailed discussion of clothing styles, past and present, in Xunwu County.

Mao's informants were more than sources of information, however; they could also be participants in the factional and revolutionary struggles that had been rending Xunwu for over a decade. For example, Guo Youmei may have been using Mao's investigations to settle old scores. As Mao pointed out in Chapter 3 of his report, Guo Youmei's shop had been ransacked by government troops, supporting one side of a factional battle, in a disturbance in June 1916. After the collapse of Xunwu's short-lived independence from the control of a Jiangxi provincial government backed by armies from the north, Guo Youmei's shop suffered a serious financial loss. The possibility that Guo's probable opponents in 1916 were members of the Pan lineage deepens our understanding of the portrayal of the anti-Communist Pan in the *Report from Xunwu*.[30]

But these in-depth looks at local society, scattered as they are throughout the text, are accompanied by information that could not have been entirely uncollected before Mao's arrival, in particular the long lists of landlords, citing landholdings, political attitudes, and educational experience. We can find indirect evidence for this view when we study the list of middle landlords, which names 93 people whose holdings were in the southern part of the county, but only 23 from the northern half, including the county seat, which did not come under Communist control until April and May 1930. It is this information, and the probable way in which it was collected, that alerts us to the broader signficance of this text. Although we may indeed be justified in treating the text as source material for studies in the fields of, for example, history, anthropology, sociology, commerce, agriculture, and education, it is well to keep in mind its significance as a political document, as a document of a revolution-in-the-making.

I have attempted, in the preceding pages, to draw attention to some of the political, intellectual, social, and economic contexts of the *Report from Xunwu*. But there is one more interpretive key to use in opening this text: that of history. In many respects both Mao Zedong and Gu Bo confronted China's past, so embedded in the present, with a similar transformatory zeal.

We can see evidence of this dialogue of past and present in the relationship established between teacher and pupil, one of the most fundamental personal connections in Chinese society. Mao was deeply influenced by his formal and informal relationship with Yang Changji, one of his teachers in Changsha and a man whose intellectual reputation extended far beyond Mao's home province of Hunan. Yang, who had moved north in 1918 to teach philosophy at Beijing University, opened doors for the young Mao in Beijing. This was more than an intellectual affair, for Mao would fall in love with his teacher's daughter, Yang Kaihui, and eventually marry her.[31] Gu Bo's experience may have had parallels with Mao's. Our information about Gu is less complete, but we do know that he was able to persuade one of Xunwu's leading scholars, Zeng Youlan, to serve as the titular head of the revolutionary Sun Yatsen Middle School. In the late Qing, Zeng had gone to Japan to study law, becoming the first person from Xunwu to go overseas to continue his education. On his return to China, he served in government positions in Fengtian, Beijing, and Hubei. When he finally returned to Xunwu, he turned his attention to local education and politics. In fact, Zeng Youlan had taught the man who was county magistrate in Xunwu in 1928.[32] Ties such as this with an esteemed member of Xunwu's intellectual and political elite served to protect student activists like Gu Bo even as they attacked the established order. And like Mao, Gu may have married the daughter of his patron; it is possible that Gu Bo's wife, Zeng Biyi, was Zeng Youlan's daughter.

These tidbits of personal history illuminate an important feature in the personalities of men like Mao and Gu: their ability to converse on both an intellectual and a personal level with the older generation. For Mao, this became a formal part of his method of investigation: he explicitly directed cadres conducting investigation meetings to question and listen to old people, people who might be able to interpret today's reality in the light of past experience. Mao wanted more than facts; he wanted to know why things were the way they were.

Mao had found in Gu Bo a comrade in spirit, for Gu seems to have entered into a dialogue with the past in both intellectual and personal terms. Because of this, we can see in the *Report from Xunwu* how things appeared in May 1930 and we can see why they did so. Gu Bo provided an array of connections to men rich in experience, men who may have seen in Gu Bo a path to the future that reached back into Xunwu's past. For Gu Bo was, they all knew, a Tangbei Gu; that is, he was born in the village of Tangbei in Huangxiang District. Huangxiang was a beautiful valley renowned for the scholarly achievements of its sons. In the section on culture in Xunwu, Mao writes, "Of the 600 Gu in the single-surname village of Tangbei in Huangxiang, eleven are *xiucai* [imperial degree holders]. This is the place where xiucai are most concentrated. . . . In the whole county the old culture was richest among the Tangbei Gu. They occupied a central position in administration in the past." Gu's paternal grandfather, Gu Youyao, had won an examination degree (*bagong*) in 1897. So too had Gu's maternal grandfather, the powerful landlord Mei Hongxing, who had been granted an imperial degree (*lingong*) during the Qing. In a sense, Gu's collaboration with Mao in investigating Xunwu County carried on a family tradition, for Mei Hongxing had been an editor of the 1899 edition of the local history and gazetteer of Xunwu County.[33]

Lest we think that Tangbei native Gu Bo was misleading

Mao about his family's position, we can cite the words of Mrs. Lillie Snowden Bousfield on the people of Huangxiang:

> Among the many mountains and hills of the southern part of Kiangsi [Jiangxi] Province are valleys of great interest, with their towns and villages, tea gardens and rice fields. One of these valleys extends for some miles, between hills of beautiful scenery.
>
> But the most interesting part of the valley is not its scenery, but its people and their homes, unlike the ordinary, and also the family history behind them. . . .
>
> The people who lived in this valley were remarkable. In their pedigrees, a long line of ancestry, were many famous men who had won favor under ancient emperors and had received tokens of esteem. Their women were famous for their virtue, and were carefully trained, though few were taught to read and write. They had their high code of morals, and were very proud.[34]

We do not know what Gu Bo thought of this heritage, although his activities were certainly those of a person groomed for leadership. Gu had shown scholarly promise as a youth, to the delight of his maternal grandfather in whose house he was growing up. Gu's father, an impoverished teacher in a village school, had been forced to send Gu Bo from Huangxiang, to nearby Datian. As one of Xunwu's eight great landlords, Gu's maternal grandfather, Mei Hongxing, was able to nourish the precocious Gu. By 1920, when Gu turned fourteen, he had exhausted the educational opportunities available in Xunwu, and he was sent, on Grandfather Mei's money, to nearby Mei County in eastern Guangdong Province. As he continued his studies at a middle school run by American missionaries, Gu became aware of the political and intellectual changes sweeping China and soon took his place in the vanguard, joining the CCP in 1925.[35]

With his growing radicalization, Gu became estranged from

his family. He reportedly refused to use the "blood money" gained by his grandfather's "exploitation" of peasants to pay his tuition and living expenses. Instead, he supported himself by teaching Chinese at the Mei County Girls Normal School.[36] But this familial estrangement did not mean that Gu Bo cut his ties to the intellectual and political establishment in Xunwu. As we have seen, he was able to enlist the support of one of the most eminent men in Xunwu, Zeng Youlan, in sponsoring the Sun Yatsen Middle School.

All of this explains, in part, the richness of the explications of traditional institutions and patterns of power in the *Report from Xunwu*. The section on the landholdings of lineages, religious associations, and administrative bodies and the section on culture give detailed information on these topics. We can be sure that Gu Bo was an important source, or at least introduced Mao to the sources, for much of these data. In the *Report from Xunwu*, we can see the struggle between the traditional political and intellectual elite and the new forces, represented by men like Gu Bo and, to some extent, He Zizhen. The world of late imperial China was still a real presence in Xunwu in 1930. Land that had been set aside for educational purposes in the previous century was still referred to in traditional terms: Confucian Temple land, Sojourning Stipend land, or Shrine for Esteeming Righteousness land. There were still men wearing their hair in queues, the hairstyle mandated by the Qing dynasty, and some of these men, according to Mao, still hoped for the restoration of a monarchy. Hundreds of holders of Qing degrees were still alive in Xunwu; the *Report* sets the number at 400. Although most of these men had little power, it had not been long since four of their number had been pushed from Xunwu's political stage by men like Gu Bo and He Zizhen.

The *Report from Xunwu* is the earliest surviving example of a formal local investigation by Mao. He had displayed a passion for facts while attending normal school in Changsha. In the summer of 1916, Mao and a friend from school set off on a walking tour of five counties in the vicinity of Changsha in Hunan Province. Possessing no money at the outset, the two young men roamed at will, depending on the hospitality of villagers. Mao's diary of this trip circulated among friends, and several dispatches were published in a Hunan journal.[37] It was a pattern that would continue. On his way by rail to Beijing in 1918, Mao took advantage of a delay caused by the flooding of the Yellow River to make an impromptu investigation of local conditions in Henan Province.[38] Mao's continued interest in local social and economic conditions was apparent in two investigations he made in 1920. During a ten-day stop in Wuhan in early 1920 during a journey from Changsha to Beijing, Mao took extensive notes on local conditions, an effort he repeated in November of that year in Pingxiang County in Jiangxi.[39] Mao returned to Pingxiang County a year later, in the fall of 1921, and visited the Anyuan district. In an attempt to organize the miners in this area on the Hunan-Jiangxi border, Mao spent a week in the fall of 1921 investigating the lives of miners and their families. Mao made subsequent visits and investigations in September 1922 and in the winter a few months later.[40]

But the series of investigations that became the best known was made in the early months of 1927 in and around his home county of Xiangtan in Hunan. Perhaps recalling the investigation he had made during a visit home late in 1924,[41] Mao toured five counties in about five weeks early in 1927. Taking his notes on them north with him to Wuhan, Mao proceeded to write the famous "Report on the Peasant Movement in Hunan," which was published in March 1927.[42] He continued to hone his technique. Forced to flee to a mountain stronghold on the Hunan-Jiangxi border in late 1927, Mao compiled two more reports on counties in western Jiangxi.

None of the county investigations of 1927 are known to survive. Mao left his Hunan investigations with his wife, Yang Kaihui, and later surmised that her death in Changsha at the hands of the KMT in 1930 also meant the destruction of his reports. Likewise, the two reports on counties in Hunan and Jiangxi, entrusted to a colleague, were also lost, to Mao's particular regret. For fifty years the *Report from Xunwu*, too, appeared to have suffered this fate. Its remarkable re-emergence in 1982 will be discussed shortly. The *Report from Xunwu* represents the crystallization of a method of inquiry that Mao had been developing for almost fifteen years: the "investigation meeting" (*diaocha hui*), a method that would eventually become a key element in the "mass line" approach to establishing communications between the central leadership of the Communist party and China's millions. In a document entitled "The Work of Investigation" that was written in the same month as the *Report from Xunwu*, Mao instructed Communist cadres in the art of inquiry. In an "investigation meeting," a group of people, from three to two dozen, gathered to discuss a set agenda. As mentioned above, Mao stressed the importance of involving old people rich in experience, people who understood not only current conditions, but also the reasons for those conditions. Mao insisted that these investigations could not be delegated, subjects must be investigated in depth, and a record must be kept by the investigators.[43]

Mao's rural investigations, which focused on market town economies as well, were conducted during a time when international attention was directed at China's agrarian crisis. Analytical tools from the social sciences and Marxism were being used by, among others, James Yen, John Lossing Buck, Sidney Gamble, Chen Hansheng, and Xue Muqiao. The efforts of these pioneers resulted in Gamble's *Ting Hsien: A North China Rural Community* and *North China Villages*, publications by Japanese scholars associated with the Research Department of the South Manchurian Railway Company,[44] and articles by Chinese scholars in journals like *Rural China* (*Zhongguo nongcun*).

An influential work by an outsider should be added to this distinguished list. The eminent British historian R. H. Tawney, who had published a work on the transition to capitalist agriculture in England entitled *The Agrarian Problem in the Sixteenth Century*, was asked to turn his attention to twentieth-century China's agrarian problems. The resulting work, *Land and Labor in China*, originated as a memorandum for a conference of the Institute of Pacific Relations in Shanghai in November 1931. Tawney synthesized current research, including work being done at the University of Nanking, Nankai University in Tianjin, James Yen's work in North China, and John Buck's rural surveys.[45]

Mao took direct aim at the methodology of Western social science, for he feared its power to turn Communist party members engaged in research away from Marxist analysis. But even Marxist analysis had its pitfalls. What was maddening to Mao was the tendency of party members steeped in Marxist theory to become as "bookish" as scholars engaged in social science research. Mao had no problem with scholarly endeavors, but he insisted in "The Work of Investigation" that they be grounded in investigations of actual conditions.[46]

In a crucial passage in "The Work of Investigation," Mao criticized certain kinds of Communist investigators and social science–oriented scholars. The thrust of Mao's argument was to redirect the attention of investigators from the general to the particular. Mao, often accused of being a "mere empiricist" by more theoretically attuned rivals in the Communist party, disparaged some of the investigations being carried out under the auspices of the Red Army. It was as if the people in towns were being viewed by someone on a high mountaintop, he chided. Mao argued that investigators should be looking at more than land tenancy arrangements among peasant proprietors (*zigeng nong*), semi-peasant proprietors (*ban zigeng nong*), and tenants (*diannong*)—terms of analysis used in contemporary social science investigations—and he emphasized the importance of class analysis that identified rich peasants, middle peasants, and poor peasants. Mao reiterated this point in expressing his belief that trade and commerce should be analyzed not just in terms of the various trades but also in terms of the relative size and the characteristics of the strata of small, medium, and large merchants.[47]

All researchers have agendas and Mao was no exception: the purpose of research was "to determine correct tactics for the [revolutionary] struggle, to determine which class is the mainstay of the revolutionary struggle, which class we ought to make an alliance with, which class we must strike down."[48] To this end, Mao had outlined what he felt was a correct method of investigation.

In the *Report from Xunwu*, we have a record of Mao formulating this empirically based approach to revolution. Certainly aware of classical Marxist class analysis and the types of analysis being conducted by Westerners and Western-oriented Chinese scholars, Mao was attempting, in the *Report from Xunwu*, to make analyses of local power relations and politics take precedence over investigations that imposed theory on the facts.

Mao's writings of May 1930—"The Work of Investigation" and the *Report from Xunwu*—are an important conjunction of theory and practice. The *Report from Xunwu* tells us not only about Xunwu County, but also about the working out in practice of investigation methods that Mao felt were crucial to making revolution. The success of Communist mobilization efforts in the late 1930's and 1940's would rest on intimate knowledge of local power relations and politics; the theoretical definitions of class analysis could be applied creatively. What would matter was ensuring that the party's friends possessed the numbers and resources to triumph over the party's enemies.[49]

It is possible that the *Report from Xunwu* might have remained a mere footnote to history. But the fates of Mao Zedong, Gu Bo, the *Report from Xunwu*, and, significantly, Deng Xiaoping were intertwined in the early 1930's, a historical fact that may explain the publication of the report and the symbolic re-emergence of Gu Bo in the early 1980's. Gu Bo had left

Xunwu in June 1930 to assist Mao in his role as head of the Political Secretariat of the Front Committee of what would become, in August 1930, the First Front Army. This committee was responsible for southern and western Jiangxi, western Fujian, and eastern Guangdong. Gu Bo's close association with Mao contributed to Gu's demotion in 1931, when he lost his Front Committee post.[50] Sometime in late 1931 or early 1932, Gu became county party secretary in Huichang, just north of Xunwu. Gu probably stayed on in Huichang after he was replaced by Deng Xiaoping, also a victim of factional infighting, in the spring of 1932.[51] At this point, Deng was able to extend his control into Xunwu County as well as neighboring Anyuan County. Mao himself had been in Anyuan County, where, on 24 June 1932, after hearing a report from rural cadres, he ordered an armed uprising and establishment of a revolutionary base. Mao also ordered the Red Army to supply the local partisans with guns and ammunition.[52] Sometime in July, at a meeting convened in Yunmenling, in southern Huichang County, representatives assembled from Huichang, Anyuan, and Xunwu decided that a committee headed by Deng would administer all three counties.[53]

These actions would ultimately lead to more attacks on Mao, Deng, and Gu. Wang Ming and the Twenty-eight Bolsheviks, Moscow's men in China, strengthened their hold on the Central Committee. With the transfer of the Central Committee from Shanghai to Ruijin, the county just north of Huichang, in early 1933, indirect attacks on Mao and direct attacks on his allies increased. The 4 April 1933 directive by the Central Committee, attacking the so-called Luo Ming line, was an attack on men like Deng, Gu Bo, and Mao's brother Zetan. All were demoted from various posts in the Red Army and in the party and suffered the public humiliation of being stripped of their guns.[54] The Central Committee had been unhappy, in particular, with the resolutions issued by the special three-county committee headed, until his demotion, by Deng Xiaoping.[55] Gu Bo, who had been in Ruijin, was assigned to

Deng Xiaoping (from Chinese Communist Party, Central Committee, Department for Research on Party Literature, and Xinhua News Agency, eds., *Deng Xiaoping* [Beijing: Central Party Literature Publishing House, 1988])

Huichang as a guerrilla commander, but even this responsibility was taken from him on 14 December 1933. He then returned to Ruijin to take a post in the Grain Commissariat of the central soviet government.[56]

But the Jiangxi soviet was beginning to unravel. By early May 1934, Xunwu County and much of the southernmost reaches of Jiangxi had fallen to Chiang Kai-shek's troops.[57] Pressure increased as government troops moved northward, and plans were made for the beginning of what would become known as the Long March. Mao was still making his investigations, leaving Ruijin in late September 1934 to study conditions in Yudu County (Jiangxi). But by 11 October 1934, government troops had occupied Xingguo County, and on 10 November, three weeks after Mao had left Yudu to begin the Long March (18 October), government troops overran Ruijin itself.[58]

Deng Xiaoping and Mao Zedong would escape; Gu Bo was not as lucky. Left behind to wage guerrilla warfare, Gu survived for five months, though in extreme danger. Gu was on his way from southern Jiangxi to Guangdong to spread the news of the Zunyi Conference of January 1935, at which Mao began to consolidate his grip on the Communist party, when he was betrayed to the KMT and ambushed in the eastern Guangdong county of Longchuan. Gu died in March 1935.[59]

Mao would not learn of Gu's death until 1937, when he eulogized his old friend. Had the *Report from Xunwu* been published in 1937, when it was scheduled to appear in Mao's *Rural Investigations (Nongcun diaocha)*, this would have been a fitting memorial. But this did not happen. By the time *Rural Investigations* was finally published in 1941, the report had been lost, a fact Mao mentioned in his opening sentence of the 1941 preface to the collection.[60]

The status of the report seems to have been unchanged in the 1940's, but in 1950 Mao again turned his attention to a newly located copy of the *Report from Xunwu*. In preparation for the publication of his *Selected Works*, Mao revised Chapter 5, which described the policies and events of the land revolution in Xunwu. On the verge of publication again, the *Report from Xunwu* once more slipped from view. Chapter 5 was dropped from the *Selected Works* and disappeared, along with the rest of the *Report from Xunwu*, for another three decades.[61] Sometime in the late 1970's or early 1980's, however, the *Report from Xunwu* was again brought out from the archives. The fates of the *Report from Xunwu*, Mao Zedong, Deng Xiaoping, and Gu Bo had crossed again, as Deng Xiaoping used the symbolism of the *Report* in his effort to claim the mantle of legitimacy once worn by Mao.

Deng, who had been purged during the Cultural Revolution, was rehabilitated in the late 1970's and quickly began consolidating his power. On 18 August 1977 at the Eleventh Congress of the CCP, Deng exhorted his comrades to recapture the traditional work style, established by Mao, of "seeking truth from facts" (*shishi qiushi*).[62] Again, in September 1978 in the context of a power struggle with party chairman Hua Guofeng, Deng argued at a party meeting that the legacy of Mao's thought could be protected only by "seeking truth from facts" and by making sure that contemporary Marxist thought reflected knowledge of China's present circumstances.[63]

It was in this context, then, that the *Report from Xunwu* and the "Work of Investigation" were introduced as key symbols of the moment in the history of the CCP when the correct line, the one advanced by Mao, was epitomized by "seeking truth from facts." Furthermore, Deng was bringing attention to a period when he and Mao had fought together. To this end, Deng appears to have thought that the *Report from Xunwu* and the life of Mao's secretary Gu Bo would highlight a time when all three men had been on the wrong side of a factional struggle at the highest echelons of the CCP.

A chapter in the history of the CCP was being rewritten. Gu Bo, the forgotten revolutionary from Xunwu, a rising star whose early collaboration with Mao and Deng contributed to his death at the age of 29, was given, apparently for the first time, a prominent historical identity. In February 1980, the journal *The Red Flag Waves* (*Hongqi piaopiao*), known for publishing first-person accounts of revolutionary moments, presented an account of Gu's life written by his widow, Zeng Biyi. In this account Zeng mentions the important role Gu Bo played in Mao's famous Xunwu investigation. The investigation may have been famous—it had been mentioned in Mao's *Selected Works*[64]—but it was still unpublished. This situation would soon end, for the Central Committee of the CCP directed its research arm to issue a new edition of Mao's *Rural Investigations*. This effort, described in more detail below, would lead, at last, to the publication of the *Report from Xunwu* in 1982.

There is one more clue to the reasoning behind the appearance of the *Report from Xunwu*: the re-evaluation of the role of Mao in the history of the CCP. Deng Xiaoping's new orthodoxy was established in July 1981, when the party issued the "Resolution on Certain Questions in the History of the Party Since the Founding of the People's Republic."[65] In this document, Mao, the demigod of the Cultural Revolution, was shown to be merely mortal after all. Although Deng Xiaoping and other members of the Central Committee delicately distanced themselves from the now-discredited policies Mao had touted during the Cultural Revolution, they did not have the luxury of dispensing entirely with the powerful symbolic resonances of Mao's image.

One element in their strategy was to present a historical Mao whose image differed considerably from that created in the 1960's and 1970's. What could be more effective than having the historical Mao discredit the Mao of myth? In the important July 1981 "Resolution," Deng was able to ensure the inclusion of a key passage arguing that an essential element of Mao's thought was to "seek truth from facts."

The later publication, for restricted distribution only, of the annotated June 1983 version of the "Resolution" highlighted the significance of the Xunwu period in Mao's life. His essay "The Work of Investigation" was mentioned in the text of the 1981 resolution, and in the annotated version party readers were told the history of the development of Mao's work style, especially the development of the "investigation meeting," in the larger context of the importance of "seeking truth from facts."[66] Behind this was the implicit argument that if the facts required China to move away from Mao's final vision for the People's Republic of China, then so be it.

These power struggles and policy debates led, in part, to the publication in December 1982 of a new edition of Mao's *Rural Investigations*. This new edition, in which the *Report from Xunwu* was published for the first time, also included "The Work of Investigation" and the April 1931 CCP Political Bureau directive in which the famous aphorism "Without investigation one has no right to make pronouncements" appeared for the first time. The importance attached to this new edition is suggested by the prominent review of the collection by the influential historian and party member Hu Sheng that ran in the *People's Daily*, the official organ of the CCP, and in the *Guangming ribao*, a newspaper directed at intellectuals.

In most respects, this article, published on 11 February 1983, is a straightforward highlighting of the collection, with special emphasis on economic issues. But Hu Sheng's discussion at the end of the article of Mao's "Work of Investigation," which was first published in 1964,[67] made clear the political and intellectual significance of the *Collected Rural Investigations*. After pointing out Mao's emphasis on the importance of grounding Marxist analysis in practice, Hu Sheng told his readers that the methods of comrades currently engaged in social investigations could profit by drawing on the method Mao used for his research in Jiangxi.

The day after Hu Sheng's essay appeared, the editors of the *Collected Rural Investigations* discussed their work in a *Guangming ribao* article.[68] After these initial two articles, however, only occasional attention was paid to the new compilation during the rest of 1983. Of the hundreds of articles commemorating the ninetieth anniversary of Mao's birth, only a dozen or so appear to have dealt with this new publication.[69]

The larger significance of the *Collected Rural Investigations* becomes clearer when placed in the context of Deng Xiaoping's continuing efforts to re-evaluate Mao's legacy while establishing his own. On 1 July 1983, *Deng Xiaoping's Selected Works* (*Deng Xiaoping xuanji*) was published and soon became a focus of a new journal in Sichuan. In the inaugural issue published at the end of 1983, the editors of *Studies on the Thought of Mao Zedong* (*Mao Zedong sixiang yanjiu*) not only called for articles on Mao but also encouraged submission of articles on Deng's *Selected Works*, as well as on rectifying the party, establishing a socialism reflecting China's special characteristics, creating a socialist public morality, and fighting spiritual pollution.

The connection between Deng's *Selected Works* and Mao's *Collected Rural Investigations* is important. The lead article in the inaugural issue of *Studies on the Thought of Mao Zedong* was the April 1931 directive, penned by Mao, from the CCP Political Bureau about investigating land and population in soviet areas. This directive was published for the first time in 1982 in the *Collected Rural Investigations*. The key phrase in this directive, constantly discussed during 1983, was "Without investigation one has no right to make pronouncements."[70]

This directing of attention to past investigators of Chinese society was emphasized a year later when other views from the past were heard. A collection of articles originally published in the journal *Rural China* (*Zhongguo nongcun*) in 1934–43 was brought out in November 1983. This journal published work by Academia Sinica scholars like Xue Muqiao and Chen Hansheng. As their colleague Qian Junrui claimed in a statement taken down on the afternoon of 8 November 1981 in Beijing Hospital, their model for personally going to the countryside to conduct investigations was Mao Zedong's own example. It was an example that argued, Qian said, "without investigation one has no right to make pronouncements."[71]

Later the chief editor of the annotated version of the 1981 "Resolution," Gong Yuzhi, explained the epistemological import of Mao's *Collected Rural Investigations* in a 30 December 1983 *People's Daily* article entitled "The Philosophical Significance of *Mao Zedong's Collected Rural Investigations*." Gong discussed "The Work of Investigation" at length. Party members, and the general reading public, were also given another glimpse of Gu Bo in 1983 with the publication of his biography in an important multivolume collection of biographies of CCP figures, edited by a senior CCP historian, Hu Hua. In these various publications we have evidence of Deng Xiaoping's continuing effort to use the legacy of Mao Zedong to legitimate his power. These works echo the statement Mao had made in May 1930 in his essay "The Work of Investigation" on the importance of investigating before making pronouncements. Indeed, this essay was given pride of place in Mao's *Collected Rural Investigations*.

Deng's attempt to wrest Mao's mantle from the shoulders of Hua Guofeng explains, in part, the importance of the *Report from Xunwu* and "The Work of Investigation." By bringing renewed attention to a period in CCP history when Mao Zedong was his mentor, and by reminding people of the first time he had been purged, Deng Xiaoping was establishing a new orthodoxy that brought to the forefront a young Mao beleaguered on all sides, but supported steadfastly by the even younger Deng Xiaoping.[72] Deng emerged triumphant in this succession struggle. Hua Guofeng was removed from the party chairmanship in 1981 and from the Politburo in 1982. Deng's agenda went beyond personal vindication, however. It is this larger context, specifically Deng's effort to restructure China's economy, that aids us in analyzing the larger political, economic, and social significance of the publication of *Collected Rural Investigations*.

Mao's rural investigations were reissued just as China's rural economy was enjoying a period of remarkable growth. Commencing with reforms launched in 1978, Deng Xiaoping had restored a measure of autonomy and initiative to China's peasants in the guise of the "responsibility system." At the same time, some of China's economic planners were pointing to the importance of developing the tier of towns situated between China's cities and villages. In hopes of stemming the migration of underemployed peasants to metropolitan areas typical of other developing countries, they touted towns and small cities as the proper area for both economic and cultural developments that would help China synchronize urban and rural development.[73] Mao addressed these issues in his *Report from Xunwu*, in which he devoted a third of the report to analyzing the economy of Xunwu's county seat. Mao's attempt in May 1930 to persuade cadres to investigate both the rural *and* the urban sectors of the economies under their control certainly was useful in 1982 to men like Deng and his protégé at that time, Premier Zhao Ziyang, as they sought to disarm their radical adversaries.

What do we know about the *Report from Xunwu*, and how might this knowledge affect our interpretation of it? Can we glimpse the mind of the young Mao Zedong in his fledgling efforts to reconcile Marxist theory with stubborn Chinese reality? Is it fair, or more important, legitimate, to see this text in historical, political, anthropological, or sociological terms?

How wary should we be of the remarkable history of the text itself: written in 1930, scheduled for publication in 1937, reported lost in 1941, rediscovered in 1950, but not published until the end of 1982? Is the young Mao being manipulated by the current leaders of China? All available evidence, some of which is discussed below, leads to the conclusion that we are not being deceived by the text: Mao conducted the investigation and wrote the report. Although the mystery of its half-century disappearance remains unsolved, it is certain that we are dealing neither with a forgery nor a drastic contemporary alteration of a historical document.

We can cite Mao Zedong's own references to the *Report from Xunwu* in other documents dating from the 1930's and 1940's. For example, Mao's 1937 preface to his *Rural Investigations* heralds the *Report from Xunwu* as the lead item in the collection of reports. Mao's second preface to *Rural Investigations*, written in 1941 when the collection was first published, begins with a comment that the *Report from Xunwu* had been lost. But Mao mentions the people who contributed to the *Report from Xunwu*, a listing that corresponds to the people we meet in the *Report*.

Could the text have been corrupted for political purposes by the committee responsible for its publication in 1982? This is a more difficult question. As we have seen, the publication of the *Report from Xunwu* was part of a campaign associated with Deng Xiaoping that stressed the importance of "seeking truth from facts." The *Report from Xunwu* exemplified, then, the young Mao's effort to gather facts from which truth could be derived. Given the symbolism and political significance of publishing a new edition of the *Rural Investigations*, including for the first time, the *Report from Xunwu*, it seems unlikely that the text was corrupted.

Moreover, the intense scholarly effort required to prepare the manuscript of the *Report from Xunwu* for publication supports the argument for the authenticity of the text. This new publication resulted from scholarly work planned and executed within the Central Committee, the CCP's executive arm. The basis for this text was a photocopy of the manuscript in the archives of the Central Committee given to the Study Group on the Works and Life of Mao Zedong of the Research Center on Party Literature, which is subordinate to the Central Committee. The Study Group was given a text of the *Report from Xunwu* in need of careful editorial attention; the archive's manuscript appears to be a copy made by clerks whose low educational level contributed to a large number of copying errors. Moreover, Mao's detailed investigation resulted in a text replete with expressions and words in the local Hakka dialect that often mystified the editors in Beijing. The Study Group began an intensive editorial effort, drawing on scholarly resources in Beijing and Xunwu to conduct further investigations, half a century after Mao's investigations, in order to produce an authoritative text.[74]

The Study Group was finishing a burdensome editorial task that Mao began during the May 1930 investigation in Xunwu[75] and, as we have seen, returned to in 1950. In preparing a new edition of Mao's *Rural Investigations*, the Study Group conducted wide-ranging research in order to publish as accurate a collection of reports as possible. In addition to extensive work with the texts in Beijing, the Study Group revisited the five counties in the Wuyi mountains of southern Jiangxi investigated by Mao half a century earlier. This retracing of Mao's steps took 51 days and covered about 5,000 *li* (over 1,600 miles). In the course of their investigations, the editors talked to 35 organizations and fourteen families and conducted eight discussion sessions. Almost 800 textual emendations of information in categories like proper names, place-names, and names of goods and products were made.[76]

The principles of editing were clearly stated in the national press in 1983. So committed were the editors to textual fidelity that in at least one case they left what they felt was an error; in their opinion they could not find evidence to justify an emendation. In this particular example, which involved the ages of people eligible to receive land, the published text reads: "Anyone over 4 years old and under 55 is regarded as one labor unit and receives one share." The editors felt the minimum age should have been 14, based on the Xingguo Soviet Government Land Law promulgated in a nearby county in March 1930.[77] The only other available evidence of textual changes concerns the local names for products sold in Xunwu County, which, in some cases, were changed to terms familiar throughout China.[78]

These examples, which suggest a high degree of editorial care, argue against the possibility of politically motivated textual changes. Indeed, to corrupt a text being presented in the context of a contemporary campaign in China stressing the importance of "seeking truth from facts" would be extremely shortsighted, since the events described in the text are within the memory of many still living in Xunwu. A final argument rests on the text itself. This is clearly a text of its time, lacking both the anachronisms and the omniscient passages to be found in rewritten texts.

The *Report from Xunwu*, then, is an extraordinary document, far exceeding in scope and depth the other investigations Mao made in Jiangxi and Fujian in 1930–34 and published in *Rural Investigations* in 1941. This 1941 volume contains, for example, Mao's October 1930 investigation of the Jiangxi county of Xingguo and reports on the administration of two subcounty areas in Xingguo and in Shanghang County, Fujian.[79] The two major investigations in this volume, dating from 1933, are essentially reports on the current administration of subunits of two counties.[80]

Mao Zedong wrote the *Report from Xunwu* in a great hurry in May 1930 on the basis of information provided by eleven informants over a period of about two weeks during a series of investigation meetings. An enormous amount of information was gathered and written down. Moreover, we know that Mao sometimes had to rely on Xunwu natives like Gu Bo to translate the replies of informants because he could not understand the local dialect.[81] The *Report* gives the appearance of an attempt to amass as much accurate information as possible given the constraints of time and resources. This was a great accomplishment, but one whose success resulted in part from the commitment brought by various individuals to the investigation meetings of May 1930.

Mao added a preface in February 1931, and, as mentioned above, two decades after these initial efforts he edited Chapter 5 (on the land revolution in Xunwu) for inclusion in his *Selected Works*. This was never realized. The version of Chapter 5 published in 1982 reflects Mao's editorial hand, but the rest of the *Report from Xunwu* was not edited for publication until recently.

I have based my translation on the text of the *Report from Xunwu* published in 1982. The Chinese text is divided into five chapters, with headings and subheadings. The tables of contents that preface the last three chapters have not been included in this translation. The reader should consult the index for a sense of the range of information included in the text. Careful use of this index will also enable the reader to connect bits of information on selected topics scattered throughout the text.

In translating Mao's *Report from Xunwu*, I have tried to convey the text as it was written. This is not a polished report. There are obscure passages and awkward paragraphs. It was written quickly in unfamiliar surroundings. In some cases

Mao was thinking through difficult policy questions relating to land revolution, class relations, and the correlation of economic and cultural status with political attitudes. I have tried to preserve in translation some of the immediacy of his thinking. At the same time I have tried to translate the Chinese into readable English and, where absolutely necessary, have rearranged sentence order and have added, at times, words or phrases only implicit in the text.

Mao presented, it seems, as much local information as he could. The detail that makes this report so unique also presents the translator with formidable difficulties. China in 1930 was a land of great variety. Mao could not even understand the speech of some of his informants, let alone the meaning of some of the terms they were using. The voices of the people of Xunwu were being translated at the very beginning. But Mao remained true to his informants, and the editors have been steadfast in their fidelity to the manuscript entrusted to them. In this spirit I have attempted to preserve as much of the local knowledge in the report as possible. This has required the use of a number of romanized terms. For example, Mao might mention a farm implement used in Xunwu and then inform the reader of the name for the same object in a neighboring county. The specialist may refer to the character list for the variants. The list can also be consulted for bracketed romanized terms that have defied accurate translation, prompting a literal rendering. This is especially true for the hundreds of goods and products mentioned in the text. In some cases the information in this report is so local that it has escaped the grasp of the compilers of the dictionaries that have aided me in this effort.

I have decided to keep one other category of romanized terms in the text. These key terms are presented in Appendixes A–C and concern, mainly, the economic and cultural affairs of Xunwu. Many units of weight, measure, and currency, in this intensive look at Xunwu's economy, have not been translated. Nor have I given English equivalents for the civil service examination degrees still used in describing the Xunwu elders who had been granted these degrees by the Qing dynasty. These distant echoes of China's imperial past were still useful and meaningful descriptions almost two decades after the fall of the Qing. Again, should the general reader be persuaded to remember the meaning of this handful of romanized terms, perhaps it will be possible to take a step or two closer to the Chinese text.

In the final analysis little is certain about a text, but we can be sure that the *Report from Xunwu* is a product of Mao's hand. The report, however, passed through many hands before appearing in this translation. I have relied on the people who have worked on this document, in particular the editors of the 1982 version of the report. In most cases I have followed their lead in punctuation, although I have sometimes introduced paragraph breaks if I thought the understanding of the text would be enhanced. Parentheses in this translation also appear in the Chinese text; brackets are used to identify material I have introduced. In all other respects, this is Mao's *Report from Xunwu*.

Report from Xunwu

Preface

The scale of this investigation is the largest of all I have done. In the past I systematically investigated seven counties: Xiangtan, Xiangxiang, Hengshan, Liling, Changsha [all in Hunan], Yongxin, and Ninggang [both in Jiangxi]. The five Hunan counties were done during the great revolutionary period (1926–27). Yongxin and Ninggang were done during the Jinggangshan period (November 1927). I placed the materials on the Hunan investigations in the hands of my wife, Yang Kaihui. In all probability, when she was killed, these five investigations were lost. I gave the Yongxin and Ninggang investigations to a friend in the mountains when the Red Army left Jinggangshan in January 1929. These were lost when Chiang Kai-shek and the Guangxi clique both attacked Jinggangshan.[1] I am not too concerned when I lose things, but losing these investigations (especially the ones for Hengshan and Yongxin) caused me pain. For an eternity I can never forget them.

The Xunwu investigation occurred in May 1930 when the Fourth Army arrived. At this time, after the Pitou Conference[2] (the joint conference of the Fourth Army Front Committee and the West Jiangxi Special Committee held on 7 February) and before the Tingzhou Conference[3] (joint conference of the Fourth Army Front Committee and the West Fujian Special Committee held in June), I still did not completely understand the problem of China's rich peasants. At the same time, in the area of commerce, I was a complete outsider.[4] Because of this I pursued this investigation with great energy.

Throughout the time when I organized this investigation, I was helped by the Xunwu party secretary, Comrade Gu Bo (Gu is a middle school graduate, the son of a bankrupt small landlord, a former primary school teacher, and former chairman of the county revolutionary committee and of the county soviet; he is from Huangxiang District). Several people gave me many documents and always came to the investigation meetings:

Guo Youmei. 59 *sui*,[5] owner of a general store, former president of the chamber of commerce; from Xunwu City District.

Fan Daming. 51 sui, poor peasant, county soviet[6] official; from Xunwu City District.

Zhao Jingqing. 30 sui, middle peasant, former iron-founder, former small merchant, former soldier and platoon leader under Chen Jiongming,[7] now a county soviet committee delegate; from Shuangqiao District.

Liu Liangfan. 27 sui, formerly involved in county tax collection, now chairman of the Xunwu City suburban township soviet; from Xunwu City District.

Those who gave us some documents and who sometimes attended our meetings were

Li Dashun. 28 sui, poor peasant, a former district soviet delegate.

Liu Maozai. 50 sui, an old examination degree student [*tongsheng*], once operated a gambling house and had a small business; originally a small landlord but declined and became a poor peasant; was a delegate to the county revolutionary committee; now a delegate to a district soviet.

Those who came to a few investigation meetings and who gave us a small number of documents were

Liu Xingwu. 46 sui, peasant; had a small business; a delegate to a township soviet; from Xunwu City District.

Zhong Buying. 23 sui, student at Mei County Normal School, chairman of the district government; from Shipaixia.

Chen Zhuoyun. 39 sui, graduate of a local self-government school, a former worker in a tailoring shop; had a small business; a former primary school teacher.

Guo Qingru. 62 sui, a *xiucai*, participated in the imperial provincial examinations, a former primary school teacher; from Xunwu City District.

Our investigation meetings involved these eleven people and myself. I was the chairman and secretary. Our investigation, which lasted over ten days, took place when the Red Army units were organizing the masses in Anyuan, Xunwu, and Pingyuan. This gave me time to organize these investigation meetings.

Xunwu County is located at the junction of three provinces—Fujian, Guangdong, and Jiangxi. Since conditions in the neighboring counties of the three provinces are similar, conditions in Xunwu County can serve as an example.

This investigation has one great defect: there is no analysis of middle peasants, hired hands, and loafers.[8] Also, in the section "Traditional Land Relationships," there is no separate discussion of the landholdings of rich peasants, middle peasants, and poor peasants.

—*2 February 1931, Xiaobu, Ningdu County [Jiangxi]*

·1·

Administrative Jurisdictions in Xunwu

There are seven districts, which include four wards in Xunwu City and twelve *bao*.[1]

The seven districts are

Xunwu City District: including East, West, South, and North wards; this is the administrative center of the county.

Renfeng District[2] (or Huangxiang bao): there are two administrative centers in this district, Gongping and Changpu (or Huangxiang), with a bureau in each center.

Shuangqiao District (or Shuangqiao bao): divided into thirteen *duan*, with Liuche the administrative center.

Nanba District: two bao, Nanqiao and Bafu, with Niudouguang the administrative center.

Jiansan District: three bao, Xiangshan, Yaogu, and Zixi, with Jitan the administrative center.

Chengjiang District: three bao, Xunwu, Dadun, and Guiling, with Chengjiang the administrative center.

Sanshui District: two bao, Sanbiao and Shuiyuan, with Sanbiao the administrative center.

There was no county government in Xunwu before the Wanli period [1573–1620] in the Ming dynasty; Xunwu County was established during the Wanli period. Before that time, part of Xunwu was under the jurisdiction of Anyuan County in Jiangxi Province. This was Shiqi bao, which comprised the present Chengjiang, Sanshui, Renfeng, and Xunwu City districts; the other part was under the jurisdiction of Pingyuan County in Guangdong Province and comprised the present Shuangqiao, Nanba, and Jiansan districts.

JIANGXI PROVINCE

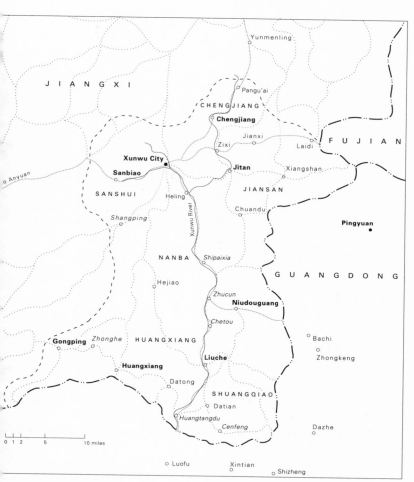

JIANGXI

Yunmenling

Pangu'ai

CHENGJIANG

Chengjiang

Jianxi

Zixi   Laidi   FUJIAN

Xunwu City   Jitan

Sanbiao   Xiangshan

Anyuan   JIANSAN

SANSHUI   Heling

Chuandu

Shangping   Pingyuan

NANBA   Shipaixia

Hejiao

GUANGDONG

Zhucun

Niudouguang

Chetou

Zhonghe   Bachi

Gongping   HUANGXIANG   Zhongkeng

Huangxiang   Liuche

Datong

SHUANGQIAO

Datian

Huangtangdu

Cenfeng   Dazhe

0 1 2   5   10 miles

Luofu   Xintian

Shizheng

UNWU COUNTY

·2·

Transportation and Communication in Xunwu

WATERWAYS

The Xunwu River originates in the Pangu'ai area of the Gui-ling Mountains. Passing through Chengjiang, Jitan, Shipaixia, Chetou, and Liuche, it merges into the Longchuan River, which goes down to Huizhou [in Guangdong]. The Xunwu River is a tributary of the Dongjiang [East River], and ships can go as far upstream as Chengjiang. There are three big market towns [*xu*] along the river: Chengjiang, Jitan, and Liuche, with Jitan the biggest.

Ships can also go from Shipaixia to Heling in Xunwu City District (10 li [3 miles] south of the town).

LAND ROUTES

With Shipaixia being the hub, there are four main roads. One road goes to Yunmenling (110 li) via Jitan (30 li), Chengjiang (60 li), and Pangu'ai. This is the main road to Guangdong Province for Xingguo, Yudu, and Huichang counties. Another goes to Anyuan City (140 li) via Xunwu City (30 li), Sanbiao (60 li), and Taiyangguan. This is the main road to Mei County for Xinfeng and Anyuan. Another road goes to Bachi in Pingyuan County (45 li) via Zhucun and Niudouguang (20 li). This is the main road to Mei County for Huichang and Anyuan. The roads from Huichang and Anyuan merge at Shipaixia and then go to Mei County together. Another road goes to Xingning and Wuhua counties via Chetou (20 li), Liuche (35 li), Huangtangdu (60 li), and Luofu (95 li) and Luogang (125 li) in Xingning County. This last road is the main way from Xunwu to Huizhou.

There are some other, smaller roads. One goes from Chengjiang to Luotang (30 li) in Wabujie of Anyuan, then from Luotang south to Xiaba and then north to [Yun]Menling. Another road goes from Jitan to Pingyuan (60 li) via Xiaotian, Chuandu, and Shuyuan. Another road goes from Xunwu City to Wuping (180 li) via Daluxia, Zixi, Jianxi, Liche, and Laidi. Another road goes from Xunwu City to Hushan (60 li) in Nanxiang in Anyuan County via Shangping, then north from Hushan to Anyuan City (60 li), and then west to Taiping (36 li) and Egong (60 li). Another road goes from Xunwu City to Xinxu (60 li), then from Xinxu to Egong (80 li) in Dingnan, passing through Gongping (3 li) and Liangguangting (45 li), then south from Egong and then west to Dingnan City, passing through Hezi on the way to Xinfeng.

The following roads are even smaller: one from Xinxu to Longchuan City (240 li) via Changpu (20 li) and Aipaikou; and another road from Changpu and Aipaikou to Xingning City (180 li).

Xunwu City is 90 li from Menling, 180 li from Wuping, 240 li from Mei County, 240 li from Xingning, 110 li from Anyuan, 310 li from Longchuan, and 160 li from Dingnan (via Shangping, Hushan, Taiping, and Egong).

TELEGRAPH

The Telegraph Bureau was moved from Jitan to Xunwu City in 1922. The telegraph line goes from Jitan to Xunwu City to Yunmenling and to Pingyuan.

POSTAL SERVICE

There is a third-class post office in Xunwu City. One post route goes to Menling via Jitan and Chengjiang. Another route goes to Bachi via Niudouguang and then from Bachi to Mei County. Another route from Bachi goes to Pingyuan. Another route goes to Anyuan via Sanbiao. There are "postal agents" in Chengjiang, Jitan, and Niudouguang and "receiving offices" in Sanbiao and Shipaixia. There is postal service on the Menling route on the second, fifth, and eighth days of the [ten-day cycle of the] lunar calendar.[1] The Bachi route has service on the first, third, fifth, seventh, and ninth, and the Anyuan route on the second, fourth, sixth, eighth, and tenth. Letters to Ganzhou are sent via the Anyuan route, and those to Yudu and Xingguo via the Menling route. Usually, amounts up to 200 yuan can be remitted through the post office in Xunwu City. With advance notice up to 500 yuan can be remitted. But otherwise not.

During the 25 March uprising the year before last [1928],[2] the director of the post office was seized and fined 500 yuan.[3] This time the new director, fearing capture, fled first. The director of the Telegraph Bureau was killed during the 25 March uprising.[4]

THE MEANS OF LAND TRANSPORTATION

Just as in Guangdong Province, there are no vehicles on any roads. The major means of land transportation are the shoulders of humans, and next mules and horses. There are many mules and horses on the road from Xunwu City to Mei County and some on the roads from Xunwu City to Menling and Jitan but none on the other roads. There are more mules than horses, but they are generally called "horses." The goods carried by horse are mainly salt and soybeans.

·3·

Commerce in Xunwu

Of the goods brought from Shicheng and Ruijin counties, rice and soybeans are the most important, with an [annual] worth of several hundred thousand yuan. Tea-oil is the major item of trade from Xingguo County,[1] although some rice (not much) is imported from there. No goods are brought in from Yudu or Huichang counties.

Four boatloads of oil come from Menling to every market in Chengjiang (the oil is carried by humans from Menling to Chengjiang and then loaded onto boats). Every boat carries 12 dan[2] of oil, and each dan is worth 30 yuan [*xiaoyang*].[3] Figuring 100 markets a year, the oil traded is worth 150,000 yuan.

Most of the rice coming from Shicheng and Ruijin to Menling goes to Mei County via Luotang, Xiaba (in Wuping County [Fujian], at the common boundary of the three provinces), and Xinpu (in Jiaoling County [Guangdong], 30 li from Mei County). The amount transported is about 300 dan a day. Rice bound for Mei County usually does not pass through Xunwu County, but oil and soybeans do. The amount of beans is almost double that of oil. Some dan contain 5 dou, and some contain 3 dou; the amount is not very regular. One dou is worth 1.5 yuan [*xiaoyang*]. There are five boatloads of oil and beans at every market (one market every three days); each boat contains 14 dan, and the value of each dan is 6 yuan (assuming 4 dou in each dan). So the value of the oil and beans at each market is 420 yuan, and the annual total is 42,000 yuan for the 100 markets held each year. The amount carried by porters is 20 dan per market, for a total of 2,800 dan annually, with a value of 16,800 yuan. So the sum of these two categories is 58,800 yuan.

BUSINESS FROM ANYUAN TO MEI COUNTY

Chicken. The most important good transported along this route is chicken, with oxen next, and pigs third. Most of the chickens come from Tangjiang, Nankang, and Xinfeng, although some come from Anyuan, and even some from Suichuan. The transport route for chickens runs through Wangmudu, Jinji, Xintian, and Banshi but avoids Anyuan City, passing 5 li to the north, and enters Xunwu County on the way to Mei County. From Mei County, the chickens are shipped to Songkou [Jiaoling County] and then to Shantou for export. Most of the chickens passing though Xunwu are from Anyuan, with some from Menling. Since between 100 and 300 dan are shipped each day, if each dan weighs 60 jin, then a daily amount of 100 dan is equal to 6,000 jin. Chicken dealers carry chickens from the Tangjiang area to Mei County or Xinpu to sell (from Xunwu the route to Xinpu runs through Dazhe; after being loaded on boats, the chickens go directly to Songkou without passing through Mei County) and get a price of 0.5 yuan per jin (0.4 yuan in Xunwu). With 6,000 jin every day, the value of the chickens is 3,000 yuan a day or 1,080,000 yuan each year. Since the chicken guild in Mei County sells chickens in Songkou at the price of 0.7 yuan or more a jin, we can say the profit is great.

Oxen. The first day of [each ten-day] cycle is the "ox market day." The ones in November are most prosperous, with 700 to 800 oxen at each market; the ones in January and February are the next most prosperous, with 100 to 200 oxen at each market. Those in March, April, May, June, and July are the slackest, with 3 to 5 or 10 odd at the most for each market. The first day in August is the "opening day"; business becomes more prosperous from this day, with 40 to 50 or 60 to 70 oxen sold per market. There are almost 100 oxen at each market by September and October.

How many oxen each year?

January		100
February		100
March		60
April		
May	no markets	
June		
July		
August (3 fairs)		250
September (3 fairs)		250
October		300
November (3 fairs)		2,100
December (2 fairs)		160
TOTAL		3,320

The average price of an ox is 40 yuan, making the total value each year 132,800 yuan.

Like chickens, most oxen come from Tangjiang and Xinfeng, with some from Anyuan, but none from Xunwu. The difference is that chicken only pass through Xunwu, but oxen are sold here. The ox market is held on the riverbank outside the East Gate of Xunwu City. The sellers are from Tangjiang, Xinfeng, and Anyuan; the buyers are from Mei County, Wuping, Jiaoling, and Pingyuan. The middlemen (brokers) are from Xunwu.

Oxen not exported through Shantou via Songkou are usually bought by ox dealers to sell to families for plowing farmland or sold to other towns for slaughter.

The fee for brokers is a half mao from both the buyer and

the seller. The ox tax paid to the government by the tax farmer is 1,740 yuan each year. In the past "bidding" (*toubiao*) [for the post of tax farmer] took place annually, and the one who offered the most obtained the bid. But recently, the bidding has been held once every three years. The tax is figured by the head, at 0.4 yuan for each ox and 0.5 yuan for each water buffalo. The tax is called *xiang*. After the tax [is paid], the character *xiang* is burned on the hide of the ox with a lime stamp, and the buyer can lead the ox away. Besides this tax, a levy of 0.1 yuan per ox was added recently. The tax that the tax farmer sends to the government plus his own income totals 2,000 yuan or more each year. Based on a tax rate of 0.4 yuan per ox, more than 4,500 oxen should be sold in Xunwu each year; thus, the figure of 3,320 cited above is a low estimate.

Pigs. Most come from Xinfeng; some are from Anyuan. Pigs arrive by two routes: most come from Anyuan County to Mei County via Xunwu City, Niudouguang, and Bachi. Some come from Nanxiang in Anyuan County to Mei County via Gongping, Xinxu, Liuche, and Zhongkeng in Pingyuan County. A total of 5,000 pigs, valued at 225,000 yuan, arrives via these two routes. The average weight is 100 jin, and at a price of 0.4 yuan a jin, the [average] value of a pig is 45 yuan. The Xunwu government levies a tax of 0.2 yuan per pig.

BUSINESS FROM MEI COUNTY TO [YUN]MENLING

Most business is in the following five categories.

Foreign goods. Tooth powder, toothbrushes, flashlights, rubber shoes, soaps, foreign umbrellas, lanterns, and foreign iron [tinned iron] are major trading items. Some of these items, for example, tooth powder and toothbrushes, are made in China, but are usually called foreign goods.

Sea delicacies. Kelp, sea slugs, fish maw, squid, mussels, and salted fish are all major trade items.

Salt. Ten years ago it came mostly from Huizhou, but three or four years ago most of it began coming from Chaozhou. This is because merchants began using a different route. Right now most salt is again coming from Huizhou because of the blockade set up by reactionaries in Bachi and Zhongkeng against Red areas. The blockade also stops salt from arriving from Chaozhou. After arriving in Menling, most salt goes directly to Xingguo.

Kerosene. Mostly Asia Brand.

Textiles. Most textiles come from Xingning; a much smaller amount comes from Mei County. Both places purchase foreign yarn to make into cloth. The weaving industry in Xingning is well developed, and the businesses there are generally larger than those in Mei County. Foreign yarn (from foreign countries) [is also imported over this route].

A good quantity of sugar and flour is also traded.

There is no transportation service from Mei County to Menling. Most goods are carried by people. All salt is carried by horses; the only transportation service is to Chengjiang by boat. Part of the flour is also carried by horses.

Porters carry a dan of goods from Menling to Mei County and then bring back another dan of goods.

BUSINESS FROM MEI COUNTY TO
ANYUAN AND XINFENG

The goods traded are the same as those to Menling, but in lesser amounts. The ratio is about four to six. This is because Anyuan and Xinfeng comprise a small area, whereas the goods going to Menling are sold in Ruijin, Shicheng, Yudu, and Xingguo—a very large area.

PRODUCTS FROM HUIZHOU

The only major trade is in salt. Apart from a little salted fish and sugar sold to Xunwu, there is nothing else.

XUNWU'S EXPORTS

The goods listed in the sections above are imported to or pass through Xunwu. In this section exported goods are listed.

First is rice. Mei County is short of rice; so it is twice as expensive there as in Xunwu, and a lot of rice is supplied by Xunwu to Mei County every year. Rice from Chengjiang, Sanbiao, Jitan (in Xiangshan) and Xunwu City District is exported to Mei County through Niudouguang, Bachi, and Dazhe. Rice from Longtu, Yutian, Liuche, Fangtian, and the upper half of Huangxiang District is exported to Mei County via Zhongkeng. Rice from Datong, the lower half of Huangxiang District, Datian, Lantian, and Douyan, and Longchuan [County] is exported to Mei County via Cenfeng and Shizheng. The amount carried over these three routes is almost equal—about 100 dan a day or 36,000 dan a year. At a price of 8 yuan a dan, the value is 288,000 yuan.

The second is tea. Tea grows in Shangping and Xiaping in the West Ward, and Tuhe, Gangsang, and Ezihu in the South Ward. Tea is picked in March, April, May, July, and August. Twenty dan (70 jin per dan) are exported at each market, for a total of 2,000 dan at the 100 markets held each year. With a total of 140,000 jin at a price of 0.5 yuan per jin, the total value is 70,000 yuan. Eighty percent or more is exported to Xingning, and 20 percent or less is shipped to Mei County.

When tea is being picked, the traders from Xingning come to the countryside and buy freshly picked tea shoots and process the tea themselves. Among the tea shoots, the "tea before rain" (picked before 20 April,⁴ also called "first spring tea") can be sold at the price of 1 yuan for 8 jin, a jin of tea can be made from 5 jin of tea shoots. This tea before rain is expensive, with a price of 1 yuan per jin. As for the "second spring tea" (picked in March and April) and "autumn tea" (picked in July and August), 15 jin sells for 1 yuan. Tea made from these tea shoots can be sold for 0.5 yuan per jin.

In the tea trade, profits can be made from the second spring tea and autumn tea, but very little money is made from the first spring tea. Some tea can be made from the tea picked in December, which is called "snow tea." The snow tea is as expensive as the tea before rain and is also sold to the same upper-class families. Not much snow tea is [produced], and traders cannot make much money from it.

Besides the Xunwu City District, some tea is also grown in Yanyangping in Shuangqiao District, although not much is produced (just over 100 yuan each year). The quality is very good. This is because tea plants are grown in gardens instead of on hillsides.

The third is paper. Paper is made in Huangxiang and exported to Xingning (via Luofu and Luogang), Mei County (via Zhongkeng, or some via Cenfeng), and Longchuan (via Beiling). On the average 60 dan is traded at each market. With 100 markets a year, a total of 6,000 dan at 8 yuan per dan is worth 48,000 yuan.

The fourth is timber. It is produced in the West Ward (Shangping and Xiaping) and South Ward (Ezihu) of the Xunwu City District, Hejiao in Nanba District, Xiangshan and Gaotou in Huangxiang District, Xiaomukeng and Zhaitangkeng in Sanshui District, and Luofuzhang in Jiansan District. All the timber is exported to Dongjiang[5] except for that from Luofuzhang, which is exported to Chaozhou and Shantou. The timber shipped from Luofuzhang to Chaozhou and Shantou is very expensive, but that shipped to Dongjiang is very cheap. The total value is more than 10,000 yuan a year. Twenty years ago much more was produced.

As for timber exports, the traders from Longchuan make investments, assisted by the local timber merchants. They all go to the hills to check the trees and then give the money to the "mountain lord" (the money is only for the trees that they are agreed will be felled). The trader employs some workers to fell the trees, and the local merchant takes care of those trees already felled so that they will not be stolen. Most of the trees are felled in April and May, with fewer and fewer after June and none after September. The tree bark is peeled off as soon as the trees are felled; they are then laid on the ground for at least two months and dried. If, after two months, the price is good and selling is to the trader's advantage, the timber is bound together to make rafts and then transported down the river. Sometimes the timber is held for three or four years there. The position of the local merchants, relative to the lumber dealers (outside traders), is like that of workers; so they call the lumber dealers "boss," whereas the lumber dealers call them "raft chief." The profit is divided so that 90 percent goes to the boss and 10 percent to the raft chief.

The fifth is [dried] mushrooms. The most important places for production are the hilly areas in Sanbiao; places along the boundary with Anyuan like Dahudong, Xiaohudong, Zhaitangkeng, Shangba, and Xiaba; and places along the boundary between Xunwu City District and Anyuan like Shangping and Xiaping. Next is Yeziche on the boundary between Shuangqiao District and Pingyuan. The price of mushrooms is 2 yuan a jin, and an amount worth 10,000 yuan is produced each year. More mushrooms are produced in Anyuan than in Xunwu. Mushrooms from Anyuan are sold to Nanxiong, and those from Xunwu to Xingning. There are no traders to buy mushrooms. Rather, Xunwu natives buy them and sell them in other places.

The sixth is tea-oil. It is produced in Datong, Douyan, Huangtangdu, Lantian, and Datian in Shuangqiao District. The amount is about 15,000 jin a year, which, at 25 yuan per 100 jin, brings in a total of 3,750 yuan. Tea-oil is exported to Xingning and Mei counties via Luofu and Cenfeng.

Here is a list of the six products and their values (only for export):

1.	Rice	288,000 yuan
2.	Tea	70,000
3.	Paper	48,000
4.	Timber	10,000
5.	Mushrooms	10,000
6.	Tea-oil	3,750
	TOTAL	429,750 yuan

THE MAJOR MARKETS OF XUNWU

First is Jitan. Salt, rice, oil, and soybeans are the main trade items. The second is Niudouguang. Less salt and rice is traded here than in Jitan, but about the same amounts of oil and soybeans are handled here as in Jitan. The third is Liuche. The major item is textiles imported from Xingning; oil and soybeans are second. The fourth is Xunwu City. The largest trade is the oxen trade, followed by oil, salt, and rice; the third is textiles. (There used to be textiles from Ganzhou, but none were brought in after 1928. This is because those textiles, made from local thread with "one ply big, another ply thin," were replaced by textiles made in Xingning and Mei counties from foreign thread. Those textiles from Xingning and Mei counties are very good, "very smooth.") The chicken business is large, but chickens are only passing through and are not traded [in Xunwu], so do not count. The fifth market is Chengjiang. Oil, soybeans, and salt are the major goods passing through here; rice is next; there is also a large trade in opium, which comes from Xingning and Yudu. The sixth is Shipaixia, which is the general port for oil, salt, rice, soybeans; but most of these goods are only in transit. There is some trade in salt and rice. Chicken, pigs, and oxen also pass through here.

There are some small markets, such as Cenfeng (rice), Gongping (paper), Huangxiang, and Sanbiao.

XUNWU CITY

What Is Xunwu City?

A person who is completely ignorant of the inside story of the world of commerce is bound to fail in choosing proper tactics to deal with the mercantile bourgeoisie and in attempting to gain the support of the poor urban masses. It is extremely clear that gaining the support of the poor is deemed unimportant by some comrades, but the high-level organs of the leadership feel that it is important. However, even they have never been able to give comrades concrete tactics to follow and have particularly failed to indicate a concrete work method. Doesn't this phenomenon result from a lack of understanding of what a market town is?

I have resolved to understand the town problem, but I have never been able to understand it because I have never found people who could supply sufficient data. Now in Xunwu, through Comrade Gu Bo's introductions, I found two old gentlemen, Guo Youmei and Fan Daming. Many thanks to these two gentlemen for allowing me to become like a young student and to begin to understand a bit about town commerce. I was overjoyed.[6]

If my findings can pique the interest of comrades (particularly those comrades in the rural movement and those doing Red Army work) to study the town problem and encourage them to study towns in addition to studying the rural question, then this will have been a valuable experience. Our study of the town question is the same as our study of the rural question; *we must spare no effort in studying one place thoroughly* [emphasis in original]. Afterward, it will be easy to study another place and to understand general situations. If one rides a horse to view the flowers, like a certain comrade's[7] so-called "going to a place and asking questions randomly," then one cannot understand a problem profoundly even after a lifetime of effort. This study method is obviously incorrect.

Among Xunwu's many markets, because of this convenient opportunity, we can take Xunwu City's market as an example to investigate. In speaking of Xunwu City's market, one truly longs for the past to replace the present. Compared with the present level of business in Xunwu City, twice as much was done in the past. The most flourishing years were 1901 and 1902. At that time not only did people from Chengjiang and Jitan in the northern half of the county come to Xunwu City to buy things, but people from settlements in the southern half of the county like Huangxiang and Liuche and even people from Bachi in Pingyuan County [Guangdong] came to Xunwu City to buy things. This is because during the Qing products from Ganzhou passed through Xunwu on the way to eastern Guangdong. If the inhabitants of eastern Guangdong wanted to buy Ganzhou products, it goes without saying that those of Liuche and other places would. Because of this, the trade in Xunwu City, occupying a central position, naturally was quite well developed.

But since the development of the trade in foreign-style goods in Mei County and of the textile trade in Xingning, the decline of the trade in native products from Ganzhou kept people not only from eastern Guangdong and Bachi from coming to Xunwu City but also from Liuche and other places in the southern half of the county from coming to Xunwu City to buy things.

And in 1901 and 1902 it was still the so-called Age of the Degree Holders. The New Policies[8] hadn't yet been implemented, and the major trade in Xunwu City was in silk goods from Ganzhou. But from that time on things changed, the need for silk decreased, and the imperial degrees were abrogated in the first year of the Republic [1912]. The market for silk goods was virtually wiped out, and trade in Xunwu City declined greatly.

Xunwu is the kind of place where the competition between handicraft products and capitalist products expresses the drastic force of the cycle of boom and bust. How can it not be worthwhile to pay attention? Moreover, until now [i.e., before the town was occupied by the Red forces], Xunwu City had both shops and stalls that were open every day and periodic markets on the first, fourth, and seventh days [of the ten-day cycle]. Approximately, 2,700 people live either inside or just outside the stout walls of the city. The aspect of the city is quiet and deserted; only on market days does it become lively and then only for a few hours. Is not Xunwu, then, an excellent source of data?

In order to analyze living conditions and the organization of Xunwu City, we will look at all kinds of goods and services in Xunwu City.

Salt

Goods are sold mostly to people from the four wards of the city and people from Sanbiao and Shuiyuan, two bao in Sanshui District. People from other localities rarely come to Xunwu City to buy things. The only exception to this is salt. Most of the salt is sold for export to Anyuan and Xinfeng; only a small part is sold in Xunwu City District and Sanbiao. Also, because it is an item used daily, it is the number-one good traded in Xunwu City. There are five salt shops in Xunwu City. Each shop can do as much as 20,000 yuan of business or as little as 6,000 or 7,000 yuan. The five shops together can have 100,000 yuan of business in a year.

Salt is divided into Chaozhou salt and Huizhou salt. Chaozhou salt is good, but expensive. A yuan [*xiaoyang*] buys 10 to 11 jin. The color of Chaozhou salt is dark green, and since it is pure, it can prevent spoilage. The color of Huizhou salt is white, but it is less salty. Because of this, the price is relatively low; a yuan buys 16 to 17 jin. Only those who want inexpensive salt eat Huizhou salt. In the past most salt sold in Xunwu was Chaozhou salt; not much Huizhou salt was used.

Two of the shops (Huitong and Xinfachang) selling Chaozhou salt are run by natives of Xunwu; one shop is run by Han Xiangsheng, a native of Pingyuan; another is run by Zhou Yuchang, from Wan'an County [Jiangxi]; and one (Wanfengxing) is run jointly by a native of Xunwu and by someone from Taihe County [Jiangxi]. Huitong has 3,000 yuan of capital and is considered the largest. Zhou Yuchang previously had 2,000 yuan, but last year, because the paper trade was disrupted by bandits, he lost over 900 yuan of capital. Now he has only about 1,000 yuan left. These two businesses were started over twenty years ago. The number-three shop is Han Xiangsheng's, with capital of around 700 yuan; he started business some ten years ago. The number-four shop is Wanfengxing, with 200 yuan invested four years ago. Now its capital is 400 to 500 yuan. The number-five shop is Xinfachang, begun more than ten years ago. Although its owners have tried every tactic, its capital does not exceed 100 yuan.

The proprietor of the Huitong Shop is Zhong Zhourui. He is a landlord (among those who run salt businesses, he's the only landlord). His shop is inside the East Gate, and his family lives outside the South Gate. He owns rice paddies with rents of 220 dan. Every year there are two crops, and every crop yields 220 dan of grain. One crop goes for the rent; one crop is kept by the peasants. His family consists of his wife, three sons, three daughters-in-law, and one bride-in-waiting (she was purchased and is now five sui; because she does not have a husband now and must wait for the boss's wife to bear a son, she is called a bride-in-waiting, which elsewhere is referred to as a daughter-in-law raised from childhood).[9] Including himself, there are nine people in the household [lit. nine people eat there]. He does not hire any clerks, and he directs his sons and daughters-in-law himself. He was the first "capitalist" [zibenjia] in Xunwu City.

Han Xiangsheng is from Bachi in Pingyuan County. He supports three people: his wife, one child, and himself. He does not hire anyone, and every year he can make a little money.

The owner [*zhuren*] of the Xinfachang Shop is Kuang Mingkui, a Chetou man who was a civil *xiucai* during the Qing. He opened his shop more than ten years ago and does a business of several dozen yuan. In his household are his wife and one child. Because he does things fairly and justly, he has twice served as president of the chamber of commerce: once for a term of two years in the Qing and again from last year until the present. He is 60-odd sui and is a white-haired old man.

General Goods

There are sixteen or seventeen general stores, of which ten or so are large. The names of the thirteen largest stores and the places of origin of their owners are

Name of business	Origin of owner
Zhicheng	Xingning
Luntaixing	Ji'an
Yitaixing	Ji'an and Xunwu
Yicheng	Xingning
Pan Yueli	Xingning
Wang Runxiang	Xingning
Pan Dengji	Xingning
Xiangxing	Xingning
Yongyuanjin	Xingning
Junyi	Began by a porter from Xunwu
Luo Jinfeng	Xunwu (with 300 dan of rents, the only landlord among these owners)
Fan Shunchang	Fujian
Huang Yufeng	Fujian

Among them, the Huang Yufeng Shop's business is mainly tobacco and paper. The most important trade for the others is in textiles, followed by foreign goods. Foreign goods of all kinds are sold in small markets. Here is a brief list of 131 items sold:

tooth powder*
rubber overshoes*
rubber boots*
slippers
pens (fountain pens)
ink sticks
inkstones
brush covers
brush racks
exercise books
plain paper
textbooks (there is no
    separate bookstore;
    books are sold in the
    general goods stores)
toilet water
woolen towels*
foreign enamel wash basins
foreign enamel bowls (with a
    handle)*
gloves
mufflers*
cosmetics
flashlights*
imported matches*
cigarettes (there are many
    brands: Jinzi, Zhongguo,
    Sanpaotai, Hademen, Shan-
    mei, etc., with Jinzi and
    Zhongguo more popular)
visored caps
cotton blankets
woolen hats (for children)
kapok pillows
Zhongshan buttons
black bone buttons
snaps
suspenders

toothbrushes*
leather shoes*
sport shoes*
pencils
chalk
writing brushes
ink boxes (for Chinese
    calligraphy)
paste
red paste for seals
printing ink
calligraphy and paintings
small towels
soap*
perfumed soda
perfumed toilet water[10]
foreign socks*
foreign enamel bowls
hair oil
hair cream
rouge
big or small combs
vanishing cream
batteries*
Magu cigarettes
cigarette holders
foreign umbrellas
straw hats
formal hats
imported enamel cups
imported felt
woolen blankets
nightcaps
leather pillows[11]
white bone buttons
conch buttons
rubber bands
silk belts

imported belts
undershirts
clocks
alarm clocks
envelopes*
mirrors
foreign knives
German razors
safety razors
shears
hair scissors (this and
    the three preceding
    items are for hair-
    cutting)
copper locks
iron locks
copper net hooks
kerosene*
rush-wick lamps*
enamel table lamps
foreign lamps
six-cornered lamps
round flints
flat flint steel (this and
    the preceding item are
    for lighting lanterns)
pipes
copper pots (for tea)
iron trays
tiles
dominoes
jujubes
various canned foods (beef,
    mixed vegetables, duck,
    winter bamboo shoots,
    loquats, sand pears, *lizhi*,
    longyan, pineapple, milk)
galvanized wire

talcum
fans (black and white paper)
watches
letter paper*
diaries
eyeglasses
toys (small guns, trains,
    roly-polies, dolls, small
    rubber balls, whistles, etc.)
leather suitcases
rattan suitcases
indigo* (blue)
dyestuff (red, black, gray,
    pinkish red)*
foreign copper locks
foreign iron locks
bone net hooks
storm lanterns*
covered lamps
lamps with lotus lids
square lamps
ink
bone chopsticks
lacquer chopsticks
abacuses
water pipes
nails*
iron pans
iron spoons
various pieces of china*
mahjongg tiles
dried *longyan*
couplets
foreign candles
white foreign wax
raisins
foreign thread
iron wire

These 131 products are all called "foreign goods" and are sold at general stores. The 23 asterisked items are sold the most; the items not asterisked are sold in lesser quantities.

One hundred eight of the 131 items come from Mei and Xingning counties. Most of the goods are from Mei County; only Western-style socks, mufflers, and other woven goods come mainly from Xingning. Tiles and couplets come from Ganzhou. Leather pillows, letter paper, envelopes, copper bowls, kerosene, fans, water pipes, and writing brushes— these eight items come from both Mei County and Ganzhou. Most leather pillows, letter paper, envelopes, enamelware, fans, and water pipes come from Ganzhou and are of the highest quality. The stationery from Ganzhou is made of paper manufactured in China; that from Mei County is made with foreign paper. Kerosene and cigarettes come mostly from Guangdong; smaller amounts come from Ganzhou. Cigarettes come from Mei County, Xingning, and Ganzhou. Writing brushes come mostly from Ganzhou; only a few come from Mei County.

The foreign goods of secondary importance are as described above; below I discuss the most important item traded in the general stores—textiles.

The textiles include native cotton cloth (blue, white, printed, gray, red, green, and striped cotton); glazed [i.e., shiny, smooth] cotton cloth (blue, white, gray, black, red, glazed, green, and printed); fine cotton (white, gray, black, blue, striped, and indigo blue); silk goods (all kinds of silk with patterns, all kinds of satin, brown-colored raw silk, and gambiered [i.e., dyed yellow] Guangdong gauze); woolen cloth (thick woolen cloth, rough woolen cloth, fine glazed woolen cloth); Chinese linen (white, blue, black, off-white, light green).

Native cotton cloth is made from foreign yarn by Chinese. It is shipped from Xingning. Glazed cotton cloth and fine cotton are called foreign cloth and are shipped from Hong Kong via Mei County. As for the silk goods, patterned silks and brown-colored raw silk come from Hangzhou via Ganzhou and Mei County. Xunwu women use it to make bonnets. Every woman wears this type of bonnet. The textile business is worth some 100,000 yuan annually in Xunwu City. The marketing area is Xunwu City District and Sanbiao District.

General stores, in addition to the two main categories of textiles and foreign goods, also sell tobacco, pastries, incense and candles [for ancestor worship], and also a bit of [cooking] oil and salt.

In the Qing the general goods business within Xunwu City was worth around 150,000 yuan annually; now it is around 120,000 yuan. The 120,000 yuan is divided among:

textiles	80,000-odd yuan (native cloth: 70,000 yuan; foreign cloth: 10,000 yuan, of which, woolens, 2,000 yuan, Chinese linen, 1,000-odd yuan)
foreign goods	20,000 yuan (each business sells at most 1,100–1,200 yuan; at the least 200–300 yuan)
tobacco	about 10,000 yuan
pastries	about 400 yuan (only two businesses sell pastries on the side)
incense, spirit money, firecrackers	about 500 yuan (two businesses sell incense and spirit money on the side; thirteen businesses sell firecrackers)

In order to understand general stores better, let us look at the concrete details of a few.

The shopkeeper [*dianzhu*] of the largest general store is a Xingning native, Chen Zhicheng, who owns a shop in Xunwu City, in Jitan, and in Chengjiang. The shop in Xunwu City has capital of 3,000 yuan. He himself had only about 1,000 yuan. He borrowed the rest. The annual interest each year on 3,000 yuan is 900 yuan. Apart from paying wages, food, and fuel costs, he uses his profits for interest payments. Chen also likes to use his money for whoring and gambling.

The second largest business is Luntaixing, whose capital, comprising three shares, is 2,000 yuan. After expenses, it makes profits of 300 to 400 yuan every year.

The third largest business is Yitaixing, whose capital, comprising three shares, is more than 1,000 yuan.[12] Every year it makes a profit of 100 to 200 yuan.

The fourth largest business, Luo Yicheng, is owned by one person with over 1,000 yuan of capital. Every year he can make 400 to 500 yuan. He's very economical: vegetables for food; native cloth for clothing. There are two apprentices. His family is still in Xingning. He is a Xingning person who, when he first came to Xunwu, peddled sweets from baskets he carried in Xunwu City and the four wards. For one copper cash[13] he'd break off a piece of candy. (Now a piece of candy costs one copper cent.)[14] Sometimes he exchanged candy for every type of salvage goods (hair, scrap copper, scrap iron, pig and ox bones, scraps of padded cloth). He is the kind of person who started from scratch. He came to Xunwu more than thirty years ago, made good, and opened a general store more than fifteen years ago.

Guo Yihe is the general store with the least capital, about 100 yuan. It sells tobacco, safety matches, eggs, red rope (red cord), silk thread, strips of embroidery (used on shoe quarters), writing brushes and ink, towels, towels made with foreign yarn, bone buttons, and other items. The store shopkeeper is Guo Youmei (he is participating in our investigation meetings), and he and his wife have clothing, food, and tax expenses each year of over 100 yuan. His business is barely sufficient for those expenses. He is a Wan'an native who came to Xunwu when he was twelve sui; he is now 59 sui. Before he came, his uncle had traded in Xunwu for sixty years. Together these two have been in business in Xunwu for 100 years. The store has always dealt in textiles.

Business was best in 1899 and 1900; they had capital of 3,000 yuan and from elsewhere they received on consignment [*jiao*] (when merchants borrow goods and then sell them, it's called *jiao*) goods worth 5,000 to 6,000 yuan. He himself consigned to other people goods worth 4,000 to 5,000 yuan. So at that time, although he only had 3,000 yuan of capital, he could do around 20,000 yuan of business. This was the number-one store in Xunwu City. Now one can go to Liuche, Bachi, Niudouguang, and Chetou to buy things, but at that time the merchants from shops in those places all came to Xunwu City to buy things. The most important source of goods was Ganzhou (textiles, silk goods, paper, writing brushes and ink, straw hats, and straw mats from Suzhou); there was also trade with Ji'an (purple cloth and silk thread). At that time one could go to Ganzhou and buy 300 yuan of goods with only 100 yuan of cash and take them away. Now this is impossible. This kind of impossibility is not limited to the Guo Yihe Shop. Almost no shops consign goods. No goods are being consigned in Ganzhou or in Mei County and Xingning. This is a great change in the economy. Just recently (1928), the "world went out of kilter."

As for goods consigned by merchants to peasants, the peasants are exploited by heavy rents and interest. Originally the peasants' lot was hard, but the year before last locusts ate the grain and there was also a drought. Peasants could not pay the bills held by Xunwu City merchants. Because of this, Xunwu City's merchants cannot pay the bills of merchants in Mei County and Xingning. Mei County and Xingning merchants are nervous about consigning goods to people.

In 1916 the Guo Yihe Shop suffered a great attack (the Guangfu faction led more than a thousand peasants to Xunwu City and attacked many other stores). After government troops recovered the city, they launched a great attack upon Guo Yihe and plundered more than 6,900 yuan worth of things.[15] From that year until now, one year has been worse than the last, until things have reached the present state. Guo [Youmei] served two terms as president of the chamber of commerce: from 1925 to 1927.

Here I want to talk about the system of employees in general stores and look at the origins of their class connections, which are so obscure.

To become a master [*chushi*] after being an apprentice for three years in a general store, according to established practice one must help the boss for a year. At the beginning of the year, the person takes the old clothes worn during his apprenticeship that he no longer wants and exchanges all of them for new ones, because now he has some money. Moreover, his status is not the same. After helping for a year, if he is capable, the boss continues with him in place. If he is not capable, the boss dismisses him. The boss says to him: "Our store doesn't need so many people; next year you must find other work." But he can turn around and go to a new shop, where his status becomes a bit higher and the clothes he wears become a bit better, and his salary (not called wages) is increased each year. In society he is not referred to as an "apprentice" any more. Rather, people respect him as a "gentleman" [*xiansheng*].[16] During the year that he is helping, the boss does not give him a fixed salary. Also, he does not have a "salary" label. But the boss gives him every kind of winter and summer clothing. If he returns home to get married, the boss, besides sending more than 10 yuan of travel expenses (if his home is far away), must also send him more than 10 yuan of gifts like fruit and sea delicacies, so that when he returns home he can give a fine banquet. If he is going home not to get married but only to see his father and mother and if his home is far away, then he is given some "traveling expenses." The least amount of traveling expenses is 10-odd yuan, although the amount can reach 24 or 25 yuan. If he is someone from close by, without a doubt, he is sent 10-odd to 20-odd yuan.

After helping for a year, he formally has a salary. The lead year he gets 40 to 50 yuan; the second year more than 50 to 60 yuan. If he does well and the shop makes money, his salary increases each year. During the Guangxu period [1875–1908] when business was good, the highest "gentleman's" salary was 120 yuan, but now because business is bad, the highest salary does not exceed 80 yuan. If a gentleman is loyal, dependable, smart, and capable, the boss may turn the business over to him completely and, in some cases, return home to live. When the profit is divided, a bonus is given to the gentlemen. In most cases it is ³⁄₁₀'s of the profit; in a few cases ²⁄₁₀'s; and in a very few cases ¹⁄₁₀. When the boss of the Guo Yihe Shop, Guo Youmei, returned home to Wan'an to live, for example, he gave the business to a dependable and esteemed gentleman. There are undependable gentlemen to whom a business cannot be turned over, because of their whoring, gambling, and cheating.[17]

Oil

The third largest business in Xunwu City is the oil trade. The oil comes from Menling and Anyuan and is sold in Xunwu City District and Huangxiang and a bit in Sanbiao. The only broker for oil is Liu Fuxing, whose capital consists of 100 silver dollars [dayang]. He paid a license fee for the oil monopoly. As an agent for buying or selling oil, he receives 0.2 yuan for each dan of oil traded. Business is greatest in November and December, when a large market (first day in the market cycle) has a trade of 100 dan; so in two months 600 dan are traded. In the small markets (fourth and seventh days) maybe 30, 40, or 50 dan are traded; so in two months 400 dan are traded. From January to October the trade in each market does not exceed 3-odd dan, so altogether the trade does not exceed 300 dan. The total for the whole year is 1,300 dan; so the brokerage fees are 260 yuan. Everyone has to buy oil from him since his license grants him a monopoly. This license is granted by the provincial government in Nanchang after the county government sends a document stating the license was paid. Then and only then is one issued. Besides the $100 fee for a license, one must also pay a $5 administrative fee. A license is good for eight years, after which it expires and a new one must be obtained. Licenses are not limited to oil brokers [hang]; they are also required for salt brokers, [soy]bean brokers, and livestock brokers.[18]

[Soy]beans

There is also only one broker. In the public area of the City God Temple, beans are bought and sold. He Zizhen, a leader of the reactionaries in Xunwu who was head of the Public Security Bureau and who recently become head of the police, bought a license in 1927 and opened a soybean business. Business is greatest in November and December, when there is a trade of 800 dan. One thousand dan of business is done a year. The broker's fee is 2 sheng per dan (1 dan = 5 dou; 1 dou = 10 sheng). The price of every dan of beans is 7.5 yuan (every sheng is 1.5 mao). This figures out to 4 percent; so every year one can make 300 yuan.

He Zizhen is a native of Xunwu City and lives outside the East Gate. He had a deprived childhood but graduated from a middle school in Pingyuan and studied two years at a Henan mining school. He returned to Xunwu and became a schoolteacher for eight or nine years; both Gu Bo and Pan Li were his students. Around the time of the KMT's purge of 1927, the Cooperative Society faction led by Gu and Pan clashed with the New Xunwu faction led by He Zizhen. There was a clash in April 1927. He Zizhen fled Xunwu during the 25 March uprising in 1928, but by April he had regained his power. Afterwards he also became head of the Public Security Bureau and police chief.

He gradually became wealthy and bought land near Xunwu City. Before 1925 and before he was struggling with the Cooperative Society faction, he represented the power of merchant capital. He organized the Society of Fellow Students Studying in Guangdong and began the Commoners Charitable School in 1921. In June 1925, when the Cooperative Society faction held a big meeting in Xunwu City and showed an increase in its revolutionary strength, he cooperated with feudal bullies and gentry and attained a leading position among the feudal faction. He Zizhen became the worst reactionary leader. This time when the Red Army came to Xunwu, he led the retreat of the Pacification and Defense Militia [*jingwei tuan*] to Xiangshan.[19]

Butchers

There are only three butcher businesses, which are set up along the side of the street; there are no butcher shops. The three are Liu Ener, Chen Laoer, and Liu Shiwei. Liu Ener once had 100 yuan of capital, but now he has nothing. Chen Laoer and Liu Shiwei have no capital at all because no money is needed to buy pork [for butchering]. They take the pig on credit, butcher it, and sell the pork. Then they pay the [pig's owner]. On the average one can butcher two pigs a day. If a pig weighs 100 jin, then every year the total weight of the slaughtered pigs is 72,000 jin. At present, a pig can be bought for 0.25 yuan per jin, and pork can be sold for 0.28 yuan per jin. So there is a profit of 0.03 yuan per jin. So every year one can make 2,160 yuan. This is not a bad trade. But one must pay a large slaughter tax. In the past these three men paid 100 yuan of taxes a month or 1,200 yuan a year. Recently, because business has been relatively bad, only 1,000 yuan has been paid; so each man pays a bit more than 300 yuan. Because the three men must collect the slaughter tax, no one apart from these three can sell pork or slaughter pigs, except for personal use. After the Red Army entered Xunwu City, the number of butchers increased to seven or eight, and the activity around the market increased markedly. Because no tax was collected, you earned what you got. All the butchers liked this. Before the Red Army came, the price of pork was 0.32 yuan but now it is 0.28 yuan per jin.

Wine

Chen Guihe, Gao Yuanli, Yuan Lizhan, Zhou Yuchang, Liu Shuangsheng, Ling Wensheng, Peng Tongfu—these are the seven largest wine businesses. Fan Guangchang, Kuang Hongsheng, and Luo Deli are the smaller businesses. The four largest businesses, with capital not exceeding 100 yuan, are those of Zhou Yuchang (Ji'an native), Gao Yuanli (Ji'an native), Liu Shuangsheng (Xunwu native), and Chen Guihe. Ling Wensheng (Xunwu native), Yuan Lizhan (Ji'an native), and Peng Tongfu are businesses whose capital does not exceed 40 or 50 yuan. These seven businesses all sell sweet wine made of polished glutinous rice, which is called *shuijiu*. It is also called yellow wine because of its color. Because it has a mellow taste, does not harm people, and is relatively inexpensive, peasants and the poor people in Xunwu City like to drink it. It is divided into double [*shuang*] wine and single [*dan*] wine (these terms are used only in Xunwu City; in the countryside, instead of *shuang[jiu]* or *dan[jiu]*, they say "good" or "weak"). Since fermented glutinous rice wine has more fermenting agent, it has a higher proof.

Wine is sold by the bottle, not the jin. Double wine [sells] for 18 coppers a bottle; it is the best of the yellow wine. When common people invite someone to dinner, they drink it, but they also use it for their own meals. Drunkards have to have a little at every meal, but if they have some wine, they do not even care about eating. Single wine, which is 10 coppers a bottle, is bought by poor people when they are thirsty; they drink it like tea [i.e., in great amounts]. The business in double wine is greater than that in single wine.

Fan Guangchang, Kuang Hongsheng, and Luo Deli are all run by natives of Xunwu City. Their capital does not exceed 10 yuan. They all sell white wine. Zhou Yuchang also sells white wine. This kind of wine is made with sticky rice. It is stronger than yellow wine. It is not sold by the bottle, but by the cup; each cup costs two coppers. A jin sells for 0.16 yuan. Yellow wine outsells white wine nine to one. Whether speaking of white wine or yellow wine, both are part of the wine business. But the purpose of these businesses is not just to sell wine. The mash that is left after making wine is fed to pigs; this is an even more important purpose. If there is too much for your own pigs, you sell the leftovers. It takes two coppers to buy one small bowl of wine.

During the best season for yellow wine shops (March through August is the thirsty season), every shop can sell 5 yuan of wine a day. In the off-season (September to February), a wine shop can take in 2 yuan. Yellow wine shops can make 1,020 yuan a year. The seven shops together do a business of over 7,000 yuan. In the hot half of the year white wine shops can take in a yuan a day, and in the cold half of the year they can take in 0.5 yuan a day. So every business makes 270 yuan a year. Together the four businesses make around 1,000 yuan.

A wine tax must be paid. Depending on whether business is good or bad, the large wine shops can pay about 0.4 yuan a month; the small wineshops about 0.2 yuan a month. There are also ones that pay 0.15 yuan.

Marine Products

The items in the marine products stores are plentiful. "Delicacies from the hills and seas" is their slogan. The gains and losses of the marine product merchants are quite interesting. First I illustrate the categories of items sold and then observe the merchants' gains and losses.

Salted fish. The most sales [lit. the first category]. These include mandarin fish, mackerel, sea horses, perch, skinned fish, rockfish, golden carp, sturgeon, spotted butterfish, carp, big-eyed sea bream, salamander (big body, small tail), flounder (also called *bingbeiluoshishi*, it has eyes only on one side; thus it needs to collaborate with another fish when seeking food. For this reason, occasions when people rely on one another are usually called *bingbeiluoshishi*; so this kind of fish has become a metaphor), spiny dogfish (it has two horns on its head). These salted fish all come from Chaozhou and Shantou.

Seaweed. Second in sales. It includes green seaweed and kelp. Green seaweed, also called Jiangxi seaweed, is of the highest quality and comes from Ganzhou. Compared with green seaweed, less kelp is sold, its quality is lower [lit. next], and its price is cheaper. It comes from Mei County and over a thousand jin are sold each year. The price is 0.2 yuan per jin.

Sugar. Also carried at the marine products store; third in sales. It is divided into white sugars, brown sugars, rock candy,[20] and slabs of sugar-preserved kumquats. The white sugars include snow powder, nice-looking but not sweet, which comes from Mei County; rough white sugar, very sweet, from Huizhou; and white-rice sugar,[21] a medium-quality sugar that comes from Huizhou. These three kinds are all imported sugars; one jin sells for 0.17–0.18 yuan.

The brown sugars are taro sugar, which is ball shaped and comes from Mei County; loaf sugar, which is sold by the block, is the best, and comes from Huizhou; loose-sand sugar, which is mixed with sand, is the worst, and comes from Huizhou. In the past, brown sugar was cheaper than white sugar; now brown sugar is expensive and white sugar is cheap. Previously brown sugar was not more than 0.16 yuan per jin; now the price has risen to 0.23–0.24 yuan per jin. The old price for white sugar was 0.26–0.27 yuan per jin, and now it is only 0.17–0.18 yuan per jin. Brown sugar is native sugar, and white sugar is imported sugar. The annual sale in Xunwu City of white sugar is over 1,000 jin, and of brown sugar (available only during the winter season) 6,000–7,000 jin. Since brown sugar is sweeter [than white sugar], it sells better. Rock candy [for cooking] comes from Mei County, and annual sales amount to only several dozen jin, at about 2 mao and a few fen per jin. Sugar-preserved kumquats in slab form come from Mei County. There are annual sales of over 20 or 30 jin at 0.3 yuan per jin.

Of the above sugars, loaf sugar sells the best. This is because it is an important ingredient in rice cakes. At New Year's, it does not matter whether a family lives in town or the countryside or whether it is poor or rich, every family makes rice cakes.[22]

Bean flour. Fourth in sales. Most of it comes from Yunmenling; some comes from other counties. It is made from sweet potatoes and sold in powdered form, not yet made into noodles. It is an ingredient for meat balls and the like. Annual sales are a few thousand jin at about 0.15–0.16 yuan per jin.

Pigskin. Fifth in sales. It is used in ordinary meals as false fish maw. It comes from Mei County. Annual sales are over a thousand jin, 0.1 yuan for 3 liang, 0.55 yuan per jin.

Fujian[23] *bamboo shoots.* These come from Mei County and Anyuan; "Fujian bamboo shoots" is just a name. Sixth in sales. They are used not only at banquets, but also at ordinary meals as well, especially during the harvest and field-weeding periods. There are some bamboo plantings in Xunwu itself. In March and April, peasants go to Mei County and sell it. In July and August Xunwu people want to have some, but there isn't enough; so they buy some from Mei County. Annual sales are 500–600 jin, one jin sells for 0.23–0.24 yuan.

Squid. It is used at banquets and at ordinary meals. Seventh in sales. It comes from Mei County. The annual sales are around 300–500 jin. One jin costs 0.7–0.8 yuan.

Fermented soybeans. Annual sales of about 3,000 jin at one jin for 0.14 yuan. The inhabitants of Xunwu can also make this and use it to make soy sauce, but the locally produced product is not sold commercially. It is a very common food, almost every household eats it. Add some oil and then steam it. One bowl of it can be served for several meals; so for frugal people this is very economical.

Mianhui. That is, flour. Coming from Mei County, much of it is foreign-style flour. Buns, Chinese ravioli, noodles, and cakes are all made with it. Cakes are most popular. Egg cakes, cookies, *pang* cake (*pang* means hollow in the center), five-seed cake,[24] and lard cake are all made of flour. At 0.2 yuan per jin, annual sales are about 100 packages.

Foreign wax. It comes in white chunks. One jin costs 0.25–0.26 yuan. There are annual sales of 500 jin or so.

Yufen. This is also called *xifen*; it is made from sweet potatoes. It is different from bean powder because it comes in the form of noodles. It comes from Mei County. All the common people eat it. At 0.1 yuan for about half a jin, there are annual sales of about 600–700 jin.

The above eleven items are used the most; the following are less commonly used.

Top Quality [lit. unsurpassed in the market]. This type of squid is the best and is only served when guests are invited. It comes from Mei County. It is not used much; each year squid worth 200–300 yuan is sold. The common squid is called "foreign[-style] squid."

Preserved vegetables. This is a turnip and is similar to a radish. This preserved vegetable comes from Xinfeng. There are annual sales of 200–300 jin. It is sold only after the Dragon Boat festival,[25] but after August no more is shipped in. One jin costs 0.2 yuan; it is a little more expensive than *xifen*.

Shark fin. One liang costs 0.4 yuan; it is rarely used. Annual sales amount to only 10–20 jin.

Sea cucumbers. With annual sales of 200–300 jin, business is greater than for shark fin. One jin costs 2.8–2.9 yuan.

Fish maw. Annual sales are 200–300 jin, and the price is about the same as for sea cucumbers. Normally, if a meal has sea cucumbers, you would certainly serve fish maw instead of the false fish maw made from pigskin.

Cuttlefish. There are annual sales of only 40–50 jin. One jin costs 0.7–0.8 yuan, about the same as squid.

Scallops. Annual sales are about 20 jin, one jin sells for 1.2 or 1.3 yuan.

Dried gongyu [lit. tribute fish]. Annual sales of about 8–10 jin. Each jin costs 0.2 yuan. About 70–80 jin used to be sold.

Big shrimp. Annual sales are 70–80 jin. One jin sells for 0.6 yuan. "Big shrimp" are not really shrimp that are big. They are also called "dried shrimp" and are smaller than Chaozhou shrimp, which can weigh as much as 4 liang apiece.

Pressed shrimp [lit. shrimp shells]. Tiny shrimp pressed as flat as shrimp shells are called shrimp shells. Annual sales are over 100 jin. During New Year's and [other] festivals, every household makes [Hakka-style] stuffed bean curd.[26] This involves making a hole in [the middle of] a piece of bean curd, inserting ground pork, fish roe, and dried mushrooms mixed with the pressed shrimp or adding garlic and leeks. All these are diced and stuffed [into the bean curd]. One jin of pressed shrimp costs over 0.1 yuan.

Jellyfish. One jin goes for 0.3 yuan, and annual sales aren't much—20–30 jin.

Dried mussels. The big ones are called *haoshi* [dried oyster]. They are also called *xili*. Annual sales of dried mussels are 40–50 jin, and one jin costs a bit over 0.3 yuan. No dried mussels are sold in Xunwu City.

Tianqingpu [lit. reddish-black ray]. This is a kind of marine fish, and big ones are as big as a fan. They are rarely sold in Xunwu City.

These products, from Top Quality to *tianqingpu*, are marine products that come from the Chaozhou-Shantou region.

Day lily. Also called golden needles. Two mao per jin; annual sales of 40–50 jin.

Cloud ears.[27] Annual sales of 50 jin; a jin costs 1 yuan. During the Guangxu period, these cost no more than 0.5 yuan a jin. They have since doubled in price. They come from Mei County.

Dried mushrooms. Annual sales of 100 jin. Winter mushrooms are better and cost 2 yuan per jin. Spring mushrooms are not as good, with one jin going for 1.2–1.3 yuan. They are local products.

Shredded preserved cabbage [lit. winter vegetables]. This canned food is made with cabbage. It used to come from Tianjin, but recently it has also been made in Mei County. There are annual sales of over 100 jars at 0.4 yuan a jar.

Dried bean curd roll [lit. curd bamboo]. This is made of thin sheets of bean curd rolled into tubes. One jin costs 2 mao and several fen; annual sales are 40–50 jin. It comes from Xingning.

Doufumei [lit. bean curd mold]. This is fermented bean curd that comes from Mei County. It is made from three items: soy-bean milk, taro, and flour. It is not made the way the dried bean curd used by the common people is made.

Pepper. For white pepper, annual sales are 10 jin at 1.2 yuan per jin. In the Guangxu period the price was under 0.4 yuan. Now the price has tripled. Annual sales of black pepper are 20–30 jin, and one jin costs 0.5–0.6 yuan. It used to be not more than 2 mao and a few fen per jin during the Guangxu period. All pepper comes from abroad.

Dried Chinese olives. Dried Chinese olives are made by boil-ing fresh olives, taking the seeds out, and then curing them. In Xunwu these are called *lanjiao*, and in Mei County they are called *lanshi*. Annual sales are ten-odd jin at 2 mao and a few fen per jin.

Soy sauce. Produced locally and in Menling. This is how to make soy sauce. First steam the soybeans and then dry them halfway, spread them flat and wait until they ferment, and then boil them again. Add some spices and salt to the boiling liquid, and soy sauce is the result. After boiling, the soybeans become fermented soybeans [*doushi*]. However, the quality of this type of fermented soybeans is not good. Good fermented soybeans are made by boiling down the soy sauce. Fermented soybeans and soy sauce sell well in March, June, and Septem-ber. Monthly sales for fermented soybeans are 200–300 jin; an-nual sales are over 3,000 jin, one jin sells for 0.14 yuan. Annual sales of soy sauce are over 300 jin, one jin goes for 0.15 yuan.

Persimmons. Annual sales are about 100 yuan; a small one costs three coppers, two large ones cost a mao.

Red and black dates. Annual sales for both are 100 jin or so. Black dates cost 0.4 yuan per jin, red dates 0.2 yuan per jin.

Longyan. Annual sales of 10–20 jin. One jin of those with a skin costs a little over 0.3 yuan. Peeled ones are called *yuanrou*, cost 1 yuan per jin, and are available only in herb stores.

Lizhi [lichees]. This fruit is rarely sold. The price is about the same as that of longyan.

Dried star fruit. Annual sales are some 10 jin, one jin sells for 0.4 yuan.

These products, from persimmon to dried star fruit, all come from Mei County.

Melon seeds. Melon seeds come from both Xinfeng and Menling. One jin costs a little less than 0.3 yuan. Annual sales are 200–300 jin.

All 39 products listed above are part of the trade of marine products shops. In addition, marine products shops also supplement sales with kerosene and tea-oil. The general outline of marine products shops in good times and bad is related below.

The stores with the most business are Shunchang Laodian, Shunchang Xingji, Lu Quanli, Tang Yaojie, Rong Chunxiang, Luo Jieci, and Zhang Junyi. In addition, there are a number of small stalls that sell marine products. Among these stores, Shunchang Laodian and Zhang Junyi are both general stores and marine products stores.

Shunchang Xingji is a branch of Shunchang Laodian; it has the best marine products business. It has capital of 1,000 yuan and consigns 200 to 300 yuan [of goods] to Mei County each year. The store proprietor, Fan Zuxian, is a native of Xunwu City and supports over twenty people in his family. Business profits are barely sufficient for living expenses and consignment fees.

Lu Quanli is the proprietor of the second largest marine products shop. He is a Mei County native, and his store has capital of 1,000–2,000 yuan. Besides marine products, he sells tong oil, tea leaves, mushrooms, and tea-oil of various kinds and ships wholesale to Xingning and Mei County. His marine products business is not as good as that of Xingji, but Xingji does not engage in the side trades he does. He also consigns goods to Mei County. Because he is a native of Mei County, his business is very good. He has no problem doing about 1,000 yuan of business. His supports a wife and hires two men (annual salary of 60 yuan each). After expenses, he has at least

200 or 300 yuan of profits annually. In years with a good business climate, he has profits of about 1,000 yuan.

Tang Yaojie, a native of Jiaoling, has capital of 2,000 yuan. He has no hired employees. He covers consignment fees and living expenses but makes no profits. Many years ago [when there were] brokers for oil and salt, he made a lot of money; but two years ago he started losing money, so he changed to marine products.

Rong Chunxiang, a native of Xunwu County, has capital of 700 to 800 yuan. His family has several dozen dan of paddy land. He supports seven or eight people. He has no employees. As for his expenses, he uses his business profits to pay for them. The grain from the family's land outside Xunwu City is saved up. Among the marine products businesses, his was the best. After the soviet was established, one part of his land was confiscated. Needless to say, he seethed with anger. His childhood was difficult; he helped a local bully with his accounts and made some money and got a start.

The proprietor of the Shunchang Laodian is Fan Xingfu, a Xunwu City native; he has 300 to 400 yuan of capital. He has more than ten family members and hires one gentleman at an annual salary of 50 to 60 yuan. His marine products business makes just enough to supply [his family's] needs. His grandfather Fan Yuanfu was a large landlord with three children and an extended family of 140-odd people. He received 800 dan of rent a year. Later their wealth declined as their land was dispersed, and Fan Xingfu's family had land with rents of only 30 to 40 dan. Under the soviet's division of land, his family was eligible to receive a bit of land. But his brother Fan Laoba still received over 100 dan of rent; so this year during the land redistribution most of his land was distributed. Fan Laoba does not engage in business. The Shunchang Xingji was started by his cousin. He had 40 to 50 dan of paddy land and over twenty family members. When the soviet divided the land, they received some land. From the final years of the Qing through the

early years of the Republic, his family and his brothers together had seven stores—Laodian, Xingji, Daji, Maoji, Junji,
Hongchang, Lufeng—which dealt in silk, textiles, general
goods, and marine products. Their businesses were known far
and wide. They could consign to Ganzhou 4,000 to 5,000 yuan
[of goods]. That is about what the Guo Yihe Shop could do
back then. In 1922 business gradually fell off, and in 1925 they
had only two businesses: Laodian and Xingji. The most
important reason was the changing market—foreign [and
foreign-style] goods replaced native goods. When Mei County
business replaced Ganzhou business, the southern half of
Xunwu no longer required native goods supplied from Ganzhou. The Guo Yihe Shop declined for the same reasons.

Another reason has to do with the large number of children
born and raised in feudal families (large landlord and nascent
mercantile capitalist families). Much whoring, gambling,
feasting, and wearing of fine clothes—their ostentatious behavior impoverished their families. Before 1921, the primary
school in Xunwu City (some landlords raised shares to build
it; 5 yuan for one share) was a famous "diploma mill." The
children of landlords throughout the county, ostentatious but
without prospects, spent money to go to this "mill" for three
years, obtained a diploma, and then put on airs. They used the
words "graduate of Xunwu City East Primary School" on their
namecards, returned home, and swindled their ancestors.
Why do we say they swindled their ancestors? First, just after
they graduated, their ancestral halls, in accordance with precedent, awarded the graduates some money. This is called
"grabbing the bonus." Second, every year, along with *xiucai*
and *juren*, they receive an equal part of the educational allowance [lit. study grain]. Third, every year after the ancestral sacrifices are completed, they, along with the degree holders, receive a part of the sacrificial meat. The Fan family has 60 or 70
young scions who had entered that diploma mill. In addition
to grabbing the bonus and obtaining grain, after they gradu-

ated, they got 100 jin of meat from their ancestral trusts [*gong-tang*],[28] large and small, during the division of meat each year.

Luo Jieci, a native of Xunwu City, has 200 to 300 yuan of capital. He supports four people [including himself], has no employees, makes wine, and sells marine products. After expenses, he makes a profit of 100 to 200 yuan. His is a fine business. He liked to whore in the past, but now he has stopped on account of his wife (her brideprice was 500 yuan). He is honest and hardworking. He uses mash [from wine making] to feed pigs. So things have gotten better year by year, and the family now has more than 10 dan of paddy land.

Zhang Junyi trades in both marine products and general goods and has 200 yuan of capital; the rest is borrowed. He does not hire anyone, but his children are in the trade. Every year he makes some profit. He is a native of Xunwu County. Five or six years ago, he was a porter and helped Xunwu City merchants ship grain and mushrooms to Mei County. From Mei County he shipped back cloth and salted fish to Xunwu. He shipped things himself, and at the same time he was a head porter, a job that allows one to make a profit. Xunwu County merchants gave him money to go buy things. Xunwu City merchants and Mei County merchants tipped him money, and from this he became rich.

As for the marine products business carried on from stalls, no business exceeds several dozen yuan of capital, or at most 100 yuan. These [peddlers'] goods come from Xunwu City's large marine products stores and from petty traders [*xiaofan*]. [People in] this kind of stall trade often can get rich if they work hard. Xunwu City has many shops that began as stalls. Pan Dengji, He Xiangsheng, Luo Yisheng, Liu Hengtai, and Fan Laosi had a business but no shop. On the first, fourth, and seventh days [of the ten-day market cycle, peddlers] take goods on a pole to the market in Xunwu City; on the third, sixth, and ninth days, they take goods on a pole to the market in Jitan. [In this way] they can make some money.

Herbs

The seven herb stores in Xunwu City are Baihetang, Yang Qingren, Xin Desheng, Tian Renhe, Wang Putai, Huang Yuxing, and Fuchuntang.

Baihetang is the number-one store. The proprietor, a certain Chi, is a native of Chaozhou. But originally he was a native of Huangxiang named Liu. When he was young, his family was very poor; so his father and mother sold him to the Chi family, herb merchants from Chaozhou. Later he came to Xunwu to open an herb shop with capital of about 1,000 yuan. He became the boss. Guangdong merchants have a common saying: "Not afraid of difficulties; only afraid of not having progeny." Those people who are without children can certainly purchase children to carry on the family line; this is because they are "afraid of not having progeny." The need for labor power also prompts the purchase of children. When children are bought, usually the intelligent and capable ones are adopted as sons. The dull ones are kept as servants [*nugu*].[29] Baihetang's manager, who was himself purchased, had a child who died young; so he bought a son. He supports seven people [including himself]: [the son just mentioned], the two sons and two daughters he fathered, and his wife. He has also taken on three apprentices. He makes some profit.

The herb business is very profitable. One buys in bulk and sells in small quantities. There are two categories of herbal medicines: common and special. The common category (water medicine) is for curing illnesses, and everyone needs them. The special [lit. delicate] kinds are used as supplements [to food], and only local bullies are able to buy them. One can bargain about the prices for special kinds, but the prices of common herbal medicines are set by the herb merchants. Among the seven herb stores, only three businesses—Baihetang, Yang Qingren, and Wang Putai—have the special types of herbs.

Yang Qingren, a native of Zhangshu, used to have capital of

500 to 600 yuan, but last year his son gambled away several hundred yuan and now he only has 200 to 300 yuan.

Wang Putai, who is also a native of Zhangshu, has capital of 100 yuan. He works hand in glove with the evil gentryman He Zizhen and the Catholic father Chen (a Mei County native).[30] Father Chen loaned him 400 yuan. Furthermore, he borrowed 200 yuan from the local prostitute Lai Fengzi. In addition to the herb shop, he also opened a foreign-goods store. Where did Lai Fengzi's money come from? She became the mistress of one of the company commanders subordinate to Lai Shihuang[31] and returned to Xunwu last year with 300 ill-gotten [lit. do evil] yuan. Wang Putai thought of a way to flatter Lai Fengzi in order to borrow this money. When the money was received, Wang Putai sent Lai Fengzi perfume, terry-cloth towels, and many other gifts.

Xindesheng is owned by a certain Du, who is also a native of Zhangshu. It has 400 to 500 yuan of capital.

Tian Renhe, Huang Yuxing, and [the owner of] Fuchuntang are also from Zhangshu, and all have capital of 100 yuan.

Annual herb sales are

Baihetang	3,000 yuan
[Yang] Qingrentang	800
Xindesheng	600
Tian Renhe	600
Wang Putai	400
Huang Yuxing	300
Fuchuntang	300
TOTAL	6,000 yuan

Wang Putai has participated in counter[revolutionary] organizations. When this faction meets, he certainly attends, although on the surface he does not appear to be an official. General goods merchant Chen Zhicheng, marine products merchant Bao Huaxiang, and the manager of the boarding house Tonglaian are all involved in local politics. When

Xunwu City came under the influence of the soviet, the businesses of these four were confiscated.

Tobacco

Two shops in Xunwu City process tobacco. One shop is Huang Yufeng's, a Shanghang native whose family has operated a shop in Xunwu for two generations. In the past they had capital of 3,000 yuan. By selling tobacco, paper, and general goods, they made a profit of more than 10,000 yuan, which they took back to Shanghang to buy land. More than 1,000 yuan of capital was retained by the Xunwu City shop. Another shop is Yongquanhao, which also processes its own tobacco. This shop, opened by an Anyuan native the year before last, has capital of 300 to 500 yuan.

Huang Yufeng has two workers, one who shaves the tobacco [blocks] and one who makes the packages. Yongquanhao hires one worker. The workers' annual salary is 60 yuan. They eat the boss's food. Their lot is about the same as the "gentlemen" in the general goods and herb stores. What differs is that the workers do not usually eat meat or drink wine and have a special dinner only on the first and fifteenth. The gentlemen usually have meat to eat; hence they do not have special dinners.

Moreover, gentlemen usually eat at the same table as the boss. Workers, when few, eat together at the table with the boss. If there are a lot of workers, the boss and the gentlemen eat at one table and the workers eat at another. These examples all show that the status of the gentlemen is higher than that of the workers. Workers are generally not called workers, but "master workers" [shifu].

Most of the tobacco in general stores and marine products stores is purchased from this type of tobacco shop.

Tailoring

Altogether there are thirteen shops with sewing machines and three shops that use hand labor. Liu Qinying, Huang

Saozi, Liao Jiefang, Liu Senhe, Liu Shifu, Xie Shenbao, Fan Laizi, Xie Qilong, He Xianggu, Xie Shifu, Huang Laowu, and Huang Shangxian all use machines. Every shop has one *chezi* (sewing machine). Every shop's boss is also a worker. Every person has an apprentice to do finishing work like hemming and making buttons and hooks.

The capital of this type of sewing shop is in the machine. First-quality machines cost more than 200 yuan; second-quality around 70 to 80 yuan; third-quality (secondhand) about 30 to 40 yuan. Before 1920 there were no sewing machines in Xunwu; without exception sewing was done by hand. In 1920 a Xingning man, He Shifu, opened the first shop with a sewing machine. He originally opened a shop in Liuche, and in 1920 he moved to Xunwu City. Because his "scissors were very sharp" (when Xunwu people want to say that the tailor steals the fabric, they don't say he steals; rather, they say his scissors are sharp), and because he also liked prostitutes and did not stay put, he took his sewing machine back to Xingning.

The year before last (1928) there were still only four machines in Xunwu, but last year the number increased to thirteen. This number includes several used machines bought from other people. Among the tailors, Huang Laowu's handiwork was the best, and his business was the largest. He worked hand in glove with officials and powerful gentry and had a monopoly in making fine clothes. Because of this, he had profits that he used to buy land. During the 25 March uprising he expressed opposition, and when the revolution reached Xunwu City, he fled with the reactionary faction.

[As for clothing styles,] in 1920 He Shifu started using a machine. He popularized "Shanghai-style clothes" ([shirts] cut down the center with rounded bottoms and embroidery).[32] In 1923 the Shanghai style fell from favor, and a type of shirt cut down the center with a square bottom and embroidery became the style. Last year the "Canton style" (seven buttons, four pockets, cut long) became the fashion. A small number of people liked to wear this kind of clothing, but most people were still wearing the embroidered style. In the past clothing was uniformly made in the old "large lapel" [*dajin*] style. The new style of center-cut [shirts and jackets] coincided with the introduction of new-style education. In 1918 or 1919, this style gradually began to be worn by more and more people. But even last year, if we speak of the population of all of Xunwu County, most people still wore old-style clothing. Wearers of new-style clothing were in a minority. But in the past two years, particularly after the victory of the land revolution, the wearing of new-style clothing has increased daily, especially among the young people. Young students, of course, began wearing the new-style long ago, but [now even] the majority of young peasants and young workers wear new-style clothing. Only in the case of the very poor, who lack the money for new clothes, are old-style clothes still worn.

Last year in the summer, with the victory of the rent resistance movement in the southern half of the county, and in the winter, when the land was divided, among the young people in the countryside under 30 sui, over 70 percent wore rubber-soled shoes and sport shoes. (The soles for these kinds of shoes come from Canton to Xingning. The shoes are completed in Xingning, and each pair costs around 1 yuan.) Cadres in the Red Guard and soviet not only, without exception, wear new-style clothing and new-style shoes, but also want to use electric flashlights and wear scarves. Some want to wear pants padded with down.

There are still three hand-tailoring businesses in Xunwu City.

To compare hand sewing and machine sewing of clothes, in the time it takes to sew one item by hand, someone using a sewing machine can sew about three items. To compare prices, a pair of pants produced by hand costs 0.7 yuan; by machine 0.6 yuan. To compare quality, machine-made is better than handmade. How can machines not drive out handicraft workers?

The most important markets in the county are these ten places: Jitan, Chengjiang, Shipaixia, Chetou, Niudouguang, Liuche, Huangxiang (sewing machines were used here earlier than in other places), Gongping, Huangtangdu, and Cenfeng. All these places have sewing machines. Because of this, 30 percent of the county's population has given up handmade clothing for clothing made by machine, especially in the southern half of the county, in which the speed of mechanization has been very fast.

Umbrellas

Peng Wanhe and Li Xiangren are shops that make paper umbrellas. Peng Wanhe was from Wuping [Fujian] and opened an umbrella shop in Xunwu City more than a hundred years or three generations ago. When Peng first came to Xunwu, he had only 100 to 200 yuan of capital, but he gradually accumulated profits from making umbrellas. As of the year before last (1928), before the 25 March uprising, the shop's capital, including land, was 1,000 to 2,000 yuan. The shopkeeper, the fifth Peng brother, and his father, Peng Sheng-xiang, bought 60 dan of paddy land in the Tianbei area outside Xunwu's South Gate. They built a new house. The fifth Peng brother's third and seventh brothers lived in Tianbei. He himself manages the business in [Xunwu] City. The Tianbei land was rented out to peasants for cultivation for 50 percent of the year's crops. His family originally consisted of seven brothers, but four have died; so there are three brothers left. There are also six sons and nephews, one mother, three wives, and five daughters-in-law; so altogether he supports eighteen people. The sons attended a primary school. Among his three brothers, he is the one who manages the umbrella business. He is 30 sui. He employs two workers. The seventh brother is over 20 sui and studied at the Sun Yatsen Middle School established by the Revolutionary faction, for over twenty days. Then when the 25 March uprising occurred, the reactionary faction said he was a "thug" [baotu][33] and confiscated the family property in Tianbei and burned its buildings in Tianbei. The third and seventh brothers both graduated from the East School in Xunwu City. Nevertheless, the third brother studied at the East School during the "diploma mill" era. The seventh brother was at the East School after the school had been reformed, when it was run by the revolutionary Sun Yatsen Middle School faction. Because of this, after the seventh brother graduated from the East School, he entered the Sun Yatsen Middle School and joined the "thugs'" forces [*duiwu*]. After the third brother graduated from the East School, he served as a teacher in an elementary school in Wuping. Now the seventh brother has fled to Wuping. The fifth brother's shop now only has 40 to 50 yuan of capital.

In the time of his father, Peng Shengxiang (during the Guangxu period), paper umbrellas were still popular. At that time about 30 percent of the people used foreign-style umbrellas and 70 percent used paper umbrellas. From the beginning of the Republic until now, this has turned around: foreign-style umbrellas now constitute 70 percent of the market, and paper umbrellas only 30 percent. It does not matter whether one is speaking of towns or the countryside, worker or peasant, merchant or student—all young men and women almost without exception use foreign-style umbrellas that come from Mei County and Xingning. Because of this, those in Liuche and Niudouguang who, during the age of Peng Shengxiang, would come to the Xunwu City shop to buy paper umbrellas, always go to Mei County and Xingning to buy foreign-style umbrellas. In the past the Peng Wanhe Shop made and sold 3,000 paper umbrellas every year. Now yearly production does not exceed 1,200–1,300 umbrellas. Previously (in the Guangxu period), the Peng Wanhe Shop hired six or seven workers; now it employs only two people. In the past the price of umbrellas was 0.25 yuan; now it is 0.45 yuan.

Li Xiangren, from Nankang, is over 40 sui. He began as an umbrella craftsman and then became a boss in the early Republic. He has 40–50 yuan of capital, and every year he sells around 2,000 umbrellas. He hires two workers: one carves bamboo into frames and one mounts the paper; he puts on the lacquer.

There are two kinds of foreign-style umbrellas: silk umbrellas and foreign-cloth umbrellas. All silk umbrellas are made in Japan; China cannot make them. The cloth for foreign-cloth umbrellas and the iron rods come from abroad. Chinese take the cloth and pull it tight over the umbrella frame. The price of a silk umbrella is more than 1.5 yuan. The price of each foreign-cloth umbrella is 1.2–1.3 yuan. The proportion of sales of paper umbrellas, foreign-cloth umbrellas, and silk umbrellas is paper and foreign-cloth umbrellas, 30 percent each, silk umbrellas 40 percent.

The umbrella business now has no apprentices. In the past ten years, no one in Xunwu City has wanted to learn how to make umbrellas for the following reasons: (1) there is no future in the umbrella business; and (2) the situation of apprentices in umbrella shops, compared to that in general stores, is much worse. The craft must be studied from the age of thirteen or fourteen sui and then and only then can it be mastered. The apprentices must cook meals for shop personnel and must also buy food. They also must sweep the floors and do odd jobs around the shop.

Wooden goods

In the past there was only one business, that of Hu Donglin, a Ganzhou man who did a business of 400 to 500 yuan. He has been in business for over twenty years and makes every kind of wooden item for sale: desks, benches, chairs, tables, beds, foot basins, clothesracks, water buckets, cabinets, wash basins, urine buckets, serving trays, signs[34] (for religious festivals, birthdays, and congratulatory occasions), couplets, bookcases, suitcases, clothes bureaus, blackboards and other items used in schools, and boxes [suspended from carrying poles] used for sending gifts.

The carpentry trade can be considered a larger business. Hu's wooden goods were sold not only in Xunwu City District, but also in each district and every county. But items in his store were generally not sold to workers, peasants, and poor people. Rather, they were sold to the landlord class, mid-level merchants, and rich peasants because workers, peasants, and poor peasants cannot afford these things except for a bride's dowry [lit. when marrying off a daughter]. Then they buy clothes bureaus and small cabinets.

Hu's family was in straitened circumstances in Ganzhou. Twenty years ago he came from Ganzhou to Xunwu to help in a workshop as a carpenter. He saved some money and opened a small wood shop, which slowly developed. At its height he hired four or five workers and made profits of 1,000 yuan. He sent half of it back to Ganzhou and what was left—400–500 yuan—he used for the business. The year 1928 marked the beginning of the period when business fell off. He kept only one worker, and he himself worked. His son helped a little; he had enough to feed his family. The reason for his declining business lies in the land revolution. The northern half of the county did not experience revolution, but it was influenced by the revolution. The landlord class and others who had money no longer celebrated birthdays. They also no longer celebrated auspicious occasions and festivals or held honorific gatherings. Most schools closed. How could Hu's business not have declined?

All his furniture—all that was sold to feudal landlords—is in the old style. But some of it was progressive; these were the items used by schools and churches. Because he knew Pastor Bao, the wood sections of the church and hospital built outside South Gate were done by him.[35]

His relative, a certain Xie, last year asked ten people to form a "monthly loan society." Every person contributed 5 yuan, and altogether 50 yuan was raised. Xie opened a very small wood shop at the side of the City God Temple. No workers were hired; just the father and son. In one year not only did they make no profit, but they lost their capital. The business is almost dead.

The wooden items used by the workers, peasants, and poor people are sold at periodic markets. On the first, fourth, and seventh days of the ten-day market-cycle, one can buy from artisans [*jiangren*]. They are called "those who make round wooden objects." They live deep in the hills and carry their goods by pole to market. These goods are commodes, carriers, water buckets, foot basins, rice buckets, rice pots, rice scoops, water dippers, wok lids, bowl covers (to cover food bowls and cooking pots), chopping boards, cutting boards (for vegetable cutting: the round one is called a chopping board and the square one is called a vegetable board), dish-washing pots, grain buckets (to carry cut stalks to the threshing area for threshing), grain flails (to beat the grain), rice hullers,[36] and ladders.[37] All are sold by these craftsmen who come out of the hills. Of course, these items are not available on every market day, but depending on the season or needs, there is a market for these things. Rice hullers must certainly be ordered. Windmills must be made by master craftsmen from Shanghang. In the whole county, there are ten master craftsmen from Shanghang. Every year master craftsmen from Shanghang visit the county once or twice. Waterwheels are owned by only one in a hundred peasant families in Xunwu County because this county has many irrigation ditches in the hills. Because droughts are rare, waterwheels are not used.

Outside the South Gate are two coffin-making shops. Each shop has only 40 yuan of capital. They make the "firewood" (also called *huobanzi*, or kindling) used by poor people. Landlords and capitalists and tenants and workers with even a little money usually hire a carpenter to make coffins. Only by the poorest households, or in emergencies [*doujin*],[38] will this "firewood" [coffin] be bought. Those people who have lost everything or have had things taken always curse loudly: "I hope you are wiped out and lose all your children. I hope you end up packed into a cheap coffin." This refers to coffins that are made of kindling wood and are used only by nameless people. Families with money hire carpenters to make coffins.

Such carpenters, except for Xunwu natives, come from Shanghang. The master workers who make windmills also make coffins.

Boarding Houses

There are Liu Wanli, He Changlong, Liu Hongxing, Wen Deli, Pan Fali, Pan Jinli, Tang Riheng, Tonglaian, Zeng Jitao, Jiu Saozi, Dazhi Sisaozi, Gu Liufang, Liu Ener (also sells white wine) and Gu Yuchang: some ten-odd boarding places. Eighty percent of the boarders are porters; the remaining 20 percent are ox dealers, people carrying bundles wrapped in cloth (these people are traveling to look for a job), people of neighboring villages coming to Xunwu City because of lawsuits, people passing through here to Ganzhou to attend school there, acrobats and trick performers, plaster vendors, fortune-tellers, monks who beg for alms, medical practitioners, geomancers, beggars (they sing folk songs called *lianhualuo*). Among those 80 percent of customers who are porters, most carry chickens or ducks in baskets suspended from poles on their shoulders; a few carry tobacco skin (tobacco skin is tobacco leaf).

It requires little capital investment to open a boarding place. A number of quilts, some rough mats, a little rice, and some firewood will do. The rent for the place can be paid after a few months of operation.

The profit comes from those customers with long gowns and those who carry umbrellas. They are customers who are treated to better food and a nicer quilt. However, they are charged a lot more when they check out. The porters and poor people are charged lower fuel and meal fees. They pay by the bowl of rice instead of by the meal, as does the first type of customer; this is much cheaper. One bowl of rice costs half a mao (people with larger appetites can consume about one and a half bowls, half a bowl is enough for people with smaller appetites). One pot of wine costs the same as a bowl of rice, for those who drink. The fuel fee for one night is three coppers, which includes fuel for lighting and wood to heat the water for bathing. In the winter it costs each customer two coppers to have a quilt. The money obtained by selling food and wine is about 40 percent of the overall profit. Essentially, the ultimate source of profit for the boarding place is pig raising, because boarding houses always have table scraps and garbage, which can be used as pig food.

The enemy of a boarding house is the police and underlings from the yamen. They often come to check customers' luggage on the pretext of investigation, and thus harass the customers or steal their belongings. For example, when they come to the boarding house on the pretext of checking for opium, they rob the money that belongs to customers. During curfew, the customer might get into some unnecessary and unexpected trouble because of a reply the police do not like. Therefore, customers are afraid of coming to the boarding places in Xunwu City. They seek to find places in Huang'ao, Heling, Changju, and Xinzhai, towns that are three to ten li from Xunwu City, long before it gets dark. This, no doubt, negatively affects the boarding place business a great deal.

Among the boarding houses, the Tonglaian Boarding House is reactionary. The owner, Chen Dengqi, comes from a poor peasant family in Liuche, where he could not keep his whole family fed. He knew some martial arts; so he taught these in the Liuche countryside. In 1918 or 1919 he went to Xunwu City and became a bailiff. In 1925 he opened the Tonglaian Boarding House and sold oil at the same time. He colluded with government officials and was friends with the evil gentryman Chen Tufeng of Liuche. During the 25 March uprising, he sheltered county magistrate Xie Yin in his escape and got into Xie's good graces. After [Xie's] political power was restored, Chen was promoted to captain of the Pacification and Defense Corps.[39] He led corp members to Shuangqiao District to kidnap people for ransom and burn down the houses of the revolutionary masses. After the county magistrate left, he went back to the boarding house. This time the soviet confiscated his house.

Bean Curd

The population of Xunwu City is under 3,000, and yet there are more than 30 bean curd stores. Nine out of ten meals in this city are served with bean curd. Bean curd is popular because it is cheap and convenient. In Xunwu's villages, people also like bean curd—it constitutes half the peasants' daily diet—but it is not as popular as in Xunwu City.

One tray of bean curd is made with 2.5 sheng of soybeans. The cost of 2.5 sheng of soybeans is 0.5 yuan. One tray of bean curd sells for 0.65 yuan. The profit is 0.15 yuan. "One tray of bean curd" means 46 pieces of big dry bean curd. The retail price is seven pieces for 0.1 yuan; one piece for three coppers. One tray of small dry bean curd contains 92 pieces. The retail price for fourteen pieces is 0.1 yuan; two pieces for three coppers.

There are four varieties of bean curd: regular soft bean curd, fried bean curd, dry bean curd, and stuffed dry bean curd. The regular soft bean curd sells the most, fried bean curd ranks second, followed by dry bean curd. Stuffed dry bean curd sells the least because it is used only for special occasions. The profit of a bean curd shop comes from the soybean residue, for it is used to raise pigs. Because the bean curd store sells an average of one tray of bean curd a day, maybe two trays when something special is going on, its profit ranges from only 0.15 to 0.3 yuan a day. In raising pigs, a "sow and piglet" can usually be produced twice a year. The profit is about 40 yuan each time. If a store raises pigs to be sold as pork, each store can raise four pigs a year, which averages 400 jin of pork. This makes a profit of 100 yuan. However, this type of pig raising requires more rice, and it is not as profitable as raising the sow and piglet.

Bean curd businesses operate out of the owner's home; people who sell bean curd also farm at the same time.

It is not easy to make bean curd. It is said: Learned easily, mastered with difficulty. It is also said: Few people claim to be masters of making bean curd and liquor.[40]

Barbers

There are eight barber shops in Xunwu City. Before 1912 all the tools were traditional ones, and the queue was the only style. In 1912, Western scissors began to be used (shears and hair scissors) and only the monk style was in fashion. In 1913 the "Japanese-style" cut started becoming popular. Large mirrors, plastic combs, and lightweight metal combs had not appeared yet. In 1917 and 1918 the "crew cut" and the "army style" were quite popular. But the tools remained those used traditionally, not the ones like the large mirror. In 1921 some of the local young men who attended school in Ganzhou returned to Xunwu and brought back with them the "Ph.D. style." In 1923 the tall, large mirror (eight or nine inches wide; thirteen inches tall) appeared, and rattan chairs replaced the four-legged bench (one foot tall). In addition, the lightweight metal comb was brought into the city. All of the new-style tools were from Mei County. During the great revolution of 1926–27, plastic combs appeared.

The Japanese-style cut was renamed, and the Ph.D-style cut went out of fashion. Nevertheless, crew cuts and army-style cuts, originally widespread among students and merchants, spread widely among young workers, peasants, and poor people. New hairstyles also became popular among the petty bourgeoisie and student masses (these masses accepted capitalist culture and opposed landlord culture): the "cultured style," "American style," and "round-headed style" (Mei County people laughed at this style, calling it the "Thai pomelo").[41] The cultured style was also called the "Western style." The American style is called the *huaqi* style.[42] It spread from Southeast Asia to Mei County and then from Mei County to Xunwu. Nowadays, in Xunwu City and other big market towns no one wears the shaved-head style, although a large portion of the peasants in the countryside still wear this style. Only a small part of the population wears fashionable styles like the crew cut and the army-style cut. This minority, moreover, is made up of young men.

As for prices, the shaved-head style costs a mao whether one is shaved or sheared. All other styles cost 1.5 mao; a shave costs half a mao.

To open a barber shop requires capital of about 40 to 50 yuan. The master barber usually hires two people, although a few hire one or three people. The wage for half a year is at least 30 or 40 yuan; a regular wage is 50 to 60 yuan; 80 yuan is maximum. When business is good, each person can make a yuan [a day]. Normally the boss and the two workers, on the average, bring in 3 yuan a day; so in a year they can bring in 1,000 yuan or so. Except for the expense of wages of more than 100 yuan, the rest goes to the boss. Expenses are fuel and food (75 yuan for each of the four people), rent for the shop (about 30 yuan), and the cost of the tools (not more than 100 yuan). So the boss can make a profit of around 400 yuan (including his own wage). How is this money used up? By whoring and gambling.

Very few barbers and tailors, whether workers or bosses, save up enough money to become rich. The reason is that these two types of people, though generally bright and capable, indulge in whoring and gambling and are fond of fine food and nice clothing. Why are they like this? It is probably because their social position is low. During the Qing dynasty, barbers were regarded by society as one of the "nine low classes." As elsewhere, the social position of tailors is also very low. Even though they are married, tailors still frequent brothels. Eight of ten barbers do not have wives, but they do not feel miserable at all. They are quite content to frequent brothels.

The "nine low classes" are opposite the "nine high classes." The nine low classes are (1) pedicurists, (2) masseuses (those who massage backs), (3) musicians (those who play drums and instruments), (4) chimney sweeps, (5) folk performers [lit. tea pickers] (men and women singing tea-picking songs [*xi*] together), (6) opera singers [*changxi*], (7) yamen clerks and runners [*chairen*], (8) barbers, and (9) prostitutes. The nine high classes consist of (1) degree holders [*juzi*], (2) doctors [*yi*], (3) fortune-tellers [*kanyu*],[43] (4) geomancers, (5) painters [*danqing*],[44] (6) craftsmen, (7) monks, (8) Daoist priests, and (9) performing artists [lit. *qin* players] and chess players [*qi*].

Blacksmiths

There are three blacksmiths: Master Ye, Master Yang, and Master Li. Master Yang comes from Anyuan, Masters Ye and Li both come from Yudu. Each of them has invested about 50 yuan. They make different kinds of firewood cleavers, axes, hoes, iron rake heads, weeding rakes, harrows (pulled by an ox), planes, shuttle spears (in the Xunwu dialect these are called *baozi*, in Mei County *tiaohaozi*, in Dongjiang *jianchuan*), kitchen cleavers (vegetable cleavers), spatulas (for frying vegetables), shovels (to ladle food out of woks),[45] fire [charcoal] tongs, fire [charcoal] shovels, hooks (for carrying water pails), iron ladles (to scoop rice and oil), all kinds of iron tools used by carpenters (various kinds of iron planes and rulers, oblique shovels, iron awls, carpenter's pincers, drills, choppers), irons (to press cotton cloth when making a shirt), knives for cutting cloth (for the tailor), sickles, sabers, and double sabers (*kazidao*), small rakes (*xiaoba*), iron nails, hinges (for mounting doors), and iron hoops.[46] All items except sickles, sabers, and double sabers are household items that are sold in the city and the surrounding area. Traditional tools and methods are used to forge iron.

Iron is produced in six places locally: Huangshashui in Xunwu City District's South Ward; Tiezashui and Shiduankeng in Shuangqiao District; and Chetou, Hengjing, and Dabeijiao in Nanba District. Every place has furnaces and casts iron ingots as well as woks, plowshares, and moldboards (*libi*). The locally produced iron is also sold outside Xunwu

County; most of it is sold in Huizhou, Shilong, and Menling. Some of the woks are sold in Xunwu County, but about half are sold in Huichang and Ganzhou, and a small number are sold in Chaozhou and Shantou. Plowshares and moldboards are sold only in Xunwu County.

Altogether about 200 people are required for one furnace for casting iron. Every furnace needs those who carry the *xiangtan* (charcoal [*mutan*]; this is used in casting iron and casting woks; about twenty men are needed to carry it), those who make charcoal (to turn wood into *xiangtan* requires three men per kiln; the charcoal from five kilns supplies one iron furnace; so fifteen men are needed altogether), those who transport the sand (sand for iron production comes from landslips; peasants carry it and sell it to those who run the furnaces; these workers are difficult to count), and those workers at the foundry (tall furnaces for casting pig iron require ten men; cupola furnaces for casting cast iron require twelve men;[47] casting woks requires twelve men, one man is the stoker, and three men are either managers or apprentices).

Every furnace for producing iron requires capital of 1,000 yuan as does every furnace for making woks; so [together] the furnaces for making iron and woks require 2,000 yuan. The biggest expense is for sand and charcoal, the next is for the fuel, food, and wages of the workers. Some foundries are run by one family; others are joint-share operations.

As for wages, the foreman (*gongtou*) gets 1.2 yuan a day; workers get 0.3 yuan and eat the boss's food and use his fuel. The managers get 70 yuan a year. Wages for foremen and workers are reckoned daily—they work a day and get paid for a day. A manager's salary is figured on an annual basis. There is also money for rituals, New Year's, and travel. These are all expenses paid by the boss for the workers. The status of foremen is high. If a foreman is treated poorly, he will take it easy, and the business will start losing money. A foreman can make 500 yuan a year. A foundry can produce [iron worth] 4,000 yuan a year. Six foundries yield 24,000 yuan.

Before the Republic, foreign iron had not arrived here at all, or only in a very small amount, and wages were low. Iron production was greater than at present. Foundries could produce iron worth over 20,000 yuan. Although in the Qing there were only two foundries, together their production was more than 40,000 yuan. Now the number of furnaces has increased, and the amount of production of each foundry has decreased. The primary reasons are that labor is expensive (labor is expensive because industrial products from abroad are expensive) and that foreign iron is being imported.

The current price of iron is double that of 30 years ago (1899–1900). At that time a dan (about 40 jin) of pig iron was, at most, 1.1 yuan. Now it is certainly 3.2 yuan, or 0.08 yuan per jin of pig iron. Three jin of pig iron can be made into one jin of cast iron, which is priced at 0.5 yuan.

Of the three blacksmiths in Xunwu City, two are Yudu natives; one is from Anyuan. All furnace operators in the countryside are natives of Yudu. There are many Yudu iron-founders. Since tall furnaces require four men to operate and short furnaces require three men to operate, with about 3,700–3,800 furnaces in operation, these iron-founders number about 13,000. Not only do they make iron in Jiangxi, but they work in Fujian, Guangdong, and even Southeast Asia.

Fireworks

There is a fireworks shop whose boss is a certain Zhong, a Huichang man. With capital of several dozen yuan, this shop has been around for six or seven years. He himself works along with a master he has hired to help. Every year he does a business of 400 to 500 yuan. An old custom on the first day of the year is to set off large displays of fireworks. Even the smallest shop would spend a couple yuan on fireworks. This year on the first the reactionary government announced restrictions. Not only were firecrackers forbidden on the first day of the year, but even on ordinary days, they weren't permitted. Because of this, the fireworks business has plummeted. The peasants in the areas of the [25 March] uprising in the southern half of the county have completely dispensed with superstition and do not want to use fireworks. Because of this, not only has Zhong's fireworks business in Xunwu City decreased, but also the importing of fireworks into Xunwu from Mei County and Menling has ceased recently.

Jewelry

Xunwu women are the same as women in other places where the feudal economy has not completely collapsed. It does not matter whether they are workers, peasants, merchants, or poor peasants or rich peasants, they all wear jewelry in their hair or on their hands. All of it is silver except for the gold jewelry worn by women in large-landlord families. Every woman puts silver hair clasps in her hair and wears silver earrings. No matter how destitute the woman, she has these two kinds of jewelry. Also, bracelets and rings are owned by even those of the most modest means. Silver earrings are actually silver-plated tin or silver-plated copper. More than seven shops in Xunwu City make this kind of jewelry. Each shop needs only several dozen yuan of capital.

Some of the jewelry is done to order; some is sold by peddlers carrying goods on their backs in a box and going to the countryside. Among the seven jewelry shops, four shops have a boss, a worker, and an apprentice, one shop has four people, one shop has two people, another shop only has one person. The apprenticeship system resembles the one for haircutting, but the work is harder and the clothes are a bit more threadbare.

Tinsmith

There is one shop [in this category], which is run by Liu Junji, a native of Xingning. This shop was opened in Xunwu City the year before last; there was no so-called tinned-iron before then. It has capital of several dozen yuan. The shop has three people: his wife, one apprentice, and Liu himself. The raw materials are kerosene tins. It produces small tin lamps (rush-wick lamps),[48] pots for holding oil and tea-oil, ladles for scooping oil, pots for making tea, filters for oil and wine, tea canisters, all sorts of small boxes, and other household necessities. So, this type of tin goods store is a social necessity. The business is also profitable. A kerosene tin costs 0.3 yuan and comes from general stores in Xunwu City, Jitan, Sanbiao, Chengjiang, and Niudouguang. These tins are made into tin products and sold for 0.6 yuan. This time when the Red Army entered Xunwu City, Liu Junji, for unknown reasons, fled with the reactionary faction.

Watch Repairing

Ye Gongchang, a native of Mei County, runs the one watch-repair shop. In addition to his tools, he has around 10 yuan of capital. He specializes in fixing watches and clocks. In addition to the business in Xunwu City, the only other such business in the whole county is in Niudouguang. These two businesses were started the year before last (1928). Xunwu County has 120,000 people; 2 percent have watches and clocks. Altogether there are 2,400 watches and clocks; so it is necessary to have one or two businesses that repair watches and clocks.

Periodic Markets

Xunwu City is a city whose trade is carried on in shops and in periodic markets. In Xunwu, the business in periodic markets represents the seminatural economy, and the business done by shops and stalls represents the mercantile economy. To compare the shop and stall business with the periodic market business, the shop and stall business constitutes 70 percent, and the periodic market 30 percent. It is apparent that the strength of the mercantile economy exceeds that of the natural economy by far.

The most important products sold at the periodic markets are as follows.

The first is rice. The rice trade takes place only on the first, fourth, and seventh days of the ten-day market schedule.

Shops and stalls do not engage in this trade. Not only is rice desired by most people in Xunwu City (Xunwu City's peasants have their own rice), but it is also shipped to Guangdong. Mei County or Dazhe people carry in a dan of salt and take back a dan of rice. This is called "salt coming; rice going." Because of this, the rice trade is greater than any other trade in Xunwu City. The items most traded in Xunwu City are, in order, (1) rice, (2) salt (more than 100,000 yuan annually), (3) textiles and foreign-style goods (100,000 yuan); and (4) [soy]beans (in excess of 20,000 yuan). In 1900, one dan (172 jin) of rice [cost] 4 yuan; in 1912, 5 yuan; in 1927, during a drought, over 16 yuan. This year, before the Red Army arrived, it was 8.5 yuan, and after the Red Army arrived, up to 7 yuan.

The second is firewood. Charcoal, *shuitanzi*, kindling, bundled firewood, and brushwood are carried by shoulder "to the market" from rural areas. In 1900, 100 jin of charcoal (*xiangtan*) was worth 0.5 yuan. In 1912–28, the price rose from 0.8 yuan to 1.2 yuan. Because it rained a lot last year, the price for 100 jin went up to 2.2 yuan, but now 100 jin costs 0.6 or 0.7 yuan. The price for a dan (70 jin) of kindling was 0.17–0.18 yuan in 1900. It went up to 0.22–0.23 yuan in 1912, and it was 0.4 yuan from 1921 to 1927. It has been 0.5–0.6 yuan from 1927 until now.

The third is pork. Those three butchers mentioned previously in the section on shops and stalls actually should have been included in the section on periodic markets because theirs is a business carried on in periodic markets.

The fourth is pigs. Piglets (two months old) and older piglets (three to four months old) are not sold by licensed brokers. They are bought and sold in periodic markets. Since each market has about 30 of them, and there are nine markets per month, altogether about 270 are traded each month. The price per jin for piglets now is 0.3 yuan, and for [older] piglets 0.2 yuan. Pigs with much meat cost 0.25 yuan. Why are older piglets the cheapest? Because the average weight for an older piglet is 50 jin or so. Unless he needs the cash, an owner does not want to sell it. But when an owner is forced to sell an older piglet, people [know the situation and] bargain the price down. The owner reluctantly lets it go.

The fifth is chicken and duck. Not many from this area are sold at markets—normally 20 at most. Sometimes no one wants even one. This proves the poverty of Xunwu. Around New Year's and other festivals over a hundred are sold at every market. The price per jin for chicken is 0.45 yuan and for duck 0.3 yuan.

The sixth is bamboo and wooden goods. Wooden goods that are sold at the periodic markets are discussed in the section on shops and stalls under the heading of wooden goods. Here I discuss bamboo goods: grain baskets, bamboo mats [da] for drying grain, bamboo scoops (to carry ashes and manure to the field), chicken and duck cages, pig cages, baskets, bags (for carrying rice cakes and other odds and ends), mill-turning handles, threshing sieves, sieves for sifting grain, bamboo beds (sleeping chairs), dustpans, bamboo chairs, stove scoops (laoji), chopsticks, brooms, wok brushes, duoerzi (that is, kite scoops, smaller than bamboo scoops), small, square-bottomed bamboo baskets [jiaoluo] (small food baskets used by children to hold cakes), containers (fish baskets, also used when picking tea-oil leaves [chazi]),[49] bamboo fish traps (that is, the trap of "after the fish is caught, the trap can be forgotten";[50] it is called a hao elsewhere), tea baskets, bamboo hats (straw rainhats), vegetable baskets, and drying baskets.[51] These are all sold at periodic markets.

The seventh is vegetables. These are leaf mustard, celery, amaranth, Chinese onion, maizi (pulse leaves), Chinese kale, garlic bolt, bitter melon, winter melon, pumpkin (gourd), seasonal melon, sweet melon, cucumber, watermelon, sweet potato (cushaw), eggplant (Guangdong people called it diaocai), water convolvulus (also called kongxincai, it is called yongcai elsewhere), taro, puzi, turnip, leek, scallion, garland chrysanthemum, cabbage, caitou (main stem of leaf mustard), dangji (blade bean), chili, snow pea, pengpidou (hyacinth bean), kidney bean, *bayuejiao* (August bean), tiger bean, tree bean, mung bean, yellow soybean sprout, purslane, and celery cabbage. These vegetables are supplied by the nearby villages to the residents of this city.

The eighth is fish. There are grass carp, silver carp, variegated carp, shrimp, carp, crusian carp, yellow eel, loach, frog, prawn, soft-shelled turtle (*jiaoyu*), freshwater fish, and "*qiang*." Ordinary markets have only grass carp, silver carp, carp, crusian carp, yellow eel, loach, and frog; the rest are seldom seen. One jin of grass carp costs 0.25 yuan; 10 liang of yellow eel cost 0.1 yuan; a jin of loach costs 0.1 yuan; 7 liang of frog costs about 0.1 yuan. *Qiang* is a kind of rare big fish. A 40-jin qiang was sold in Xunwu last year. Some qiang found elsewhere weigh as much as 70 to 80 jin. Sometimes along rivers in the Huizhou area people who have drowned serve as food for this type of fish.

The ninth is candy. There is powder, glutinous paste, *nazi* (vermicelli), cakes (soft cake, *tielian* cake, *tieshao* cake, bean cake, *youguo*, sugar cake, fish cake, ramie-leaf cake, sweet-potato cake, and impressed-character cake[52]). Whenever the market is open, candy vendors are there; especially during a "joyous procession" (during folk dancing or a religious festival), a lot more of them appear. The capital is only a yuan or two.

The tenth is fruit. Plums sell best; water chestnuts rank second. In addition, there are loquats, pomelos, red bayberries, persimmons, peaches, oranges, and tangerines. The fruit trade is not a small business.

Prostitutes

There are 30 to 40 brothels in this town of 2,700 people. The best known among the hard-bitten lot of prostitutes, young and old, are Chang Jiao, Yue E, Zhong Simei, Xie Sanmei, Huang Zhaokun, Wu Xiu, Run Feng, Da Guanlan, Xiao Guanlan, Zhao E, Lai Zhao, Yu Shu, Wu Feng, and Yi E. Except for

Da Guanlan and Yi E, all are young prostitutes. Run Feng, Wu Xiu, Yue E, Wu Feng, and Zhao kun are the five best known.

When the civil and military imperial examinations were flourishing, there were just as many prostitutes as now. After the imperial examinations were abolished, their numbers declined. Around 1904 there were only about ten prostitutes. Later the number gradually increased; so now it is the same as during the booming period of the exams. When the land revolution in the southern half of the county moved to the north and the Red Army arrived in Chengjiang, many of the prostitutes fled to the countryside. Among them it was said: "Wherever the Red Army is, not a blade of grass remains; even a broom will be snapped into two pieces." Therefore, they were frightened and ran away.

In Xunwu City most of the prostitutes are from Sanbiao. The people of Xunwu have a saying: "Prostitutes [lit. 'goods' (*huo*)] from Sanbiao; glutinous rice from Xiangshan." This means that the women of Sanbiao are very pretty.

Ten years ago, when business was flourishing, merchants visited prostitutes the most, powerful gentry were second, and the sons of powerful gentry (the "young masters") participated in this activity the least. In the past ten years the positions have changed: the powerful gentry visit prostitutes the most, their sons and brothers are second, and merchants the least. Why do merchants go whoring the least? Because business is not good now. Why do the gentry do this the most? Because they are involved in litigation and stay in brothels throughout the year. Only at New Year's and other holidays do they return home. Where does the money for this come from? In lawsuits, country folk give them 100 yuan when only 20 yuan is needed for legal fees. They pocket the 80 yuan and in this way are provided with the means to cover their expenses for prostitutes. Why are the young masters coming to the city for whoring much more than in the past? Because an increasing number of "diploma mills" are being established.

The young masters break away from the warmth of their families when they go to town to study; so they feel quite lonely and leave a lot of footprints leading to brothels.

United Welfare Society

In 1901 or 1902 the manager (boss) of the Hengfu Silk Store in Ganzhou, a certain Xiong (a native of Nanchang), came to Xunwu to start the United Welfare Society.[53] He was a so-called Heavenly Blessing Master. At that time the director [shanzhang] of the society was Gu Hefu, a xiucai who lived in the city and whose family circumstances were deteriorating. Later the director of the United Welfare Society was Pan Mingdian, a holder of a bagong degree, whose wealth was about 1,000 yuan and who served as a clerk in the county court in Jiujiang [Jiangxi]. Guo Youmei joined the United Welfare Society in 1901 or 1902 at a time when the society had 80–90 members. Afterwards many more people joined, and during the most flourishing period there were more than 200 members of the United Welfare Society.

The United Welfare Society originated in Sichuan, where the society sent formal letters to each provincial capital asking them to initiate United Welfare societies. Once permission was granted by the government in each province, the society spread to counties, where branches were set up. The Heavenly Blessing Master of Ganzhou Prefecture received official approval from the provincial government in Nanchang. After he arrived in Xunwu, paid respects to the county magistrate, and [secured] the magistrate's approval, the magistrate issued a proclamation protecting this society. The United Welfare Society could then carry on its activities.

Joining the society required approval by the gods. Pieces of paper rolled into balls, some with the word "permitted" and some blank, were placed in a bamboo container. The deity of the United Welfare Society was Bodhidharma.[54] A person wanting to join the society was led by the person introducing him before the deity, to whom he kowtowed and paid respect. Then he picked a paper from the holder; if he picked one that said "permitted," he was allowed to join. If it was blank, then he was not allowed to join. One butcher drew a blank three times, and a local bully drew a blank four times. "You couldn't say there is no god; actually you could say there is a god."

Lin Hu[55] arrived in Xunwu City as a big-headed and ferocious man of 27 or 28 sui. Xu Chongzhi[56] also passed through once. Seven or eight company commanders under Lin Hu, stationed in Xunwu for over a month, joined the society.

The membership fee was 1 yuan. Later, although not mandatory, you could contribute as much as you wanted. The Nanchang United Welfare Society and the Sichuan United Welfare Society asked for contributions in a letter that said, "If you contribute money, some day when you go to Nanchang or Sichuan, your name will be on the register and then you will be able to find a job." Guo Youmei contributed 3 yuan to Nanchang and 5 yuan to Sichuan. Xunwu's society had more than 200 members, of which 30 to 40 were women. Their backgrounds were merchants 50 percent, landlords 20 percent, and peasants 30 percent. But the so-called peasants were not poor peasants. All of them had "food on the table" or were "quite independent."

In 1918 or 1919 on the orders of the provincial government, the United Welfare Society was closed for a year or two. Afterwards Tang Shengzhi[57] issued a directive saying: "The Bodhisattva[58] can be worshiped; you do not have to abolish the society." Therefore it was re-established. In 1923 or 1924 a government directive ordered the society closed, and then and only then did it really cease to function.

Every day you meditated three times—morning, noon, and evening. This was called "to practice." Those who were "practicing" could not sleep with women for two days, because if they slept with women they would not be effective. The United Welfare Society had secret practices if you reached the fifth level. Then the Heavenly Blessing Master told you some secrets. Guo Youmei had only reached the second level, so he never heard the secrets.

Sichuan had a ninth-level Heavenly Blessing Master who came to Ganzhou. The United Welfare Society members there contributed 2 yuan each for a welcoming banquet for the Heavenly Blessing Master. Fang Benren[59] also came.

Every year the United Welfare Society had two *Longhua hui*: all members came and were charged 0.2 yuan per person when they arrived. They kowtowed toward the Bodhidharma, music was played, and they ate a vegetarian meal.

If you joined the United Welfare Society, you could make friends and become an official.

The Xunwu magistrate went to the United Welfare Society three times and kowtowed [to the god] together with United Welfare Society members.

Status Within Population and Positions Within Administration

Having analyzed the composition of the population in Xunwu City, we know that it is a city based on agriculture and handicrafts. The percentages of the population in and around the city in various occupations are as follows.

Occupation	Number of persons	Percentage
peasant	1,620	60%
artisan	297	11
loafer	270	10
prostitute	162	6
merchant	135	5
government	100	4
landlord	78	3
religious leader	22	<1
TOTAL	2,684	100%

From this list, we can see that peasants and artisans [*xiao shougong*] constitute 71 percent of the population. It is apparent that agriculture and handicrafts are the major activities in the city. The majority of the residents in adjacent areas also get their livelihood from farming and handicrafts. The so-called artisans include workers, owners, and store clerks. The so-called handicraft industries include shops for tailoring, tobacco, liquor, umbrellas, firecrackers, haircutting, wooden goods, bean curd, jewelry, tinned-iron, watch repair, and slaughtering.

Those 22 religious leaders include ten Protestants, three Roman Catholics, six Daoists, and three Buddhists.

In Xunwu City there are twelve households surviving totally on land rents. There are 78 people in these households.

The five merchants who are also landlords are included in the category of merchants.

Merchants include people who are salt, oil, or soybean brokers; merchants dealing in general goods, textiles, marine products, and herbs; or those who run boarding houses. Altogether there are 135 people in this category.

There are over 30 brothels, with over 30 prostitutes. These prostitutes, combined with people they support, number 162. Those loafers who are neither workers nor peasants nor merchants specialize in gambling, blackmail, or being lackeys [lit. running dogs] for the rulers [tongzhi]. The total number of these people is, surprisingly, twice the number of merchants. They almost equal the total number of artisans. The number of loafers and prostitutes is about equal to the number of merchants and artisans. This shows the stunning number of jobless people.

The 100 government workers are the 40 people of the new Xunwu County soviet government and the Xunwu City District government along with the 60 people in the county soviet's Red Guard. Here we do not mean the former government workers, although the number of them was about the same as that of the new government.

When we talk about the leaders of the masses, we mean the leading segment of the ruling class in the old society. Naturally these were not the peasants, workers, loafers, and prostitutes constituting 87 percent of the whole population. These were the people led by the ruling class. The rulers consisted only of the landlords, merchants, and Protestant pastors and Catholic priests, constituting 13 percent of the population. The chamber of commerce did not have much power. However, some of the merchants participated in the county-wide government. Nevertheless, those few merchants did not speak just for the mercantile bourgeoisie. They did things at the instruction of the landlords. This is because the scale of commerce in Xunwu is very small; moreover, it has gradually been declining.

First among the merchants in political influence was He Zizhen, who was a soybean broker, having used a false name to obtain a license and then having someone else run the business. He was a teacher, director of the Public Security Bureau, head of the police [*jingcha duizhang*], and a KMT deputy. His father was a tax farmer for the ox tax who exploited the ox dealers. Just after he returned to Xunwu, He Zizhen behaved as a bourgeois and was a member of the New Xunwu faction. Later, he cooperated with landlords. Now he has fled the county. The second [in influence] was Huang Guangfu. He was the boss of the Baohuaxiang marine products store and the secretary of the chamber of commerce. He was able to influence the yamen. He fled and his store was confiscated. The third was the boss of a boarding house, Chen Dengqi. He first worked as a bailiff and later was promoted to captain of a pacification and defense corps. He hung out at the yamen. He fled. The fourth was the boss of a general store, Chen Zhicheng. He was not an official and yet consulted with the reactionary faction on all their affairs and attended their meetings. He fled, and his store was confiscated.

The following is a list of the twelve landlords who collect rent.

He Dexin. He previously collected 600 dan [in rent] but now collects 100 dan, just enough to feed his family of seven or eight members. County folk who had business with the yamen would ask him to intercede for them. His son, He Tingba, graduated from Pingyuan Middle School and is one of the main members of the New Xunwu faction.

He Chengzhi. He previously collected over 300 dan. With very few family members, he could sell 300 dan and thus became the richest landlord in the city. After he died, his widow managed household affairs. His son was purchased and cannot influence the yamen.

Liu Forong. He collected over 200 dan and sold some of it because his family was small. He was the second richest landlord in Xunwu City. [He was known as] *shui jin niupi,* which means he was very stingy. He pays no attention to outside matters.

Liu Duanxuan. He collected only a few dan in rent and belonged to the Sun Yatsen faction. He exhausted his fortune in a lawsuit against He Zizhen. His son is still in jail in Ganzhou. His son is a graduate of Ganzhou No. 4 Middle School and is the new principal of Xunwu City East Primary School.

Fan Laoba. He collected over 100 dan and had a surplus. His elder brother managed the Shunchang Laodian store. He collected rent at home and did not hang out [*zou*] at the yamen. This time [the soviet] imposed a contribution of 300 yuan on him. The peasants confiscated his property.

Fan Jiasheng. He collected over 100 dan and had a surplus. He is about fifteen or sixteen sui and is a student at Sun Yatsen Middle School. He Zizhen imposed a fine on him. This time he was also assessed a contribution of 1,000 yuan by the soviet.

Zhang Sanyu. She collected over 100 dan and had a surplus. She is a widow and is in charge of household affairs. She is not interested in other things.

Kuang Sisao. She collects less than 100 dan and has a surplus. She has one son and one grandchild. She is not a reactionary.

Wu Laosi. He is dead and is survived by a wife, one son, and one grandchild. He collected over 100 dan and had a surplus.

He did not meddle in politics. Wu Laosi was in charge of tax collection for the county government during the Guangxu reign in the Qing dynasty. All the county grain levies were managed by him. He died four years ago.

Fan Mingcai. He used to have a general store, but he closed it over ten years ago. He collected 80 dan and had some surplus. He was a head of a protection militia in 1912 and was an evil gentryman who indulged in whoring and gambling. He fled.

He Xiangsheng. He used to be a street vendor and became rich selling marine products. During the 25 March uprising, he was fined and his business was shut down. His adopted son, He Jiachang, whom he purchased, graduated from East Mountain Middle School in Mei County. He Jiachang was one of the leaders of the 25 March uprising and a Communist party member. He went to Southeast Asia and now is in Fujian.

He Xuecai. The father of He Zizhen. He worked as a clerk in the Judicial Section in the [former] county government. Later he worked as a geomancer. He was a tax farmer for the ox tax and bought a piece of land that produced some 10 dan of income. He was a very evil member of the gentry.

These twelve households subsisted on land rents alone. Among them, He Dexin, Fan Mingcai, and He Xuecai are active reactionaries; Liu Duanxuan and Fan Jiasheng are sympathetic with the revolution; He Xiangsheng's son, He Jiachang, is a Communist party member; the remaining six are households that "care only about making a fortune and don't want to mind other business."

The following five households have characteristics of both merchants and landlords.

Zhong Huitong. He was the first salt broker in Xunwu City. He collected over 220 dan and had a surplus of over 100 dan. He hung out at the yamen and influenced the people there.

Luo Jinfeng. The household was split into four separate households. Altogether their income was 6,000 to 7,000 yuan. The second child is the richest one; he had 250 or 260 dan. He was honest and did not try to influence the yamen. The oldest son is dead; he had over 10 dan. That was not enough to support his family. The third child had 30 to 40 dan, just enough to feed his family. The fourth child (a former president of the chamber of commerce and the main teacher at the United Welfare Society) had only several dozen dan, just enough to feed his family.

Rong Chunxiang. He had several dozen dan of income. He saved all of it and made a living doing business. He did not try to influence the yamen.

Wen Rongji. He saved all of his 80 dan of income and made a living doing business. His third son, Wen Xichun, colluded with the New Xunwu faction.

Lin Bili. He manages a marine products business. He collected over 100 dan and had some surplus. He minds his own business.

These five households have characteristics of both merchants and landlords. Among them, Zhong Huitong and Wen Rongji are members of the reactionary faction. The rest of them are the "mind their own business" type. Among these five households, Zhong Huitong and Luo Jinfeng are middle landlords; the remaining three are small landlords.

·4·

Traditional Land Relationships in Xunwu

RURAL POPULATION

Large landlords (receive more than 500 dan of rent)	0.045%
Middle landlords (receive 200–499 dan of rent)	0.4
Small landlords (receive less than 200 dan of rent)	3.0
Bankrupt families	1.0
Newly rich families	2.0
Rich peasants (have surplus grain and capital for loans)	4.0
Middle peasants (have enough to eat and do not receive loans)	18.255
Poor peasants (insufficient grain and receive loans)	70.0
Manual workers (craftsmen, boatmen, porters)	3.0
Loafers (no occupation)	1.0
Hired hands (permanent and day laborers)	0.3

OLD DISTRIBUTION OF LAND[1]

Corporate	40%
Landlord	30
Peasant	30

ANCESTRAL TRUSTS

There is much corporate land in Xunwu, a phenomenon spread throughout each district. There are many kinds of trusts [*gonghui*]. Trusts belonging to ancestral halls are mostly those of this deceased "esteemed person" or that deceased "esteemed person."[2] As long as there are descendants and the descendants have money, each will certainly contribute a share from his own family's property to establish a trust. This method of making contributions toward establishing a trust is widespread. Generally that which is contributed as a share is land; money is not used. Furthermore, if that esteemed person is still alive, he himself can make bequests and establish a trust [in his own name or in the name of an ancestor]. This type is more prevalent than the previous type.

After this type of corporate land [*gongtian*] is established, the rent is collected year after year. [After some of the] rent money is used for ancestral sacrifices, there is generally a surplus, which is set aside. Money is saved, not grain. Thus, every year the surplus grain is sold to poor people, and the money accumulates. After a certain number of years, the savings yield a sum of money, and land is bought. In this way, the trust land gradually increases quite a bit. But using income to increase the total resources of a trust constitutes only a portion of the disbursements; there is also a portion that can be distributed to the descendants of the one [who established the trust]. When most of the descendants are poor, then and only then do they emphasize division. When the descendants are mostly well off, they do not concern themselves with division.

When does the division happen? Also, what is the method of division? At New Year's and at other festivals, grain and meat are divided at the ancestral hall. The men all get a share; the women do not get any (in some lineages widows get a share). Every person gets a share of several dou of grain and several jin of meat. This grain is called the annual grain allowance [*hongding gu*]. There are four ways to distribute meat.

1. *Meat for sacrifices.* In the past shares were given to those who had won a *xiucai* or *juren* degree. Afterwards graduates from new-style schools were added.

2. *Meat for branches.* Every branch [in the ancestral trust receives] one share.

3. *Meat for old people.* Every person over the age of 70 receives one share.

4. *Meat per capita.* Every male gets one share.

The order of the division is as follows. First, the meat for sacrifices [i.e., for degree holders] is distributed and then the meat for old people. Because these two types of people are quite respected, every person gets about one jin. Next is the meat for branch families. Every branch gets about eight or ten jin, but there are also ones who get as much as twenty jin. After this division is completed, a smaller division is made to the members of the branches.

Why do some want a division of the meat by branches? This is a kind of struggle. Those in a branch with few people want to distribute the meat by branches; those in branches with many people oppose distributing the meat by branches and advocate a per capita division of the meat. But the result is that in every area most of the meat is divided by branches; thus the division occurs in accordance with the viewpoint of the branches with the fewest people. Why do the small branches prevail? Because in this kind of property trust, every branch originally had equal rights [and an equal voice].

Next is the division of the meat per capita. Not every trust makes this kind of division. Most trusts lack a per capita division of the meat, because trust monies are few or because there are too many people. A small number of trusts do not divide the grain and meat equally but rather in rotation. This is called "collecting in turn" or "the one in charge" [*guantou*]. That is, the members of the trust take turns collecting the ancestors' rent. When the rent is collected, every year a small part is used to pay the expenses for sacrifices to the ancestors. Most of the rent money lines the pockets of the one in charge but this certainly is not cheating,[3] because this is the economic basis for the trust. Why? While the patriarch is still alive, he takes the family land and divides it among his children. But because he is afraid that his descendants will later take their share and sell it and there will be nothing left to eat, he takes from his land a part that cannot be divided. This becomes corporate land, forever inalienable. On the one hand, it provides sacrifice money after his death, and on the other hand, it provides relief for his descendants in difficulties. This is called "providing security." His descendants quite approve of this method because this is their security.

When most of these patriarchs are alive, no trusts are established. After the patriarch dies, the descendants, provided they are moderately well off, certainly establish a trust. Nominally this is called "sacrificing to the ancestors," but actually it is for themselves. So the practice of taking turns in receiving the rent is ostensibly collecting rent on behalf of the patriarch, but it is actually taking turns collecting rent on behalf of oneself. Under the circumstances, those poor descendants always clamor to divide the corporate land, whereas the rich descendants are opposed. This becomes a kind of class struggle within a lineage. The poor people clamoring to divide the land do not want to till the land after it is divided. They want to divide the land and sell it to obtain money to pay off loan sharks or to buy gruel for tomorrow's breakfast. In this situation, we can see the poor masses, because of their suffering and inability to get food, gradually abandoning the feudal thought associated with the sacrifices performed for ancestors. Their life compels them to dismiss such treasures.

To sum up ancestral lands, they constitute 24 percent of all land and 60 percent of corporate land.

RELIGIOUS TRUSTS

There are six kinds of "religious trusts"; god and shrine associations, village communities, temples, Buddhist monasteries, and Daoist monasteries. Every kind and type of god [*shen*] can have an association [*hui*]; for example, the Duke of Zhao Association, the Guanyin Association, the Guanye Association, the Dashen Association, the Zhenjun Association, the Potai Association, the Laiye Association, the Gongwang Association, the Bogong Association, the Wenchang Association, and the like. None of these have temples.[4] In this category is also a type of sacrifice association [*jiaohui*] that makes sacrifices to a god.

Among the various kinds of gods described above, there are some for whom a shrine [*tan*] is established. A shrine is a place where a stone is set up or [where] several stones are placed to form a small room. Inside is an efficacious god. Because of this it is called a shrine.

Whether a god or a shrine association, all associations have trust lands. Rich peasants and landlords put out the money to set up these god associations. Ninety-five percent of the property of these god associations consists of land; 5 percent consists of [contributions of] grain or money. This kind of land, grain, and money is called an association endowment. The purpose is (1) for the god, because the god can protect the health of a contributor's family and livestock and ensure the prosperity and wealth of his family and descendants, and (2) for eating. On the god's birthday, a meal is eaten. At New Year's and other festivals, there is also some meat for those members who contribute dues. Those who contributed membership dues but later become poor can give up their share. For example, if every share consists of a five-yuan endowment, when someone is given a five-yuan "replacement," he is considered to have resigned from the association.

A community [*she*] has a kind of community shrine [*shetan*] that is different from a shrine association. Every village has one. Even if a village only has three families, there is a community shrine. Why do they want a community shrine? To ensure that their crops are not devoured by insects and that their livestock do not get sick, and to ensure the health of the people. Every community has an association.

From the beginning of February to the end of October, there is a meeting each month. The meeting is usually scheduled for the second, but in some places it is on the sixteenth. On the day of the meeting, one person from each family in the community comes. Rich or poor, all have a share. A pig is killed and wine purchased for a big feast. After the feast, a meeting is held to discuss affairs like building terraces and water channels, prohibiting livestock from harming fields, and prohibiting careless use of wooded areas. The regulations are numerous, and everyone has his say. Also, there is no chairman; nor is any record [of the proceedings] desired. The discussions are chaotic, but there is a kind of natural order. So when the so-called elders or the enlightened ones voice a reasonable view, then everyone says their words have "been spoken well." [When this happens,] a decision has been reached.

This community of the masses is totally different, even though they both believe in gods, from the shrine associations of the rich peasants and landlords.[5] The peasants run this kind of community discussion, not the bullies or the powerful gentry. Nor is it completely run by rich peasants. The informal chairman is the person whose reasonable manner causes people to trust him. Very few community shrines have public halls. In the majority, when they hold the meeting on the second of every month (to worship the god), everyone contributes money. Each time everyone pays 2, 3, or 4 mao; but if a person is not going to eat, he does not have to pay.

As for "temples" [miao], they have rooms with images. A temple has a temple caretaker, called a temple elder [miaolao] in the local dialect, who is an old man who takes care of the image and tends the lamps and incense. Generally speaking, most temples have land, the rent from which is used to support the temple elder. Elders of the temples without land get their food and sundries from contributions of money and food from the masses. Among the temples are the City God Temple, Guandi Temple, Three Forces Temple, Three Sages Temple, Lailao Temple, Dragon God Temple, Guan[di] and Yue [Fei] Temple,[6] Yanggong Temple,[7] Eastern Mountain [Dongyue] Temple, and Jiangdong Temple. These temples honor "persons whose contributions or virtues caused people to worship them as gods."[8]

Shrine associations are needed by landlords; the community shrines are needed by peasants; temples are needed by both landlords and peasants. The land income of the temples is low, and the rent is not enough to pay for the cost of incense, spirit money, and the needs of the temple elder. These are not places engaging in serious exploitation.

"Monasteries" [si] are different in every respect. These caves of bonzes are places of extreme exploitation. All monastery land is derived from the "bequests" of large landlords, who are called "benefactors." Why do large landlords bequeath land to the monks? Because Buddhism is the religion of the large-landlord class. Large landlords, in order to "benefit" their sons, grandsons, and themselves, bequeath land to the monks. All the following Buddhist monasteries, convents, or temples [heshang si] are near the Xunwu City District: Wufu an, Huilong si, Zhengjue si, Guanyin ge, Dongbi shan, Dabei ge, Ehu an, Xizhu shan, Tiantai shan, Shizi yan, Sanjiao dong,[9] Jiaogong yan, Fahua an, Xihua shan, Nanyang shan, Fanhui si, Ganlu si, and Jiulong shan.

Daoist vegetarian halls are called "monasteries" [guan];[10] for example, Yungai dong,[11] Dashan li, Chuantang keng, and others. The origin of the property of these monasteries and their exploitative characteristics are the same as those of [Buddhist] monasteries.

To sum up, the landholdings of religious trusts (shen, tan, she, miao, si, guan) constitute 8 percent of all land and 20 percent of corporate land.

ADMINISTRATIVE TRUSTS

These are divided into two kinds: (1) land set aside to fund institutions connected with the traditional examination system, the Confucian Temple, and education; and (2) public works–related lands associated with bridge societies, road societies, and tax societies.

The examination hall lands [*kaopeng tian*] of Xunwu City bring in about 650 dan of rent. The powerful gentry [*haoshen*] managers skim off 180 dan for feasting, which leaves 470 dan for the examination hall [account].[12] The examination hall lands originated in the Qing when buildings were constructed and big landlords contributed much grain for the building. Funds not needed for construction were used to buy land, the income from which provided monies for repairs. A Shrine for Esteeming Righteousness [Shangyi ci][13] was built, and the names of the large landlords who contributed were put on tablets. The tablets of those who contributed the most were put at the top of the display case, and the tablets of those who contributed the least were put on the bottom of the display.

Sojourning stipend lands [*binxing tian*] were also contributed by landlords.[14] These lands are dispersed in every *bao* throughout the county. Most are still managed by the original owner. Half of each year's income is given to the Xunwu City Sojourning Stipend Shrine (Bingxing ci). This shrine has a branch bureau in every district to manage the property. Income from the property was used to provide travel money for those taking the provincial- and metropolitan-level imperial examinations and stipends for juren and jinshi degree holders. (Most was disbursed to provide traveling money for those going to the provincial [*xiangshi*] examinations or awards for those who won degrees at the provincial exams). These awards were also called stipends [*huahong*, lit. flower red]. The county Sojourning Stipend Shrine can collect 1,500–1,600 dan of rent grain annually. The provincial examinations occurred once every three years, in the *zi*, *wu*, *mao*, and *you* years.[15] Over a hundred Xunwu men took the provincial exam each time. Each person received 24 yuan for travel expenses. Those who won a juren degree received a stipend of more than 100 yuan. Within the Sojourning Stipend Shrine are over a hundred tablets on which are written the names of all the powerful gentry who contributed money. After the examination system was abolished, everyone who graduated from the No. 2 Normal School in Ganzhou received travel money of 30 yuan to travel in Jiangsu and Zhejiang [to broaden his knowledge]. Furthermore, everyone who went overseas to Japan to study received an allowance of 360 yuan for his trip. When Xunwu City built a preliminary normal school and an upper primary school, money from the Sojourning Stipend Shrine [account] was used.

A Confucian temple [*xuegong*] was also built with money contributed by landlords. Just like the Shrine for Esteeming Righteousness and the Sojourning Stipend Shrine, a Shrine for Loving Righteousness [Haoyi ci] was built to commemorate these contributions. Later, more than 1,000 yuan was donated for the annual worship of Confucius—this was in currency, not land.

Educational lands were contributed by every surname group of landlords in order to encourage the young people of their surname group to take the [Qing] examinations. Every surname group has these lands. For example, the Gu of Huangxiang contributed land that yields rent of 100 dan. The Kuang of Chetou gave land yielding over 200 dan. At the least, the contributions amounted to several dozen dan. Furthermore, Xunwu City District, like every other district, has a teacher salary association [lit. fuel and water association]. Throughout every district there are also literary societies. These resemble associations for encouraging people to study for the examinations, but they are a kind of local form in which a group of families or a whole district unites together. Also, a certain landlord in the Gu family of Huangxiang (Gu Bo's paternal grandfather) contributed land yielding 100 dan of rent to build a Hall for Recognizing the Educated [Zunyu tang].

This rewards students from throughout the county, but this is a special case.

To sum up, land connected with education amounts to 4 percent of all land and 10 percent of corporate land.

A rather considerable amount of land is associated with public works–related organizations like bridge associations, road associations, and tax associations. Not only do large bridges and long bridges have associations, even small bridges in villages have associations. If there is a bridge, then there is land, because landlords and merchants contribute to maintain bridges. When a bridge is first built, there is little money [in the bridge fund], but year after year enough rent is collected and saved so that land can be bought. Every year in December, an accounting is made and the bridge god is worshiped. This is called "gathering for the bridge association." The contributors all come together to eat, and afterwards they divide up the pork. Actually the bridge association is an organization for exploitation. Larger bridge associations, such as the Fu Bridge Association in Liuche, have 8,000 yuan, and their property brings in 500 dan of rent each year. Smaller ones get 2–3 dan of rent—these are the smallest of the small bridges.

There are not many road associations, and no association owns much land. In the whole county there are more than fifteen such associations. Each road association only takes in about 7 or 8 dan of grain. Why do bridge associations [have more assets] than road associations? Because, unlike a bridge, a road in disrepair is easy to fix; even if it is not fixed, it does not ever get to the point that people cannot use it.

There are only a few tax associations in the county. For example, the Yan of Huangxiang have one, as do the Mei of Datian, the Kuang of Chetou, or the Liu of Chuanxia in Jitan, and each association has some land. The richest is that of the Kuang of Chetou. Their tax association has land with rents of 500 dan. Originally it was called "army land," but now it is called a tax association. The purpose of the tax association is to be responsible for an entire lineage's tax quota in order to counteract the government's grasping taxation of every family in the lineage. With every type of extortion and blackmail, tax collecting was harmful to all involved; to prevent this, a tax association would be established, or money would be collected from small ancestral trusts. If [a lineage] has a tax association, then the authorities collect taxes only from the tax association, and hence every family avoids harm. Without a tax association, the authorities take more than the quota. If the payment is late, then interest is computed and it is really high. Because of this, tax associations are started. When a tax association is organized, it has little money, but after several years it mounts up.

To sum up, public works–related land constitutes 4 percent of all land and 10 percent of corporate land.

LARGE LANDLORDS

Above I discussed the land held by trusts. Now I turn to the land of individual landlords. The land owned by individual landlords constitutes 30 percent of all land, which is much less than the amount of land owned by the trusts. Of this land, small landlords (rents under 200 dan) own the greatest part; middle landlords (rents of 200–499 dan) are next; and large landlords (rents over 500 dan) own the least. In the whole country there are eight pre-eminent landlords:

Liu Tuyuan	Xunwu City District
Luo Hanzhang	Huangxiang District
Xie Jie	Nanba District
Kuang Wenrong	Nanba District
Mei Hongxing	Shuangqiao District
Pan Mingzheng	Jiansan District (nicknamed "Uncle Shitcrock")
Lin Chaoguan	Chengjiang District
Wang Juyuan	Chengjiang District

Each receives rents of 1,000 dan or more. The greatest among these is considered Uncle Shitcrock, who is from Xiangshan bao in Jiansan District. The value of all his holdings—land, buildings, forests, livestock, and his herb store and general store in Jitan—is 300,000 yuan. His land rents are about 10,000 dan. He is the leader of the powerful gentry throughout the county. In the early Republic, his third son, Pan Mengchun (an illiterate scoundrel who did not pass the civil service exam or attend a new-style school), became chief of the county Tax Collection Bureau (national taxes). In 1917 or 1918, his eldest son, Pan Yiren (a xiucai who is more or less literate), finished his three years as chief of the Tax Collection Bureau (local taxes, managing funds from the examination hall and Sojourning Stipend Shrine lands, the ox tax, the gambling tax, the business protection tax, and others). In 1924 or 1925 Pan Mengchun became the head of the All-County Protection Militia and controlled the militias of all seven districts. All true power was in his hands. He was head of the All-County Militia and needed money [for it]. At the same time the Beiyang Army's Deng Ruzhuo[16] came to the county to ask for money, and Pan issued a lot of paper money. After these bills had been in use for several months, a middle landlord named Lai Aoxu in the provincial capital brought suit against him and only then was this practice stopped. In 1926, when the KMT's influence reached Xunwu, he lost his clout. But he immediately united with the New Xunwu faction, which, although it originally had the character of the bourgeoisie, was cooperating with the landlords at that time. He became a member of the KMT's county branch. In March of this year, the powerful gentry brought down Magistrate Hu Zefan, and Pan became magistrate. When the Red Army arrived, he fled to Wuping. His seventy-odd guns were taken over by Zhong Shaokui of Wuping.

Liu Tuyuan is the second great local bully, but he is not active. He is a graduate of a middle school and has no power in the county.

Xie Jie is a graduate of the Jiangxi Army Academy and was a division commander under Lai Shihuang. Now he is in Shanghai organizing the South Jiangxi Mining Association in order to encourage [Chinese-operated] mines. He has joined the Reorganization faction [Gaizu pai][17] that organized the Jiangxi Self-salvation Society [Zijiuhui] and publishes the *Self-salvation Daily* [*Zijiu ribao*] and opposes Chiang Kai-shek. He is zealous in calling for "mopping up the CCP."

Wang Juyuan is a graduate of Ganzhou's No. 4 Middle School. He is influential in Chengjiang and is on good terms with the loafers. He has opened three shops in Chengjiang for marine products, general goods, and opium. In the back of the shops he has opened opium dens and invites the loafers to come and take opium for free. Because of this, he gets their support. He messes with other men's wives but if other people have no sense of propriety and go whoring, they are severely tormented by the loafers. Those who receive this kind of torment can be completely ruined financially.

Xunwu's large landlords (500–999 dan) number twelve.

Cao Shancheng (Tianbei, West Ward). 500 dan; his grandfather [was the one who] got rich; he is from an old rich family [lit. *laoshuihu*, or old tax family].[18]

Qiu Shulie (Tuhe, West Ward). 500 dan; a useless person; his son is an engineer who graduated from Nanyang University and went to England for a while; now he is in Tianjin serving as an engineer for some boiler company.

Cao Yuansen (East Ward). 500 dan; a graduate of Xunwu City Upper Primary School; 40 sui; he is a power in the East Ward.

Huang Jiabin (Changju, North Ward). 700 dan; KMT member; He Zizhen wanted to use him, but he would not agree. Now he opportunistically expresses sympathy toward peasants. If they want guns, he gives them guns. If they want money, he gives them money. He said: "The KMT is useless. If I pay them, I still don't get protection; but if the money goes to the soviet, it can save my life."

Xunwu City gate

Unless otherwise identified, the photographs in this section were taken by Dr. and Mrs. Cyril E. Bousfield during their stay in Xunwu County between 1912 and 1928. Some are reproduced from Lillie Bousfield's *Sun-wu Stories* (Shanghai: Kelly & Walsh, 1932); the rest are copies of photographs in the collection of Neal D. Bousfield, Bar Harbor, Maine.

Strongholds in Xunwu. According to Mrs. Lillie Bousfield (*Sun-wu Stories*, pp. 67–68), these fortresses were up to five stories high and were used as defensive strongholds during lineage feuds or incursions by bandit gangs. In Chapter 4 of the *Report from Xunwu*, Mao cites these fortresses as the current home of this or that "reactionary" or "counterrevolutionary" and in Chapter 5 mentions that the Huangxiang stronghold had been burned, with the help of women revolutionaries. (*top*) Stronghold on the road to Jitan, in Jiansan District (from *Sun-wu Stories*, p. 24). (*bottom*) Rural stronghold, thought to be in Xiangshan *bao*, Jiansan District, the center of Pan Mingzheng's power.

Rural stronghold

Bridge near Xunwu City (from *Sun-wu Stories*, p. 40)

Village (from *Sun-wu Stories*, p. 64)

Two peasant women

A tobacco porter
(from *Sun-wu
Stories*, p. 112)

Rural valley (from
Sun-wu Stories, p. 32)

View looking south from the Xunwu City walls, showing the southern branch of the Xunwu River and the Taiping Bridge

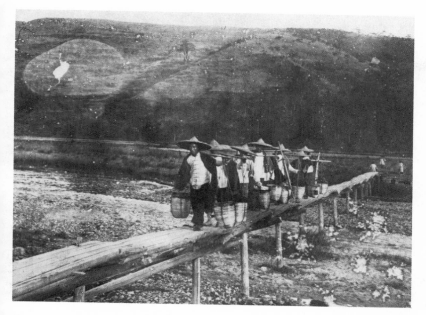

Porters crossing a simple bridge

Man plowing field

Peasant girl

Woman tending a local shrine

(*opposite*) A cabinet made by Hu Donglin, whom Mao identifies as the leading maker of furniture and other wooden items in Xunwu City. The cabinet is now in the possession of Neal D. Bousfield (photograph by R. Normand, First Exposure).

The Bousfield residence, circa 1917. Mao used this building as his headquarters during his stay in Xunwu, and the investigation meetings that resulted in the *Report from Xunwu* were held there. This structure was largely destroyed during the seesaw battle for control of Xunwu City that continued until the KMT victory during the summer of 1933. A replica was opened in December 1987. Visitors are shown Mao's bedroom and his private office, the central room where the Xunwu investigation meetings took place, and an office used by Fourth Army Personnel.

Xunwu City, during the 1910's, viewed from southeast of the city. The mission compound and the Tremont Temple Hospital were later built in the field in the center.

View of the Tremont Temple Hospital compound, outside the South Gate of Xunwu City, facing east. This part of Xunwu County was relatively unforested, perhaps because of the proximity of Xunwu City. The building on the right was the Bousfields' house.

The main entrance to the Tremont Temple Hospital. Although most of the hospital was destroyed sometime after Mao left Xunwu, the remaining walls were used to construct a church in the mid-1930's. The building shown in this 1986 picture is reportedly being used for classrooms (photograph by Christopher Lee).

Panorama of the landscape southeast of Xunwu City, 1986 (photograph by Christopher Lee)

Soldiers awaiting treatment, circa 1916, in the portico of the first Bousfield residence (1912–17), which doubled as Dr. Bousfield's clinic.

Xie Shande (Yazimu, Sanbiao). 500 dan; he is a reader of old books and a hermit [*shanlaoshu*].[19]

Wang Fosheng (Aobei, Shuiyuan). 500 dan; his son Wang Weifan, a graduate of Chaoyang University in Beijing, is a KMT member who left and has not returned.

Lan Shaozong (Chengjiang). 500 dan; since his death, his widow has handled family affairs.

Cao Guodong (Jitan). 600 dan; in the past his was called a 10,000-dan family, but he used some money to build a mansion; a graduate of upper primary school; a relative of Uncle Shitcrock; cooperates with Pan Mengchun.

Yi Zhanliang (Guishixia, Shuangqiao District). More than 500 dan; at the beginning he was a reactionary, but his land was quickly divided and he was fined more than 1,000 yuan, so he became poor; not a reactionary.

Lai Pengchi (Danxi, Shuangqiao District). Called a 10,000-dan family; more than 500 dan; a Qing *fusheng*; very conservative, still has a queue, but not reactionary.

Kuang Mingjing (Jizijiao, Nanba). 600 dan; his fourth brother is a White army battalion commander; whole family has fled.

Chen Wanbao (Tingling). 600 dan; deals in pork and opium and runs a general store; he himself is not a reactionary, but his brother is a member of the New Xunwu faction and lives in the same household; his brother is very reactionary.

The above eight great landlords and the twelve second-level landlords together number twenty. When Jiangxi people speak of "10,000-dan families," they mean these people. Why have I listed them one by one? In order to study the class's political function. If we failed to mention examples, then we would not have substantive evidence. For this reason, I want to list examples of middle landlords. However, it is not easy to list small landlords because there are too many. Why do we distinguish middle landlords within the landlord class? Because not only is their political function greatly different from that of small landlords, but it is obviously different from that of large landlords.

MIDDLE LANDLORDS

Xunwu City District

Qiu Weiwu (Tuhe, West Ward). 400 dan; graduated from the Leather Course of the Imperial University in Japan;[20] worked as an engineer at Ganzhou Poor People's Factory for six months; returned to Xunwu in 1922 to serve as head of the Education Bureau; joined the KMT; one of the leaders of New Xunwu faction and helped make plans for the faction; tough guy; ran away with Xie Jiayou when the Red Army arrived in Xunwu.

Huang Jiakui (Changju, North Ward). Over 300 dan; Pingyuan Middle School graduate; member of KMT Executive Committee in Xunwu; member of New Xunwu faction (teacher at New Xunwu School); active reactionary.

Luo Songsheng (Changju, North Ward). 300 dan; runs the Luo Jinfeng General Store in the city; not very reactionary; his nephew is a KMT member and an upper primary school graduate who speaks badly of the Communist party.

He Tingba (outside North Gate). Over 300 dan; a graduate of Pingyuan Middle School; member of the KMT; major figure in the New Xunwu faction; energetically works against the revolution.

Liu Forong (outside Little East Gate). 300 dan; is not a reactionary; works as a doctor.

Sanshui District

Lei Changxiang (Changpai, Sanbiao). 300 dan; a "hermit"; useless.

Hu Enrong (Sanbiao *xu*). 300 dan; a religious vegetarian; uninterested in current events; tends to look for a few coppers and then stays at home and sleeps.

Hu Jingru (Sanbiao *xu*). 200 dan; graduate of No. 4 Middle School in Ganzhou; in his twenties; famous local strongman in Sanbiao; involved in county politics.

Ling Lushi (Jingshi, Sanbiao). Over 300 dan; an old xiucai; in the past served as Tax Collection Bureau chief for many years; was a section chief of something; official in charge of examinations; after working for over ten years, he accumulated some savings; built a new house in Sanbiao; in his fifties.

Yuan Dehe (Yuanwu, Shuiyuan, the most reactionary area). 200 dan or so; middle school graduate; member of the KMT; counterrevolutionary.

There are many other middle landlords in Sanshui District, but it is difficult to name them all.

Chengjiang District

Lan Ziqian. 400 dan; provincial middle school graduate; owns the Lan Xietai general goods and textile store in Chengjiang; counterrevolutionary.

Xie Jiayou. 300 dan; upper primary school graduate; in his forties; was a regimental commander under Xie Jie in the Fourteenth Army; the head captain of the Xunwu militia; member of the Reorganization faction; he was the one who wiped out the First Battalion of the Fiftieth Regiment of the Red Army; graduated from the Jiangxi Army Academy.

Ling Xixian. 300 dan; a middle school graduate; member of the New Xunwu faction; member of the KMT; owns a store in Chengjiang xinxu.

Jiansan District

Chen Yuheng (Jitan). 300 dan; graduate of Pingyuan Middle School; local strongman at Jitan; major figure in the New Xunwu faction; Uncle Shitcrock's grandson-in-law; very active.

Liu Taizang (Chuanxia, Jitan). 400 dan; a gambling boss; started as a loafer; became rich through gambling; until 1916 he was a *dangwu* (a burglar).

Pan Jindi (Xiangshan). Over 200 dan; graduate of Mei County Normal School; a member of the New Xunwu faction; an active KMT member; the commander of Jitan Pacification and Defense Militia.

Pan Mingrui (Xiangshan). 400 dan; relative of Uncle Shit-crock; owns two stores in Jitan for general goods and marine products; the leader of Xiangshan reactionaries.

Pan Guanlan. Although he is a small landlord with a 100-odd dan income, he is a reactionary leader; Pan Li died by his hand; graduated from Ganzhou Upper Primary School; worked as a primary school teacher for five or six years, he was not a reactionary at that time; was corrupted into a counterrevolutionary around the time of the 25 March uprising; his father was a gambling boss and made his money that way.

Pan Mingdian (Pingdi, Xiangshan). Over 100 dan; a Qing *bagong*; graduated from a school of law and administration during the Republican period; was a magistrate in Lufeng [Guangdong] and Huichang [Jiangxi]; was the head of the Education Bureau in Xunwu County for a few years; was assigned to many other positions; known as *Shenjianjiuzhang* [one who holds many posts simultaneously]; originally was a middle landlord; has spent over 4,000 yuan campaigning for election to the provincial assembly but still has not been elected; was the warden of Nanchang High Court last year; this year he is a clerk in the Jiujiang High Court; a bureaucratic frame of mind; speaks well; has good calligraphy; handsome appearance; very proper; resembles Confucius.

Pan Jingwen (Dali, Xiangshan). Over 300 dan, a Qing xiucai; an old scholar.

Pan Guocai (Xiangshancun). 300 dan; also an old xiucai.

Pan Guoqing (Xiangshancun). Only 50 or 60 dan; upper primary school graduate; secretary to the bandit Ye Zishe; counterrevolutionary.

Liu Hanyuan (Jianxi). Over 200 dan; good for nothing.

Huangxiang District

Li Qilang (Huangxiang *xu*). Over 300 dan; gambling background; his son, Li Hanhui, an upper primary school graduate, is an important member of the reactionary faction.

Liu Yujie (Huangxiang *xu*). Over 200 dan; his son, Liu Jinyan, went to Xinyuan Middle School in Nanchang and then to Hujiang University and Shanghai University for some time, previously was close to the Cooperative Society faction.

Liu Yulin, younger brother of Liu Yujie. 400 dan; is a mute; has four or five sons who graduated from primary school; his youngest son went to middle school; all participated in the 25 March uprising; now they are counterrevolutionaries.

Lai Shoucheng (Hongtouling). 400 dan; his son, Lai Shifang, studied at East Mountain Middle School in Mei County; counterrevolutionary.

Lai Aoxu (Hongtouling). 400 dan; xiucai; graduated from Shanghai Technical Training School; principal of the county upper primary school for one year; was a teacher for five or six years; campaigned for the provincial assembly but lost; has two sons who went to middle school; one of them graduated from Beijing Normal School and is close to the Cooperative Society faction; the New Xunwu faction attacked him during the 25 March uprising, and now both of the sons are counterrevolutionaries.

Wang Ziyuan (Shanzixia). 200 dan; reactionary leader in Huangxiang; is a great evil gentryman [*lieshen*]; was the head of a protection militia [*baowei tuan*]; the head of an educational trust.

Liu Jingxi (Sichengcun). Over 300 dan; graduated from Mei County Middle School; his father worked for Hu Qian and was killed by bandits; is not a reactionary.

Liu Quanlan (Sicheng). About 200 dan; started out as a usurer; is not a reactionary now; his son joined the peasants' association, but because of a misunderstanding he was mistakenly shot to death by the peasants.

Luo Chengtian (Xiwei). 400 dan; bargains with merchants even when purchasing a tiny bit of tobacco; a miser; values money more than life.

Luo Fushou (Xiwei). Used to have 300 dan; now the property has been divided; a counterrevolutionary.

Luo Peici (Xiwei). 200 dan; was Yudu County magistrate; is a very cunning person; before the 25 March uprising occurred, while everybody was still preparing in secret, he spied [it coming]; he walked about the countryside urging [other landlords] to pretend to reform; "Sell your family's grain at a fair price and don't try to make money. Or give the grain to poor people with the same surname. If you don't, there's going to be real trouble." He is a reactionary leader; among the powerful gentry, he's fearsome.

Luo Lushou (Xiwei). 200 dan; his son is a member of the New Xunwu faction who likes attention.

Gu Lesan (Tangbei). 300 dan (with his brother); his older brother is a xiucai and was a provincial assemblyman for two terms; he [Gu Lesan] worked under Hu Qian as a commissariat officer; was a district head in Wuhua County during the Chen Jiongming period; one of the reactionary leaders in the county; taking 30–40 guns, he fled with Xie Jiayou.

Gu Guangrui (Tangbei). Over 200 dan; upper primary school graduate; reactionary.

Gu Hua'nan (Tangbei). 200 dan; is an honest man.

Gu Guanglu (Tangbei). 400 dan; stingy; likes to take advantage of other people; haggles with a vendor over small dishes; his son is a graduate of East Mountain Middle School in Mei County; he is a fellow who cannot figure out much.

(The Tangbei Gu are Gu Bo's relatives.)

Gu Youyu (Tangbei). 500 dan; operates a paper store; sells raw opium; runs a brothel; indulges in gambling; is a miser, indifferent to current events, cares only about making money; he is the weak one in a powerful family; his family takes advantage of him; if they ask for 50 yuan, they get 50 yuan; if they ask for a 100, they get 100.

Yan Jinxiu (Gaotou).   Used to be a 10,000-dan family; he became poor after spending too much money building his house; he now has about 300 or 400 dan; owns a store in Gongping; has over ten children and grandchildren; apathetic toward the world; primary concern is money; is a "hermit."

Yan Guoxing (Gaotou).   Over 100 dan; a small landlord; main pursuit is business; runs a general store in Gongping; also sells paper; had good relations with other businesses; some merchants from Beiling and Yanxia lent him money; together with his own money he spent about 6,000 to 7,000 yuan when he ran for the provincial assembly; he lost and now is in debt; one of the reactionary leaders in Huangxiang District.

Yan Xibo (Gaotou).   200 dan; runs a general store in Gongping; not extremely reactionary.

(In the above list, several small landlords are mentioned because they are well known.)

Shuangqiao District

Huang Qingyun (Huangtian).   200 dan; not a reactionary.

Luo Shouhan (Huangsha).   200 dan; not a reactionary.

Zhao Shangqin (Yutian).   300 dan; Pingyuan Middle School graduate; reactionary.

Xie Youfeng (Yutian).   200 dan; not a reactionary.

Chen Dequan (Liuche).   200 dan; ran a salt store in Liuche; reactionary; the Twenty-first Column executed him.

Chen Jingri (Liuche).   200 dan; not a reactionary. His son, Chen Jiguang, participated in the 25 March uprising; Mei County Middle School graduate; after the failure of 25 March uprising, he escaped to Southeast Asia.

Chen Shanniu (Liuche). An inveterate gambler; over 200 dan; not a reactionary.

Chen Biaoji (Zukeng, Liuche).   Used to be a 10,000-dan family; later was divided into four households; since his death, his son "Zhuaziliu" [Sixth Claw] has 300 dan; owns a marine products store in Liuche; is a reactionary leader.

Chen Guocai (Zukeng, Liuche). 200 dan; Mei County Middle School graduate; reactionary.

Chen Tufeng (Zukeng, Liuche). Over 200 dan; an evil gentryman; one of the "Five Tigers of Xunwu." "Pan (Mingdian), Xie (Xuzuo), Chen (Tufeng), Peng (Zijing), Kuang (Tailan) are the so-called Five Tigers of Xunwu." With the rise of the two new factions, New Xunwu and the Cooperative Society, the five old tigers fell from the [political] stage. Chen, Pan, Peng, and Kuang are xiucai; only Xie is a graduate (Xunwu Preliminary Normal School).

Liao Honggui (Shijie). 200 dan; has a store that carries marine products, general goods, and pastries in Fengshan; not a reactionary.

Liu Junfu (Qiufang). Used to be a 10,000-dan family; after division, he now has 400 dan; his son Liu Hongxiang graduated from South Jiangxi [Gannan] Middle School; later he went to Culture University in Beijing; is incoherent and yet very reactionary; is one of the counterrevolutionary leaders in Shuangqiao District; he still is guarding the [Qiufang] stronghold with his life.

Liu Shifu. A brother of Liu Junfu's; over 200 dan; once donated some money to set up a primary school; is still in the stronghold.

Liu Yuanying (Qiufang). Over 200 dan; in the stronghold.

Liu Zuorui (Qiufang). 400 dan; his large family consists of about thirty members; participated in the revolution; the family property was divided. The reason was that earlier he competed with Liu Junfu in buying land; later they quarreled with each other because of an adultery case; some of his family members took part in the 25 March uprising; after its defeat, Liu Junfu brought a false charge against him and colluded with the bandit Ye Zishe and burned down Liu Zuorui's house. Now his nephew Liu Guoxiang is a soviet committee member. Liu Risheng is a township soviet committee member; he himself [Liu Zuorui] stays at home and cares about nothing. He graduated from the No. 5 Middle School in Mei County; very honest; 23 or 24 sui; even younger than his nephew; the lawsuit was handled by his nephew's father, i.e. his older brother.

Liu Baohua (Shibei). 300 dan; his son graduated from the Sun Yatsen Middle School in the county; is involved in the revolution; is a Communist party district committee secretary.

Liu Kaixiang (Shibei). 200 dan; upper primary school graduate; not a reactionary.

Tang Sixian (Xiaqi). 300 dan; graduated from Mei County Middle School, a cadre of the New Xunwu faction; a complete reactionary.

Tang Lixian (Xiaqi). 200 dan; was a student at Whampoa Military Academy; was a head of a pacification and defense corps; member of the New Xunwu faction.

Tang Foshu (Xiaqi). 200 dan; is an evil gentryman; people called him a local strongman; graduated from the Primary School Teacher Training Institute; a lackey of the New Xunwu faction.

Zeng Chaoqun (Shangqi). Over 100 dan;[21] Mei County Middle School graduate; not a reactionary.

Zeng Xilin (Fangtian). 300 dan; received a traditional education; makes extremely usurious loans; he and his nephew Zeng Guanghua (a primary school graduate) are extremely [lit. 120 percent] reactionary; they are besieged in the Qiufang stronghold by the peasants.

Zeng Juxiang (Fangtian). 200 dan; his nephew is Zeng Chanfeng; an upper primary school graduate; a member of the Communist party whose house was burned down by the bandit Ye Zishe.

Zeng Hailan (Bogongao). Used to be a 10,000-dan family; recently the property was divided, and he got 200-odd dan; participated in the 25 March uprising; he spent 1,000-odd yuan in a lawsuit brought by Zeng Xilin; Bandit Ye also fined him; one of his younger brothers was fined over 600 yuan by Bandit Ye; not a reactionary now.

Yi Songzhou (Guishixia). 200 dan, a Qing xiucai; an evil gentryman; colluded with Bandit Ye; has fled.

He Ziwen (Danxi). In the past a 10,000-dan family; land was divided, and now he has more than 200 dan; not too reactionary.

Widow Zhong (Danxi). Over 200 dan; a reactionary; fled.

Lai Rongjun (Cenfeng). Over 200 dan; was a minor evil gentryman; now he is not a reactionary.

Mei Renhua (Cenfeng). 200 dan; not a reactionary.

Mei Diaoxian (Datian). Xiucai; 300 dan; member of the reactionary faction; fled.

Lai Wenlian (Datong). 300 dan; was caught by the Twenty-first Column of the Red Army and was fined 2,000 yuan; his land was divided and distributed; not a reactionary now.

Kuang Chunlong (Yanyangping). 200 dan; a usurer; property was confiscated; not a reactionary now.

Kuang Shiyang (Yanyangping). 200 dan; graduated from Mei County Normal School; KMT member; very reactionary.

Kuang Yingshao (Huangqiangping). 200 dan; not a reactionary.

Kuang Lanchun (Huangqiangping). 200 dan; not a reactionary.

Chen (née Tao) Xianggu (Zukeng). 300 dan; widow who handles her own affairs; started as a gambler; counterrevolutionary.

Nanba District

Liu Huangxian (Longtu). 300 dan; counterrevolutionary; was executed by shooting.

Liu Tianyuan (Longtu). 300 dan; counterrevolutionary; surrendered after one of his sons was killed.

Liu Huantong (Longtu). 300 dan; was fined over a thousand yuan by the Red Army; now he is not a reactionary.

Liu Shidi (Longtu). 200 dan; a Qing xiucai; reactionary faction; the whole family fled.

Liu Zhenguang (Hejiao *xu*). 200 dan; his third son is a reactionary who fled; the other sons are not reactionary.

Liu Meirong (Hejiao *xu*). 200 dan; not a reactionary.

Zeng Yuehui (Hejiao *xu*). 200 dan; not a reactionary; his widow manages household affairs.

Zeng (née Lu) Fuxing (Hejiao *xu*). 200 dan; has some savings; colluded with Bandit Ye; whole family is reactionary and has fled.

Chen Erlaihe (Jizijiao). 200 dan; he, his sons, and his nephews were executed by shooting by the Red Army; were very reactionary.

Zhao Zhixiang (Chetou). 200 dan; old scholar; used to be a bit of an "evil" [gentryman]; not a reactionary.

Zhao Zan (Yanger) (Chetou). 200 dan; the whole family is reactionary; fled to the Qiufang stronghold; a gambler; his grandfather made the [family's] money.

Zhao Ener (Chetou). 200 dan; honest; engages in business; runs the Huaxing Store in Chetou, which was set on fire this year during the third attack by militias from the four counties;[22] his father was killed; not a reactionary.

Zhao Yinghua (Chetou). 200 dan; used to be a 10,000-dan family; he divided his land and gave half of it to his four sons, the other half is for himself and his wife; (when dividing family property, to keep a share for oneself is called *zuo zaozi*, "to sit on the stove"); not a reactionary; has temporarily given his remaining savings to the son who has the most children.

Wen Zanbiao (Qinglong). over 200 dan; upper primary school graduate; not a reactionary.

Zhong Wenfa (Zhucun). 400 dan; has both a salt and a grain business; his grandfather willed him some money; not reactionary.

Zhong Bansan (Zhucun). 300 dan; has some property willed by his grandfather; used to gamble; sometimes serves as a mediator; not a reactionary.

Zhong Jishan (Zhucun). 200 dan; studied at the Mei County Middle School; participated in the revolution; works for the Fifth Column of the Eleventh Army of the Red Army.

Zhong "Big Face" Liu[23] (Zhucun *xu*). 300 dan; old rich family; gambles; reactionary; the whole family has fled.

Zhong Yongliu (Zhucun *xu*). 200 dan; studied in Japan; was the head of the Wuxue [Hubei] police station; was a first-class section clerk, investigator, and the chief of the Industry Bureau in this county; worked for Xie Jie; one of the reactionary leaders in Nanba District; fled to Pingyuan.

Peng Zijing (Gukenggang). 300 dan; a Qing xiucai; one of the Five Tigers in the county; in the late Qing he was a police chief [*xunjian*] in Fenghuang Autonomous Sub-prefecture in Hunan; in the Republican period he was a member of the Xunwu County Tax Collection Bureau and accepted bribes from gamblers; recently has worked as a commissariat officer in a unit of a militia [*tuan fangdui*]; has participated in every rural mop-up operation. His son, Peng Bingyi, graduated from the Mei County Middle School; member of the New Xunwu faction and KMT; was the principal of the Zhichi Primary School. The whole family is extremely reactionary.

Li Zude (Gukenggang). Used to be a 10,000-dan family; suffered business losses; only 300 dan left; the whole family is reactionary; fled.

Peng Hongyun (Xialiao). 200 dan; not so reactionary; has a general store in Xialiao.

Peng Hongquan. Peng Hongyun's brother; 200 dan; reactionary; fled to Pingyuan.

Peng Jinhan (Xialiao). 200 dan; runs several businesses; has an herbal medicine store and a general store; very money-minded; not a reactionary.

Han Foxian (Mankeng). 200 dan; did some business and farming; honest man, but also fled to Pingyuan.

Zhong Yicai (Lintianba). 300 dan; upper primary school graduate; in his grandfather's time, his was a 10,000-dan family, but the land was divided among two families; did not accept the revolution and fled; now he is willing to be fined because he wants to return home.

Zhong Dingsi (Lintianba). 200 dan; has some property willed by his grandfather; some of his children are cultivators; not a reactionary; "worries about communal property" [*gongchan*].

Zhong Shufen (Lintianba). 200 dan; he is dead; his widow manages the household; fined 200 yuan; not a reactionary.

Xie Ruilin (Niudouguang). 300 dan; doctor; unwilling to accept a fine; fled.

Xie Zhaofan (Niudouguang). 200 dan; member of the New Xunwu faction; graduated from the South Jiangxi Middle School; was the head of a protection militia; recently was the captain of a pacification and defense militia; after the success of the revolution in Nanba District, he worked as a secretary in the reactionary county government; is one of the reactionary leaders in Nanba District.

Chen Chunrong (Tingling). 200 dan; honest; his son is an upper primary school graduate and served as a company commander in the White army; reactionary; the whole family fled to Pingyuan.

Chen Liuji (Niudouguang). 300 dan; had stores [selling] oil, grain, and soybeans in both Liuche and Niudouguang; colluded with Bandit Ye; very reactionary; the whole family fled.

Chen Zhongjun (Tingling). 200 dan; honest; his son was a head of a protection militia; not a reactionary.

Xie Peiqin (Fengshugang, Niudouguang). 400 dan; was a usurer; many inveterate gamblers borrowed money from him; his son was studying at the New Xunwu School; reactionary; fled.

Chen Anru (Tingling). 300 dan; trader of pigs and oxen; runs a boarding house; was fined; it is unlikely that he is a reactionary now.

Zeng Rensheng (Lianping). Over 300 dan; did farming himself; made money by gambling; did not pay his fine; fled.

Zhong Xingkui (Longhukeng, Zhucun). 200 dan; graduated

from the Pingyuan Middle School; participated in KMT affairs; graduated from Nanchang Political Tutelage Training School; major figure in the New Xunwu faction; extremely reactionary.

Altogether there are 113 middle landlords in the seven districts of the county.[24]

ATTITUDES OF LARGE AND MIDDLE LANDLORDS
TOWARD PRODUCTION

The middle landlords, who receive 200 dan in rent or more, and the large landlords, who receive 500 dan or more in rent, pay no attention to production. They do not work personally and also do not organize production—their only goal is to receive rent. Certainly every large and middle landlord has some land cultivated [under his direction], but his purpose is not to improve production methods or increase productivity. You cannot get rich on this. In order to avoid the dilemma of having no use for accumulated human and animal wastes and also to keep hired hands from being idle, the landlord selects the richest of his own land and cultivates land yielding 10–20 dan of grain. None cultivates enough land to yield 40–50 dan. This kind of landlord normally hires one worker. Only the large landlords of 10,000 dan or above and households without much manpower hire two workers. In order to make sure that workers do not loaf, landlords ask them to cultivate small plots of land in addition to doing other odd jobs.

POLITICAL ATTITUDES OF LARGE
AND MIDDLE LANDLORDS

The lifestyles of large and middle landlords can be divided into three categories on the basis of the situation in Xunwu.

The first kind is the progressives [xinde], who have been influenced the most by capitalism. Their lifestyle is comparatively luxurious. They spend freely and want to buy every kind of foreign-style good. The clothes they wear button down the middle, and they have Western-style haircuts. They are relatively keen on sending their sons to school or have themselves graduated from middle school or other kinds of schools. There are relatively few people of this type among the landlord class; most of them live near rivers or near markets. Most of them have merchant backgrounds. Wang Juyuan of Chengjiang is a good example.

The second type is the moderates [lit. half-new but not old]. They approve of new trends a bit, but right away criticize their weak points. They build schools and serve as heads of the Education Bureau, but the schools they establish are the traditional rotten ones. They become head of the Education Bureau in order to get power and money, not to "enlighten the people and promote education." In the past most of those who served as Education Bureau heads were in this category. The first type are too progressive for the job. The landlords in this group are not misers but they are not profligates either. Most of the large and middle landlords are like this. The basic characteristic of landlords is to preserve the old, so why do the second type want to jump on the bandwagon of moderation? In order to grasp the power to lead. Otherwise leadership would be seized totally by the People's Rights faction or the so-called New Study faction; so they must change their ways a bit. Because their economic connections still depend on feudal exploitation, they display all the characteristics of landlords. Their progressive attitude [*gexin*] is only on the surface. Qiu Weiwu of Xunwu City District, Pan Yiren of Jiansan District, and Xie Jiayou of Chengjiang District are examples of this layer.

The third kind [of people] have totally feudal attitudes and lifestyles. They live in the hills, far from rivers or markets. They have never ceased to hope for the restoration of the examination system; they are total monarchists. They want to use monarchical ideas to strike down ideas about people's rights, restore their political leadership, and return to the deteriorating and collapsing situation of the feudal economy. Their lifestyle is very rigid. Although most have adopted the shaved-head style haircut, some still follow the Qing practice. In Xunwu this kind of person makes up the smallest part of the large and middle landlords. An example is Mei Hongxing of Datian in Shuangqiao District.

Among the large and middle landlords, the progressives constitute 10 percent, the moderates 70 percent, and the traditionalists 20 percent. But we cannot say that the so-called progressives, who are heading toward capitalism, are revolutionary. As a whole, the large and middle landlords oppose revolution. There is also a situation that needs to be explained. The moderate part of the large and middle landlord class is not formed only by reason of locality (near rivers or in the hills; close to markets or far from markets). There is also an age factor in these formations. Within one family, most of the old people are old-fashioned, most of the young people are reform-minded, and most of the middle-aged are moderate. The age factor reflects the times one grew up in. The old folks were deeply affected by the old system. Moreover, they are going to die soon and lack the ability to speak of progressive matters; they can only preserve the old. Young people are influenced by old ways only slightly, but because they have no future without reform, they are relatively less conservative.

The middle-aged people are on both sides. For example, the large landlord Uncle Shitcrock is very conservative. His children advocated building schools, but these new-style schools are neither new nor old. His grandchildren—six or seven of them—have gone to Canton, Shanghai, Beijing, and England to study the so-called New Curriculum [xinxue]. Nevertheless, it does not matter what they have studied, they all are counterrevolutionary. Pan Zuoqin, a grandson of Uncle Shitcrock, graduated from medical school in England and returned. Now he is in Shantou, where he is considered the second best of the Western-trained doctors. Every day he earns 40 to 50 yuan;

every month he can receive more than 1,000 yuan. When he first returned home, he refused the Xunwu Education Society Clinic's offer of 1,200 yuan a year because his income at Shantou was much greater.

SMALL LANDLORDS

Small landlords (less than 200 dan) far outnumber the other two categories. Taking landlords as a whole, large landlords (over 500 dan) make up 1 percent, middle landlords (over 200 dan) 19 percent, and small landlords 80 percent. The number of large landlords is the smallest; their influence throughout the county is insignificant. The center of power in the county is among the middle landlords. Most of their children have gone to middle school. The administrative power of the county—Tax Collection Bureau, Education Bureau, Security Militia—is mostly snagged by them, especially the monies for the spring and autumn sacrifices [zhengchang],[25] which are almost totally in their hands. Small landlords and rich peasants cannot interfere. But among the landlord class, small landlords are absolutely the greatest in number, and they display these special characteristics.

1. Many have small businesses. They open small general stores and buy agricultural goods at a low price and wait until the price is dear to sell. Probably 10 out of every 100 small landlords engage in this kind of small business. Some middle landlords engage in business and their businesses are larger than those of small landlords, but the proportion of middle landlords engaged in business is smaller. Most middle landlords have a lifestyle that is part of the feudal economy, unlike the extreme mercantilization of the small landlords.

2. Particularly indicative of the mercantilization of small landlords is that they also send their children to new-style schools. All the children of small landlords go to primary schools, and almost all go to upper primary school—at least in eight families out of ten. And three families out of ten have

children in middle school. This class, compared with any other single class, has been influenced by the new culture [*xin wenhua*] quickly and in great numbers. In terms of administrative affairs, the small landlords are ruled by the middle landlord class; that is to say, they have no power. Their revolutionary demands during the first period of the revolutionary movement were expressed very stridently; their revolutionary activism advanced sharply. The Cooperative Society faction in Xunwu (Sun Yatsen Middle School faction) represents this class, but the New Xunwu faction (Young Revolutionary Comrades Society faction) represents the counterrevolutionary segment of the middle landlord class.

Why does the small landlord class, influenced by capitalist culture, become so quickly infused with the revolutionary culture of the People's Rights movement, and why are its revolutionary demands and activities so intense and so fiercely advanced? This is solely because their class in general suffers, to the point of bankruptcy, from the encroachments of capitalism and from forced contributions to the government (of large and middle landlords). Because of the struggle between these two classes (the small landlords and the large and middle landlords), which gives rise to the struggle between the peasant class and the landlord class, the New Xunwu faction, representing the middle landlords inclined in a capitalist direction, daily forms a counterrevolutionary battle line in cooperation with the large landlords. But the Cooperative Society faction represents the small landlords inclined toward the revolutionary People's Rights [movement], and daily they receive the leadership of the proletariat class. They have united with the poor peasant class and risen up, creating the recent struggle for land revolution.

These comments on small landlords do not refer to all small landlords, just to a portion of them. Generally speaking, the small landlords can be divided into two parts. One part comes from the so-called old rich families. This part originates mostly in the division of property of large and middle landlords, the so-called large share becoming small. That is why so many large and middle landlord families become small landlord families. The portion of these people within the whole landlord class is 32 percent.

In terms of economic position, the small landlords can be divided into three categories.

1. Those who annually have surpluses: the percentage of these people within the whole landlord class is 0.96 percent; during the land struggle they were counterrevolutionary. Liu Hongxiang, Lai Shifang, and Liu Ruibiao of the Cooperative Society faction belong to this layer. They are all Cooperative Society members, but since the outbreak of the 25 March uprising and even after its defeat, they have incessantly displayed counterrevolutionary [actions and ideas].

2. Those who, in years with a declining standard of living, must incessantly sell land in order to survive. This group has a very miserable future ahead. There are many people in this layer—22.4 percent of the entire landlord class. They are enthusiastic for revolution. The people in the Xunwu Cooperative Society faction are mostly part of this stratum. For example, the following are members of this group.

Those leaders of the land struggle who have died:
    Pan Li (Xunwu CCP county committee secretary)
    Liu Weilu (chairman of the Revolutionary Committee during the 25 March uprising)
    Liu Weie (CCP district committee member)
Current leaders of the struggle:
    Gu Bo (Xunwu CCP county committee secretary)
    Zhong Xiqiu (Red Army battalion commander)
    Huang Yugui (CCP district committee secretary)
Those who did not participate in the Cooperative Society but have participated in the revolution:
    Mei Ruhuang (Red Army group political commissar)

3. Those whose bankruptcy is quite severe and depend on loans to survive. This part constitutes 8.64 percent of all landlords. They are revolutionary, with many people participating in the struggle going on in Xunwu today.

Of the second and third parts of the small landlords, generally all the so-called old rich families whose circumstances are deteriorating participate in the revolution. To speak of Cooperative Society members, there are 30 middle-school students and 100 upper-primary students or teachers who have participated or are participating in the revolution. All belong to those two strata of small landlords in deteriorating circumstances; most belong to the second stratum.

Besides the old rich families discussed above, another large group—48 percent of small landlords—is the so-called newly rich. This layer, in complete contrast to the layer of the old rich, consists of peasants who get rich from farming or from small businesses. This layer is "flourishing." Its economic situation is based, on the one hand, on self-cultivation (little use of full-time hired help; mostly part-time hired help) and, on the other hand, on renting out remote arid land to others and collecting rents.

They are serious about money, and their special trait is stinginess; getting rich is their central concern. They toil all day. They have surpluses every year, and moreover, they either sell their unhulled grain or hull it and take it to market themselves, even to faraway places like Bachi in Pingyuan County, in hopes of making a lot of money. They also make loans at reprehensively high interest rates—most at 50 percent. They loan out grain and oppress poor people [by making loans that] "take the first crop for the principal and the second crop for the interest." They also make "grain-money" and "oil-money" loans.

What is a "grain-money" loan? When the last harvest is eaten and the new crop is still in the fields, they take advantage of this opportunity to loan money to the peasants and then are repaid in grain. Usually they loan out 2 yuan before harvesttime and are repaid with a dan of grain. But at that time the price of grain is almost 4 yuan per dan. This is a type of 100 percent interest. "Oil-money loans" are the same; most are of the double-interest type. Loan-sharking is almost always done by the newly rich families. Large and middle landlords loan money at a 30 percent rate; very few make 50 percent loans, and these landlords do not make grain loans or oil-money loans.

Also, there is the more severe "monthly interest" loan, with an interest rate of 10 percent a month; so that the annual interest rate exceeds that of the double-interest loan. To receive this kind of loan requires a mortgage; moreover, to save face, some borrow the term "society" [hui] like the Dingtong Society. There is also the "chop loan society,"[26] a 10 percent per month loan at compound interest, which is more severe than the Dingtong Society.

Large and middle landlords usually do not make such loans. During the Qing these reprehensible loans were relatively scarce, but they have increased during the Republican period. "Now people are more greedy" is the historically significant criticism of poor people toward loan sharks. "Today the hearts of people are relatively more greedy"—this is something one hears when one goes among the poor peasant masses throughout Xunwu. Nothing is more important than money to the newly rich families. They do not waste money [on tuition]; nor do they sacrifice the labor of their children by sending them to school. Middle-school graduates among them are few, and although there are a few graduates of primary school, there are not as many as among the bankrupt layer.

As for the bankrupt families, why have most of them gone to school? Because they inherited money and are not that desirous of it. Moreover, since those who depend on study and on their own ability for their livelihood lack other ways to raise their family's fortunes, most of the graduates come from this layer.

Some people refer to the so-called newly rich families of small landlords discussed above, not as small landlords, but rather as rich peasants, the so-called half-landlord-like rich peasant. This half-landlord-like rich peasant class is the most evil enemy in the countryside. In the eyes of poor peasants there is no reason not to strike them down.

RICH PEASANTS

There is also a relatively rich peasant who is normally called a self-cultivator or middle peasant, but actually is a kind of rich peasant. As for the so-called half-landlord-like rich peasant mentioned earlier, we did not call them rich peasants but rather small landlords. This is the viewpoint of the poor peasants. During struggles, most people do not argue for attacking this kind of so-called relatively rich self-cultivators or middle peasants because they do not have the characteristics of half-landlords. All their production comes from their own labor, not from the exploitation of others.

Actually in the eyes of poor peasants, they are a special class. Except for not renting land to other people to till, they are the same type of high-interest exploiters because they have surplus money and surplus land. They add labor to their own agricultural produce, for example, turning unhulled grain into hulled rice, and then go to market themselves to sell it. They also carry on small hoarding activities. They raise piglets, shoats, and meaty pigs. These rich peasants have all the characteristics of half-landlords, but they are not the same as the self-sufficient middle peasants. Because of this, when the land struggle develops into a mass activity, most of the poor peasants cry out [slogans like] "equal land" and "tear up debts" in opposition to this kind of rich peasant.

If the Communist party should stop this activity of poor

peasants, those poor peasants could not but hate the Communist party. Because of this, we know that not only must we decide to strike down these half-landlord-like rich peasants, but moreover we must equalize the rich self-cultivators' land, cancel loans made by the rich self-cultivators, and divide the rich self-cultivators' grain—there is no doubt that we have to do this. We must do this, and then and only then can we win over the poor peasant masses. This is the paramount policy of the rural struggle. Only those opportunists who take the rich-peasant line oppose this policy.

POOR PEASANTS
(THE FOUR LAYERS OF POOR PEASANTS)

What is a poor peasant? We can answer simply: a poor peasant does not have enough to eat (the reason is exploitation, that's obvious). But this is a conventional explanation. If we once again analyze the poor peasantry from within, then we know that poor peasants are certainly not a homogeneous class made up of one economic position, for the class has four different strata.

The first group is the semi-self-cultivators. They do not have enough to eat because of insufficient land. They must rent some land from landlords. After paying all the rent, they do not have enough to eat, but among the poor-peasant masses they are the best off, because not only do they have oxen and plows, they also have some money in their hands. Moreover, there is something that manifests their special characteristic: they own a bit of land. This level constitutes 10.5 percent of the total rural population. Among the poor peasants they constitute 15 percent.

The second level is made up of that group among tenants who are doing fairly well. They have oxen, plows, and some money, but not a bit of land. Their special characteristic is their oxen: most have one ox, and an extremely small number have two or three. Compared with semi-self-cultivators, they are poorer and have even less to eat, but compared with other parts of the poor peasantry, they are certainly better off. This level constitutes 42 percent of the rural population and 60 percent of the poor peasant population—they are the largest mass in the countryside.

The third level is made up of tenants in dire straits. They likewise have no land. They have plows, but most are in poor shape, and they have some money, but not much. They also have a special characteristic: not every family has oxen. Several families may share an ox, or if they have an ox, it certainly is not their own. It is the landlord's, who turns it over to them in order to save on fodder costs. Only under certain conditions can they use the work power of this ox. In Xunwu, they refer to this as "getting only one hoof." Their level of insufficiency with respect to food, compared with those groups mentioned above, is more severe. They constitute 10.5 percent of the total rural population and 15 percent of the total poor peasant population. They are a mass of the same size as the semi-self-cultivator.

The fourth category comprises the poorest tenants. Besides having no land, they have no money—they normally borrow rice and salt. They also lack one iota of animal power. During the busy agricultural seasons, they wait until other people have tilled, and then afterwards they join with other people (their relatives) and borrow or rent oxen. They cultivate several mu of infertile land rented at high rates. Although they have plows, they have no harrows, because to make one requires quite a bit of money. Their means are insufficient to do this. This layer constitutes 7 percent of the rural population and 10 percent of all poor peasants. They are not an insignificant mass. The clothes they wear are very ragged; they have to beg them from people. Two out of three meals they eat are *zaliang* (millet, slices of sweet potatoes). To supplement their income, they make cakes for sale, chop wood to sell for fuel, or hire themselves out as porters.

THE SYSTEM IN THE HILLS

Most hill land in Xunwu is in the hands of the lineages who first homesteaded; the lineages that came later do not have any hill land or only a little, because the land had been occupied by first-comers. Therefore, the small lineages, who settled first, have hill land, while the great lineages, who came later, don't have any.

The situation of hill lands differs from that of croplands. Cropland is bought and sold quickly. Through mortgaging, the land of small landlords and peasants can be transferred [*zhuanyi*] twice a year, and even more land is transferred once a year. Outright sales are also frequent.

Generally speaking, because of its low productivity, a lineage hill (single-surname village) is managed by an ancestral trust. Within an area of 5 or 6 li, a system of compacts is used. The so-called prohibitions not only forbid the buying and selling of land, but also absolutely prohibit tree foraging. Apart from those "who chop down wood to build a temporary hut to cover a tomb site," permission to cut timber can be obtained only for purposes of the public good, like building roads or canals and repairing bridges. Besides this, the hills are opened only twice every three years for clearing brushwood and once every two years for timbering.

The schedule for opening the hills is set by a gathering of lineage mates from a land reeve's [*jinzhang*, lit. restriction chief] village. When the time comes, every family supplies a worker who goes to the hill to collect brushwood and timber (thinning timberland is also called *luoka*, which means "to prune tree branches"). These are distributed to everyone.

There are also cases when the whole hill is divided into lots in accord with the production situation in the hills. The masses are called together to draw lots. Afterwards, based on the lots drawn, they individually take their share. This is the "lineage system" of hill "communism." But there is also a geographical system of hill communism. In most cases, the village is taken as the unit, and each lineage elects the reeve. They strictly forbid private foraging and set a schedule for opening the hills—just as in the system of family communism in the hills.

The number of land reeves varies from a minimum of three to a maximum of ten or more, based on the size of the village's forest—in most cases, there are five or six. The land reeves are all elected, and their terms are indefinite. Some serve for six months; others for four or five years. It all depends on whether a reeve fulfills his responsibility or not.

All land reeves must be absolutely incorruptible and fair-minded. "It doesn't matter if you are the old wet nurse of the emperor, if you exceed your quota of wood or licorice root, you will be punished." There was a land reeve in Longtu Township in Nanba District who came upon a woman stealing wood. The woman said to him: "I would like to chop down some wood to build a stand, you must not punish me. I am a Longtu person just like you—we are related. Why do you seem so cold-hearted." The land reeve answered her: "Be quiet, you old liar. Even if you were my great-aunt, I would penalize you. You must know that I, Liu Shilie, am just and fair."

If the land reeve does not maintain order and everyone chaotically chops trees down, not minding the public good, he must *nuanjin*. (Calling people's attention to the rules is called *nuanjin*. If anyone neglects the spirits and then once again pays respects, that is called *nuanshen* or *nuanfu*).

Every year the land reeves call a Protect the Hills meeting. All the regulations for protecting the hills are decided at this meeting. Most Protect the Hills meetings are called on an ad-hoc basis, but there are also "scheduled meetings." On the day when the Protect the Hills meeting is called, not only do the land reeves come, but also one person from every family in the area comes. Every person brings wine and rice and also pays 5 or 10 fen to buy cooked dishes and incense for worshiping

"Bogong." (Bogong is Yang Dabogong. Every place has a shrine; every tree, field, and hill has one.)

The two systems mentioned above are for public hills. There are also private hills, with mushrooms, tea-oil plants,[27] tea, bamboo, and Chinese firs. The produce can be sold for relatively good profits. These hills were originally public hills but gradually fell into the hands of the wealthy. Large landlords probably own half of them, and small landlords who are newly rich and rich peasants own the other half. Because this kind of hill cannot be developed without capital, especially when growing mushrooms and tea, the owners must be large landlords. The rest are mostly small landlords and rich peasants.

The hill lands of Xunwu are distributed as follows: lineage hills constitute 15 percent, village hills 5 percent, private hills 10 percent, and the so-called waste-hills—those that are remote from inhabited areas, inaccessible hills, and neglected hills—70 percent. There are waste-hills because in areas of low population with many hills there is no need for them. Some are delineated by lineage boundaries. Although people from other lineages might want to use such land, they are forbidden to do so by the Hill Lord. They can only let it be wasteland. This type of situation in which a person desires to develop a hill but cannot do so because of restrictions is common. After the land revolution, this kind of lineage barrier was wiped out.

EXPLOITATION

Exploitation by Land Rent

Sharecropping

There are two ways of collecting land rents in Xunwu County: "sharecropping" and "measuring rent." In the former, the peasant goes along with the landlord to the fields when the crop is ripe, and the yield is split 50–50. Moreover, the peasant is asked by the landlord to take his share to the landlord's home. In some places the landlord first takes one dan of grain before the division, and this dan is not included in the rent. The landlord's reason for this is: "When I bought this land I spent a lot, and you, the tenant, did not supply the fertilizer. If I didn't take this dan first, it would be too advantageous for you." But this method is not used by more than one family in a hundred. In another method, however, the peasant takes some grain first; this is called "taking seeds." The amount is one measure [cuosuan] out of all the land rent. The reason is that the seedlings came from someone else's land, not from the landlord's in question. The owner of the other land has no spring harvest [zaozi][28] from the seedling land and will suffer a loss. The first measure from the crop is to compensate the tenant or the other landlord for the loss. When the landlord or his agent comes to watch the dividing process, he requires a lunch with pork and fish (even duck sometimes), and the peasant has to carry the rent to the landlord's home after the lunch and the dividing of the crop. The peasant even has to put two eggs on the rent rice; this is a daily occurrence in this area. If the peasant has better relations with his landlord, he may put on seven or eight eggs.

Measuring Rent

The system of rent by measure is called "early rice six parts; late rice four parts." In Pingyuan County, the split is 50–50. Why must it be "early six, late four"? Since the yield of early rice is greater and it gets a higher price, taking 60 percent of the yield as rent does not give the tenant any advantage. But late rice yields less and its value is lower, so the rent is 40 percent of the yield. At first glance it would seem that the 60–40 ratio, when applied to the two crops grown each year, comes out to 50–50, but this is not so. The landlord usually gets 56 percent to the tenant's 44 percent. Since the yields for early rice are relatively great, the landlord gets 6 dan out of every 10 dan of early rice, leaving the tenant with only 4 dan. As for late rice, which generally yields 8 dan (2 dan less than early rice), the tenant hands over 4 dan for rent and keeps 4 dan for himself. These 4 dan plus the 4 dan of early rice [gives the tenant] a total of 8 dan whereas the landlord gets 10 dan. So the ratio is 56 to 44.

Rents based on sharecropping are figured at the Great Heat [23 July–6 August], and measuring rents are assessed during the first period of autumn [in the traditional solar calendar, 7–22 August]. Landlords notify peasants that land rents are due; if the rent is not sent, the landlord goes to the tenant's home himself to press the tenant. If the rent is still not paid, he sends some workers to take the rent. If this does not succeed, he turns the land over to someone else. Some bad landlords even bring lawsuits against tenants and imprison them, but bad landlords of this type are few.

Originally sharecropping covered 40 percent of all cases in this county, and "measuring rents" covered the other 60 percent. But recently the incidence of sharecropping has increased, and that of "measuring rents" has decreased to about 50 percent. Why has sharecropping been on the rise? Because the number of poor tenant households has been increasing, and they frequently have no seed rice left after the rent is sent. Landlords, afraid that peasants cannot afford to pay the rents, often prefer to sharecrop, causing this method to increase. At the same time, because the peasants are afraid of losing the land or of involvement in lawsuits, they prefer sharecropping too.

From the Top of the Stalks to the Bottom of the Roots, There's Nothing to Eat

"From the top of the stalks to the bottom of the roots, there's nothing to eat" means that just after the harvest and payment of the rent the tenant has nothing left to eat. This occurs in almost 40 percent of the cases in Xunwu County. Why is there no food to eat from the top of the stalks to the bottom of the roots? Take, for example, a piece of land yielding 20 dan, of which over 11 dan are paid as rent. Of the remaining 8-plus dan, 2–3 dan may be used to repay the landlord for loans of grain. These short-term (up to two years) loans, with an interest rate of 50 percent, are extended when the previous year's crop is consumed and the current crop has yet to be harvested [*qinghuang bujie*]. At harvest time, tenants have to purchase fine things for entertaining landlords. And after the harvest, they buy some cooking oil and salt and in the spring some rice. When autumn comes, everything is gone. This is what "From the top of the stalks to the bottom of the roots, there's nothing to eat" and "One year's yield is all gone" mean. During the land struggle in the southern half of the county, peasants and children everywhere sang this song:

> *The moon is shining, as if burning.*
> *We bear hardship, while others are happy.*
> *Little to eat, little to wear.*
> *Year after year of work, always living in a dilapidated house.*
> *I've no money to obtain a pretty wife; I'll grow old alone.*
> *With no schooling, we're blind even though we have eyes.*
> *Oh, God! How bitter is our lot.*
> *No other work to do but till the land year after year.*
> *The June harvest is hardly over before the landlord arrives.*
> *With umbrella in hand he looks over the rice sacks.*
> *Asking nothing but "Is the rice dry?"*
> *As soon as the destitute reply, "Not yet,"*
> *The landlord starts talking like an official.*
> *Every word he says is as mean as a tax collector's.*
> *Oh, what can we do?*
> *Bushel [luo] after bushel,[29] land rent plus interest,*
> *That's one year's yield, and it's all gone.*
> *Oh, all is gone.*
> *Being aggrieved, let us poor brothers be united and of one heart.*
> *Let's join the Red Army and kill our enemy.[30]*

Renting Land

In Xunwu landlords require all tenants to sign a lease.[31] There are no exceptions to this. In Xunwu there are small leases for periods of five years and large leases for periods of seven years. Although no formal law governs this, this is the rule between landlords and tenants. Only bad landlords find an excuse to break this rule and try to change tenants in three to four years or seven to eight years.[32] The following items are covered in a lease:

The location and boundaries of the land are clearly stated.

The amount of rent and whether it is determined by share-cropping or by measure.

The quality and quantity of the rent payment: rent rice should be dry enough, and shorting is disallowed and can be penalized by the landlord.

Tribute: a chicken every year or two.

There are leases even for land yielding only 3 dan. There are two reasons for this. First, without a lease, if a tenant does not pay the exact amount of rent, there is no proof in legal proceedings. Second, landlords are afraid that after a long period of time tenants might take over the land. A landlord never signs a lease; only tenants sign leases and give them to landlords. The following is an example of a lease:

Leasee, Kuang Shiming, rents a piece of land from Ling Jiangui. This piece of land is called Tieliaoba, it is arable and has one large mound [*qiu*].[33] After negotiations witnessed by a third party, an agreement was made to rent the land for six buckets [*tong*] of rent each year, which may be sent in two payments, one in autumn and one in winter. The rent is 60 percent for early rice and 40 percent for late rice and is to be sent to the [landlord's] home. The rice must be clean and dry; the quantity must be exact. If there is shorting, the landlord may rent the

land to someone else, and the leasee will have no cause
for complaint. Because an oral [agreement] does not constitute a lease, this lease is drawn up to establish the
agreement.

There will be tribute of one chicken each year.

Witness: Luo Changsheng
Written by: Xie Yulin
Leasee: Kuang Shiming
The sixteenth year of the Republic [1927], 24 November.

Fees, Tribute, and Landlord Dinners

There are two kinds of fees: fees-in-money and fees-in-
[kind] (a rooster). The fee-in-money is generally 0.1 yuan for
each dan of rent specified in a five-year lease and 0.2 yuan for
each dan in a ten-year lease. But sometimes, as in Huangxiang, the fee is 0.3 yuan. This fee is paid at the beginning of
the lease. The fee[-in-kind requires] one rooster for one lease,
whether a five-year or a ten-year lease, to be sent when the
lease begins. Fees-in-money or fees-in-kind should be sent
again when the lease is renewed (i.e., either every five years
or every ten years). In the southern part of the county, most
leases run for ten years. In Huangxiang and Shuangqiao, there
are no five-year leases, and although few in number, some
leases run for decades. If a landlord sells land after it is leased,
he returns part of the fee. In the northern part of the county,
most leases are for five years and fees are never refunded in
any way.

A chicken is sent in tribute each year. Although leases can
specify a "rooster," because a rooster is bigger than a hen,
most peasants still send hens. Peasants usually send one every
other year—even though the leases say one rooster a year—
around the time of the New Year's celebration or after the winter harvest. If a chicken is not sent, the landlord goes out and
presses the peasant for payment. "Did you send the tribute

rooster?" "Not yet, sir, please wait until I buy one." Or "No, sir, I can't give you one this year."

In Shuangqiao, there is a custom of landlord dinners, in which [a tenant] invites his landlord to dinner once a year. This is not common in other areas.

Grain Rent and Money Rent

Eighty percent of the rent in this county is paid in grain; the other 20 percent is paid in money. About half the ancestral, religious, temple, and bridge trusts accept money because most of their tenants are members of ancestral trusts, religious associations, and so on. Because of this, the tenants can keep the rice for their own use and use money to pay the rent (figured according to the current rice price). Most of these tenants make money through small businesses or by raising chickens and pigs for market. Some ancestral and religious trusts controlled by powerful gentry may force tenants to send rice for rent in order to pursue their exploitative practices (rice can be sold later at a higher price). The tenants have no alternative but to turn over the grain and put it in the granary. For the same reason, landlords accept only rice and do not allow the peasants to pay in money except for landlords who live far from the croplands.

Fixed Rents and Variable Rents

Eighty percent of the rents in the county are variable [lit. not-iron] rents. When there is a flood, drought, or other disaster, the rent can be reduced by 10 to 20 percent. If the yield is affected too much by a big disaster, landlords will accept some blighted grain [panggu] once they know the facts. Twenty percent of the rents in this county are fixed. In such cases there is no "no rent reduction for disaster" clause in the leases. Actually, tenants rarely follow this rule. They ask landlords to come and see the disaster, so that blighted grain may be accepted as part of the rent.

Go Sleep with Someone If You Want Some Clothing

Many peasants have no food left to eat after paying the rent and their debts, and landlords who receive their rents in grain are unwilling to sell the grain. Only around New Year's time do landlords give some grain to peasants badly in need of food. But this is for loan only, not for sale. This is because the interest on grain loans is 50 percent semiannually (the interest rate was 30 percent for money and 40 percent for grain every half-year, but recently few grain loans have been let for 40 percent, most interest rates are 50 percent), and the appeal of such loans is much greater than that of selling. Landlords sell rice only in April or May when the new crop is still in the fields and the old crop is gone. At that time the price is highest, and [in order to get a higher price] the landlords pretend to be reluctant to sell.

A peasant will come to a landlord's house and ask: "Sir, did you have your dinner?"

Landlord, "Um, yes."

Then the peasant will slowly bring up the subject of buying grain: "Could I buy a couple of dou of your grain?"

Landlord: "N . . . no, I don't have enough for my family."

Peasant: "Hey, if you don't have enough, then there's no water in the river. Please help me out; I'm waiting for food to eat."[34]

Landlord: "OK, if you really need it, I can save some for you, but will you pay this high price?"

Peasant: "Sir, please do me a favor and don't charge me too much!"

The price is set according to the landlord's wishes; afterwards he gives the grain to the peasant.

There is a story known all over the county. The landlord Liu Fulang of Huangxiang is a famous miser who always mixes blighted grain with the good to sell at times when the new crop is still in the fields and the old one is gone. One day, a peasant came to his home to buy some rice. Liu called his

daughter-in-law and daughter and said: "Go sleep with someone if you want some clothing."

Peasants have spread this sentence so that it has become a
famous joke in the whole county. Why did this sentence become a joke? Because it is customary in Xunwu for adulter-
esses to be called *lao*, but *lao* also means to mix blighted grain
with good grain. The landlord could not clearly tell [his
daughter and daughter-in-law] in the presence of the peasant
to mix blighted grain with good, so he carelessly came out
with these funny words to his daughter and daughter-in-law.
This story is still being told.

Labor

There is no corvée labor in the county now. If there is any
emergency or a wedding or funeral, a landlord may ask tenants to help him. If the landlord has some farmwork to do, he
may ask tenants to help him in the busy season, but these la-
borers are paid.

Buying or Selling Land

According to Liu Liangfan, who was a clerk in the county
yamen, 600 households sold land in this county in 1925. Since
some households bought the lands of more than one household, there were less than 600 households buying land. Sup-
pose there are 30,000 households in the county (a population
of 120,000, with four people per household). [This means that]
one household out of every 50 became bankrupt. Even more
mortgaged their lands—five households out of every 100.
(There are two mortgagees for every 100 households because
one mortgagee may have several properties mortgaged to him.)
So, in recent years 2 percent of the households in Xunwu have
gone bankrupt, and 5 percent are heading toward bankruptcy.

Price of Land

For every dan of rent, 17–20 yuan for [terraced] rice paddies
[*kengtian*] and 30–40 yuan for bottomlands [*duantian*]; gener-

ally 20 yuan for rice fields and 30 yuan for bottomlands. Rice fields can be mortgaged for 15 yuan [for each dan of rent] and bottomlands for 20–25 yuan.

There are two kinds of mortgages: *fiducia cum creditore* [*guoshou*] and *antichresis* [*buguoshou*].[35] Fiducia cum creditore means that the mortgagor gives the land to the mortgagee after receiving money from him. The mortgagee either tills the land himself or leases it to someone else. The mortgagee makes all the decisions, and the mortgagor has no say. After the transfer of the land, the mortgagee does not pay rent to the mortgagor. Apart from reserving the right to buy the land back, the mortgagor loses the rights of ownership. It is almost like selling the land because most of the rights to the land are in the hands of the mortgagee.

Antichresis means that the mortgagee pays some money to the mortgagor, but the land is tilled by the mortgagor, who has to pay rent to the mortgagee every year. The rent is the same as for other rented land: for every [2] dan of combined yield [of the early and late crops], there is a dan of rent. For example, if the land price is 20 yuan for each dan of rent, the mortgagor gets 20 yuan but has to pay a dan of grain in rent. Since the grain normally sells for 4 yuan per dan, the yearly interest is 20 percent.

Why is the mortgage rate lower than the interest rate on money charged by moneylenders? (Generally the interest rate for borrowing money starts at 30 percent a year.) This is because rich peasants (those who have just become rich) think that the low rates for mortgages are safer than the high interest rate for money loans. "Putting the money in the earth is very safe."

Why do the rich peasants buy mortgages and not land? Because the bankruptcy of peasants and landlords occurs gradually, not suddenly. "First buy mortgages and then buy land" has become a common phenomenon. "Land belongs to rich people, mortgage means selling" is also a common phenomenon. So buying a mortgage is almost the same as buying the land.

Ninety percent of the mortgages are fiducia cum creditore and only 10 percent are antichresis. Most of the antichresis mortgages are governed by fixed rents. But [in some cases], even though the land is legally transferred in the manner of fiducia cum creditore to the mortgagee, so that a lease changes the relationship of the original owner and the mortgage owner to that of landlord and tenant, the original owner still tills this piece of land. This is another layer of landlord-tenant relationships beyond the one between mortgagor and mortgagee.

Some antichresis land is mortgaged secretly. For example, when a dissolute youth owes gambling debts or lacks money for whoring, he may secretly mortgage his family's land to some big landlord and then transfer the land in the manner of fiducia cum creditore after his father is dead. Why do such youths mortgage lands to the big landlords? Because the big landlords are not afraid of complications. Even if the secret deal becomes known, a big landlord does not fear that the parents will not honor the agreement.

Antichresis mortgages present opportunities for high degrees of exploitation between mortgagee [dianzhu] and mortgagor [tianzhu]. When the mortgagor cannot afford to pay the rent, the mortgagee adds interest to the unpaid part of the rent. This adds up year by year and finally the mortgagor certainly cannot pay off the mortgage for this land. The interest rate for unpaid rent is 30 percent or higher, rather than the 20 percent rate for mortgages.

Exploitation Through High Interest Rates

The Interest on Money

The ordinary rate of interest on money loans is 30 percent [in reality 36 percent]. There are also 40 percent and 50 percent loans. Respectively, these constitute 70, 10, and 20 percent of the total money in the loan market. If a debtor has no land, all loans are secured by property, such as houses, livestock, or tea-oil fields [*muzi*], specified in the contract. Those with extra money to lend include large and middle landlords, ancestral trusts, and the newly rich (small landlords and rich peasants who have suddenly become wealthy).

In terms of the total amount of money lent, the middle landlords lend about 50 percent, the newly rich about 30 percent, and the big landlords and ancestral trusts about 20 percent. In terms of lending frequency, the newly rich are the most frequent lenders with 75 percent of the loans, and the middle landlords are next with 20 percent, followed by the large landlords and ancestral trusts with 5 percent. In terms of borrowers, as for 50 percent loans (50 yuan of interest per 100 yuan of principal per year) or 120 percent loans (a 10 percent interest charge per month, or 120 yuan in interest payments per year for a 100-yuan loan), poor peasants are the ones who usually borrow on these terms. Poor peasants seldom take out 30 percent interest loans. Such loans carry a 3 percent interest rate per month (36 yuan in interest payments per year for 100 yuan in principal). Among the total amount of money borrowed by poor peasants, 30 percent loans constitute 20 percent, 50 percent loans constitute 70 percent, and 120 percent loans make up 10 percent.

Most of the creditors lending to poor peasants are newly rich, for they are willing to lend small amounts of money such as 3–5 yuan or 8–10 yuan to poor peasants bit by bit and charge compound interest. Since poor peasants have no land, they are able to use only their houses or livestock as security. Because creditors always jump at the chance to gobble up poor peasants' houses, livestock, small pieces of land, or gardens, when poor peasants stand in need of money, creditors are always eager to lend money. Later on, they seize the security if poor peasants do not meet their payments.

Sometimes middle landlords do the same thing as the newly rich. For example, Gu Youyao, Gu Bo's grandfather, acquired three parcels of vegetable gardens and two houses from poor peasants in this manner. He might lend one yuan one day and two yuan the next day to a poor peasant. As the debt built up gradually, he came to possess the debtor's whole vegetable garden. He devotes much attention to occupying other people's property by this method. He cares about nothing else, for he thinks that taking care of local affairs and the ancestral trust will keep him from making money. He is a typical high-interest exploiter.

Most 30 percent loans occur between rich peasants and make it possible for rich peasants to start small businesses, such as trading in rice or livestock, or to establish a small shop in a market town. Why can rich peasants get 30 percent loans whereas poor peasants can get only 50 percent loans or 120 percent loans? There are two reasons: the first is the "bigness" of the loan amount. The amount of money lent by rich peasants is usually around 200–300 yuan, which can be used to do something big when it is repaid, whereas poor peasants usually borrow only a little money, which is too small to do anything with after it is repaid. The second reason is the security of the loan. Rich peasants use their land as security for loans, and, in addition, they borrow to make investments that always have the prospect of making money. But poor peasants have little property, and they frequently spend their money or use the money to pay another creditor; so their dependability is very low.

Middle landlords usually lend money, for the purposes of amassing land, to small landlords who are bankrupt or to peasants who are on the road to bankruptcy.

Few large landlords or lineages lend money. They hold on to their money because they prefer to enjoy life rather than increase their capital. They spend money on celebrating eightieth birthdays, building large houses, or educating their children (this is not a major purpose). A few of the large landlords who have become mercantilized are willing to invest their money in business. Therefore, there is no money left for lending. Some of the large landlords with extra money who do not have a business to invest in and who are not interested in lending to poor peasants or small landlords because of the risks and poor returns would rather dig a pit and bury their money in the ground than get interest by lending. Moreover, local warlords collect heavy customs and duties from those who have extra money to lend out; there is no escaping this. For instance, on several occasions Lin Hu and Liu Zhilu,[36] troop leaders under the command of Chen Jiongming, levied contributions totaling more than 10,000 yuan on large, middle, and small landlords, ancestral trusts, and religious trusts in the Huangxiang area. These levies encouraged landlords to hide their money in cellars.

Interest on Grain Loans

The interest on grain loans is much higher than that on money loans. It is the most sinister way in which rich peasants and well-off middle or small landlords exploit poor peasants. Most high-interest loans are made in December and March. Poor peasants borrow in December to celebrate New Year's and in March to sow seeds. No matter when they borrow, the loan has to be repaid in June when the early rice is harvested. The interest is 50 percent of the principal (repaying a principal of 1 dan with 1.5 dan) (three measures [*luo*]). A loan with 50 percent interest for six months or three months is a most terrible loan.

Early rice is harvested in June. After paying the rent for the use of the field and repaying the grain loan, poor peasants eat the remainder by August and have to borrow grain again from landlords or rich peasants. Poor peasants borrow 1 dan of grain in August and have to pay back 1.2 dan of grain in October. In other words, the interest is 20 percent for about two months.

If a poor peasant cannot repay the loan, he has no option but to talk it over with the creditor: "I have nothing left to repay your grain loan this year. May I repay it after I harvest my early rice next June?" The creditor answers: "Well, we must calculate the interest in a different way. The 1.0 dan of grain borrowed last August is the principal of the loan and has a 5 dou interest due by next year, the 2 dou that is the interest for the 1.0 dan of principal for the period from last August through October should have 50 percent interest too: 1 dou by next year. So the total payment should be 1 dan 8 dou of grain by next June." (The original dan had interest of 2 dou, plus the interest of 5 dou to which was added 1 dou, together making 1 dan 8 dou.) In fact, the total interest payment is 80 percent from June of this year to June of next year. If the borrower cannot repay it the following year, the principal becomes 1.8 dan, with the 50 percent interest being automatic. If the poor peasant is still unable to repay the loan at the harvest of late rice [*fanzi*], nor the next year or in subsequent years, the total payment for the loan becomes a huge amount after ten years.

Tea-oil Loan Interest

The tea-oil loan is called "double oil" and is the most odious type of loan. The so-called double oil is found in the southern part of Xunwu County, where there are many hillsides planted with tea-oil plants. There are no double-oil loans in the northern part of Xunwu County because there are no hillsides of tea-oil plants there. Why is it called the double-oil loan? Because a loan of 1 jin of oil is repaid with 2 jin, 2 with 4, and 4 with 8. This is the double-oil loan. What is its time limit? It is always repaid in September when the tea-oil seeds are gathered, regardless of when the [loan] was made, whether it was made that month or up to a year earlier.

Landlords and rich peasants own hills with tea-oil plants and rent them to poor peasants to cultivate. Then they collect half of the harvested tea-oil seeds as rent. The rent is 10 jin of oil when a poor peasant harvests 20 jin or 30 jin when 60 jin is harvested. After receiving the rent, landlords and rich peasants usually market 90 percent and lend 10 percent to poor peasants as double-oil loans.

When a peasant borrows the tea-oil, the lender always says the tea-oil is his son's or his daughter-in-law's. Sometimes it is true that it is from his son and daughter-in-law's supply of tea-oil. In fact, young people in rich peasant families who have as yet not managed household affairs frequently have their own tea-oil. After the harvest season for tea-oil seeds is over, the youths pick up the tea-oil seeds that have fallen to the ground under the tea-oil plants [*chazi shu*][37] and then squeeze oil out of those tea-oil seeds. This oil belongs to the youths. This makes it possible for the youths in a rich peasant family to make high-interest tea-oil loans:

"Sir, could you lend me some money?"

"No, I don't have any."

"Some grain."

"No."

"I have nothing to eat. Please lend something to me, anyway."

"How about some of my son's tea-oil."

The interest on tea-oil is so high that no poor peasant wants to borrow it. However, poor peasants have no choice but to take out a tea-oil loan, because neither landlords nor rich peasants are willing to lend them money or grain. Poor peasants can only sell the tea-oil they borrow and then use the money to buy grain to eat.

Sometimes poor peasants want to borrow tea-oil in order to eat. When they have harvested their crops and need cooking oil, they go to the landlord's or rich peasant's house with a bottle to borrow a bottle of oil. They borrow one big bottle of tea-oil in June and repay with two big bottlesful in September. Many poor peasants have no steelyard with which to weigh the tea-oil. Moreover, some poor peasants' wives and daughters-in-law do not know how to use a steelyard. Consequently, it is easier to measure the tea-oil with a bottle than with a steelyard. So they borrow one bottle of tea-oil and repay it with two bottles.

Selling Children

A loan in default for ten years, as mentioned above, is rare. In fact, a lender will seldom allow a borrower to extend his loan for ten years. The lender always forces the borrower to repay the loan as soon as possible and makes a new loan only after the old loan has been cleared up because he is worried about the peasant's ability to repay. Frequently a lender permits the borrower not to pay the interest on a loan for a couple of years, say no longer than three to five years, provided that the borrower repays the principal of the loan on time. By that time the interest has doubled.

How does a lender force a borrower to repay a loan? During the harvest season the lender goes straight to the borrower's cropland with a pair of big baskets and says: "You must give me your crops as repayment for your loan." The only thing that the borrower can do is watch the lender take away his crops. During the harvest season, after paying the rent and loans, "from the top of the plants to the bottom of the roots, there's nothing to eat." In these cases, many peasants wipe their tears with their sleeves.

There is a saying in Xunwu County: "You must repay your loan even if you marry off your daughter or sell your son." Lenders usually shout this out when pressing "terribly stubborn borrowers" for repayment. Their anger builds up because the borrower is unable to repay the loan.

Reader, I am not exaggerating in order to expose the evil of the exploiting class in Xunwu. All my survey reports are made carefully without any overstatement. I always doubted that the description of "selling his wife or son" appearing in articles was true. So I carefully questioned peasants in Xunwu to see whether this really happens. The result was careful interviews of three peasants who participated in an investigation meeting. The following happened in their three villages.

Liu Liangfan, from Fufushan in Xunwu City District (about

18 li from the city) said that his village consists of 37 house-holds divided into five surnames: the Liu, the Cao, the Chen, the Lin, and the Huang. Five households had sold sons [*naizi*]. (The Hakka call their sons *naizi*.) Three of the five households were from the Liu surname group and are related to Liu Liang-fan, the chairman of the Xunwu City suburban township so-viet. These were the households of Liu Changyu, Liu Chang-lun, and Liu Changchun. The other two households were those of Lin Fangting and Chen Liangyou. Liu Changyu (Liu Liangfan's uncle) is a carpenter, the other four are tenants. Liu Changyu sold three of his four sons, Liu Changlun sold one of his three sons, Liu Changchun sold one of his two sons, Lin Fangting sold two of his three sons, and Liu Liangyou sold half of his one son. All five households had become bankrupt with nothing left; consequently, they had to sell their sons to repay their debts and buy food.

The buyer was either a nearby member of the gentry of the same surname as the seller or a rich peasant. There are more gentry buyers than rich-peasant buyers. The price of a boy ranges from a minimum of 100 yuan to a maximum of 200 yuan. When making this transaction neither the buyer nor the seller call this business "selling"; rather they call it an "adop-tion." But the world in general calls it "selling a child." An "adoption contract" is also commonly called a "body deed." An "adoption contract" might read:

> X writes this adoption contract. Because he is too poor to feed his children, who have a crying need for food, and because he cannot borrow money, on the advice of his relatives and friends, he would rather give his (first, second, etc.) son to his brother, X, as a son. The biolog-ical father will get . . . yuan in payment for his son. Af-ter adoption, the adoptive father has all rights to teach and to control the marriage of the adopted son; he can even beat him. But the biological father has no right to interfere. Both parties voluntarily agree, without coer-

cion, with the contents of this contract, and no party will change his mind in the future. Because words are unreliable, we have written this contract as evidence.

Matchmaker A (signature)

B (signature)

C (signature)

Relative A (signature)

B (signature)

C (signature)

Friend A (signature)

B (signature)

C (signature)

Biological father of the boy (signature)

Biological mother of the boy (signature)

Biological older brother of the boy (signature)

Biological younger brother of the boy (signature)

Day   Month   Year

Only the seller writes up a contract; the buyer writes nothing. The so-called matchmakers are go-betweens. At most there are four or five of them [per transaction], who share a fee for services rendered amounting to 5 percent of the selling price. More than ten relatives and friends might be present and are paid a "signature fee" by the buyer. When a close relative or influential person (most are members of the gentry) signs his name to the adoption contract, the signature fee is high, from more than 10 to 20 yuan. But the fee paid to ordinary relatives and friends is less than 1 yuan.

The ages of the boys sold range from three or four sui to seven and eight sui to thirteen or fourteen sui. After the deal is made, the matchmakers carry the boy on their backs to the buyer's house. At this moment the biological parents of the boy always weep and cry. Sometimes couples even fight with each other. The wife scolds the husband for his uselessness and his inability to feed his family, which have forced them to sell a son. Most of the spectators weep too. When Liu Chang-yu sold his son, for example, his nephew Liu Liangfan was one of those who wept for Liu Changyu.

Now let us talk of Li Dashun's story. He was the second of our peasant friends to attend the investigation meeting. He comes from the large village of Huangsha, in Shuangqiao District, with 400 households. He personally witnessed five cases of households in his village selling a son. Each of the five households sold one boy. When one boy was sold to someone in the Bachi area in Pingyuan County, Guangdong, Li Dashun came across the father, carrying his baby on his back, going in the direction of Bachi. The father had tears on his face and was ashamed when he realized an acquaintance could see he was selling his son. Why did he sell his son to someone in the Bachi area in Guangdong? Because the price was higher. A boy could be sold for 200 or 300 yuan there. A child of four or five sui brings the highest price because such a child can easily "develop a close relationship." In contrast, the price of an older child, eight or nine sui or over ten sui is lower, because it is difficult to develop such a relationship and the boy can easily escape from his adoptive parents.

Mei Zhiping, the third of our peasant friends who attended the investigation meeting, is a peasant in Lantian Village in Shuangqiao District. The selling of children happened in his village also. His uncle, Mei Hongpo, is an extremely poor peasant. He has three sons: one went abroad to Southeast Asia, one is living with him, and the other was sold to someone in Pingyuan County. In the neighboring village of Anjing, the poor peasant Mei Chuanhua sold five of his seven sons.

Here were only three people—Liu, Li, and Mei—at the investigation meeting, but in their own villages so many people had sold their children. One of the three people, Liu, comes from the northern half of this county; the other two come from the southern half of the county. Therefore, we can easily imagine the situation in the county as a whole. Based on their knowledge of the places they are familiar with, they estimate that 10 percent of the households in the county have sold their sons. Liu Liangfan told us that he had seen of, or heard about, more than a hundred boys being sold in the vicinity of his village.

It is common to sell a boy, but no one has heard of wives or daughters being sold.

On hearing that a borrower has sold a son, lenders will hurry to the borrower's house and force the borrower to repay his loan. The lender will cruelly shout to the borrower: "You have sold your son. Why don't you repay me?" Why does the lender act like this? Because it is a critical point for his loan. If the borrower does not repay his loan after selling his son, the lender knows that he will never have another chance to get his loan back once the money is used up. Therefore, he considers only how to force the borrower to repay the loan without regard for anything else.

The relationship between people in the old days was one of man eat man!

Establishing a Savings and Loan Association

The purpose of establishing a savings and loan association is for mutual help, not to exploit the other members in it. A person might invite his relatives or friends to establish a savings and loan association in order to pay for wedding expenses, engage in business, pay burial expenses, or repay a debt. However, since such associations as the month association, the double-year association, and four-season association have a strong tendency to make money, the result can be exploitation of the peasants.

The one who organizes the association (association head) is seldom a person who is utterly destitute but is rather a middle peasant or a small merchant. Rich peasants do not need to take part in such associations. The utterly destitute cannot establish an association because no one will join it. Only semi-self-cultivators and tenants with their own draft animals and plows, self-cultivators, and small merchants not in danger of bankruptcy can invite people to join an association and have people come.

There are five kinds of associations: permanent associations, half-year associations, month associations, four-season associations, and double-year associations.

Permanent associations consist of six people, and one cycle lasts six years. Ten yuan is collected from every member but the organizer, who receives 50 yuan. In the first cycle there is "no principal but there's interest." [Interest rates are:] 30 percent for the first three years (15 yuan for each year for a total of 45 yuan in three years); 25 percent for the next two years (12.5 yuan for each year for a total of 25 yuan for two years); and 20 percent for one year (10 yuan). In the first cycle, the interest payments for six years total 80 yuan.

The rules for the second cycle are the same as those for the first cycle except that the interest decreases each year. For example, the recipients in the second cycle pay 30 percent interest for the first two years (15 yuan each year for a total of 30 yuan); 25 percent [for the next two years] (12.5 yuan for each year for a total of 25 yuan), and 20 percent for one year (10 yuan). The total interest is 65 yuan. The interest rate for the third cycle is much less than that for the second cycle. The saying the "first cycle loses face whereas the second cycle gets benefits" means that although the first cycle has economic advantages, the organizer has to beg people to join his association [before he gets it]. In the second cycle, however, one gets benefits, though a bit less, without begging.[38]

The interest rates for half-year associations change each half-year. The number of association members can be as few as eight, nine, ten, or eleven or more than twenty. The system of "no principal but there's interest" does not work in a half-year association. Instead, accounts are cleared up among each member of the association once each six months. (No data for month associations, double-year associations, and four-season associations.)

Exploitation Through Taxes and Levies

Money and Grain

Land tax. The total tax revenue in the county was 1,424 ounces of silver. A liability of one ounce of silver in regular taxes could be met with three silver dollars. The supplementary tax was 0.34 yuan. In fact, the land tax was collected in the form of rice, not money. Eight shao of grain were collected per dan of yield. (10 shao = 1 ge; 10 ge = 1 sheng.) According to the exchange rate, one sheng of land tax grain equals 0.642 ounces of silver and one ounce of silver equals 3.24 silver dollars, [so] 0.2 silver dollars [*dayang*] were collected from a one-dan field.

It was said that long ago Yang Xiaoyuan, a jail warden [*dianshi*] in Anyuan went to the capital city of Beijing to see the emperor. On meeting the emperor, he put a plate on his head and held a piece of paper in his hand. There were many liquor cups on the plate, which represented Anyuan and Xunwu counties, where there are many hills and mountains but few fields. On the paper he petitioned the emperor to reduce the land tax, with such words as "in ten thousand *qing* [1 *qing* = 16.5 acres] of mountains there is only a thread's width of land where it is possible for people to grow crops." The emperor flew into a towering rage and roared out: "You are such a low-ranking official that you should not be reporting directly to me. Not only do I disagree with you; I would also like to cut your head off." But after he read the paper, especially the paragraph that included "in ten thousand *qing* of mountains there is only a thread's width of land where it is possible for people to grow crops," the emperor said: "The words in the paper sound reasonable." So he approved a land tax reduction. Since then, the land tax in Anyuan and Xunwu counties has been lighter than in other counties. And to this day, the landlords and rich peasants in the two counties still hold a memorial ceremony for Yang with incense and candles at the end of each year's harvest. You can see temples to Yang in both counties.[39]

State rent. All land in Huangxiang District, part of Sanbiao District, and part of Xunwu City District is owned by the state. The land is called state land [*guantian*]. The government does not collect land tax from state land but rather "state rent" [*guanzu*], which totals about 940 ounces of silver each year. The state rent rate is nine to ten times heavier than the land tax and is about 0.2 yuan [*xiaoyang*] per dan. How did this land become state land? In the Ming dynasty there was a very powerful rebel, Ye Kai, who made his base in Huangxiang District for many years and fought against the emperor. But finally the emperor overcame him through a stratagem and took over all of Ye Kai's land. This land became state land. It was illegal to buy and sell state land, and transfers could be effected only under the guise of rent, the so-called *dingtui* between tenants of state land. Ye Kai's subordinates had occupied Sanbiao District, and so the story behind the state land in Sanbiao is the same as in Huangxiang. As for the small pieces of state land in the City District, these came from the expropriations of the land of those in the town who broke the emperor's law.

Total. In total, the land tax and the state rent should yield 2,360 ounces of silver, which is equal to about 7,640 silver dollars at the exchange rate of one ounce of silver for 3.24 silver dollars. However, because of (1) natural disasters like erosion and flooding, (2) the fact that some residents have moved out and others were without offspring, and (3) the fact that some taxpayers were too poor to pay tax or rent, the local government lost 20 percent of the figure. In fact, about 6,100 silver dollars were collected.

Bitterness. As mentioned above, a sum of only about 6,100 silver dollars was collected each year. But the county government needed more than 10,000 silver dollars each year for public expenditures on administration, justice, prisons, and public welfare. There was a big gap between revenue and expenses. Consequently, all those appointed as officials in Xunwu felt that life in Xunwu was very bitter and, as a result, collaborated with the local gentry to make up a variety of pretexts to oppress the poor people in the area in order to get money. The collection of the taxes on tobacco, liquor, and slaughtering was controlled directly by the provincial government, not the county government. The latter was able to administer only the land tax.

Customary fees. The Money and Grain Collection Department in the local government charged several customary fees. The first was the discount [*yinshui*] in the exchange rate; the person in charge of the Collection Department would get a cut of 5 to 10 percent of the money he handled. For example, the chief of the Collection Department might decide that one silver dollar [*dayang*] was equal to 1.25 yuan [*xiaoyang*], when the official exchange rate was 1.2 yuan. So he could rake off more than 300 silver dollars when he collected a little over 6,100 silver dollars in land taxes and state rents each year. These discounts were the biggest way in which taxpayers were exploited by the Collection Department. The chief of the Collection Department had no salary at all and could survive only on discounts and other customary fees.

The second fee was called the land transfer tax [lit. the after severance present] (also called the "severance grain" present). When anyone sold land, he had to pay a land transfer tax of 0.2 yuan to the Collection Department. Each year some 600 households sold land. The Collection Department would get 120 yuan from that.

The third was the [land deed] recording fee [lit. present]. When someone sold land, he had to pay not only the land transfer tax, but also the deed fee. He had to take the land deed to the Collection Department and have an official deed (issued by the Tax Collection Bureau) made. A recording fee of 0.2 yuan was charged to transcribe the information on the land deed onto an official deed. Each year the amount collected was the same as the land transfer tax.

The fourth was the receipt fee, namely, the money collected

from grain-tax receipts. The Collection Department got 0.03 yuan [*xiaoyang*] for each grain-tax receipt, or a total of 60 yuan from 2,000 grain-tax receipts each year.

All income from the four customary fees mentioned above belonged to the government [*gonggong*], except for the discounts.

When a new magistrate arrived and started his tour of duty, the chief of the Collection Department always gave him a present of 20 to 30 silver dollars. The money was called *diangui*. This meant the chief of the Collection Department hoped to be reappointed by the new magistrate. In addition, the Collection Department had to present the festival fees (for the Dragon Boat festival)[40] and the New Year's fee not only to the magistrate but also to the section chief of the Tax Collection Bureau in the county government. The former could receive things, whereas the latter received money (10 to 20 silver dollars). These expenses were derived from customary fees.

The people who are in charge of the money and grain. Three people—Liu Shihui, Liu Meifang, and Huang Shaotang—were in charge of the Money and Grain Collection Department since the beginning of the Republic. They controlled the tax registers and worked hand in glove with the magistrate. Their position was hereditary. They voted one of their number in as chief, and the others automatically became assistants. When the Red Army attacked and occupied the town, they fled with all the books.

The Tobacco and Liquor Stamp Tax

The revenue from the taxes on tobacco and liquor in Xunwu County was 60 yuan [*xiaoyang*] a month for each, or a total of 120 yuan. A merchant had contracted to collect the taxes and had established a tax bureau inside the North Gate. Once a month he went out and collected taxes in sixteen market towns: Chengjiang, Jitan, Sanbiao, Shipaixia, Liuche, Chetou, Niudouguang, Zhucun, Huangtangdu, Gongping,

Huangxiang, Zhonghe, Cenfeng, Maoping, Longgang, and Shangping.

He collected the tax from vendors selling liquor and every shop selling tobacco. He collected the taxes in accordance with the regulations from crooked vendors, but forced upright vendors to pay much more. He made 80 yuan each month based on the difference between the 120 yuan he had contracted to pay the government and the 200 yuan he actually collected. The tax bureau employed two clerks and one cook. The tax farmers were always from Ganzhou.

The Slaughter Tax

The collection of the slaughter tax was also contracted out. The amount that person contracted to pay the government was 80 yuan, but the actual money he collected was more than 150 yuan per month. So he could clear about 70 yuan each month. The slaughter tax farmer also established a bureau and employed one clerk and one cook. The clerk not only served the tax farmer, but also helped him to collect the tax. One-third of the 150 yuan came from the three butchers in Xunwu City. The slaughter tax farmers were also from Ganzhou. Although by law any rural resident had to pay a slaughter tax when he killed a pig for food, it was impossible for the tax farmer to uphold the law to the letter. He was actually able to collect the tax only from butchers with permanent slaughtering places in marketplaces.

Business Protection Tax

This was a local tax and was also called a sales tax. The funds for the KMT and the Pacification and Defense Militia came from the sales tax. Sometimes when the Public Security Bureau had a shortage of money, a certain percentage of the sales tax would be appropriated for it. The Sales Tax Bureau was under the Tax Collection Bureau and had established three branches, in Jitan, Pangu'ai, and outside the North Gate. There was a tax on all goods in transit, such as cooking oil, salt, rice, beans, chickens, ducks, oxen, pigs, sheep, dogs, marine products, general goods, and textiles. The tax payment started at 0.05 yuan and rose to a maximum of 0.5 yuan. Goods from nearby rural areas that were sold in small amounts—cakes, fruit, firewood, and [items] made from bamboo or wood—that were not being shipped elsewhere were tax free. In other words, everything shipped long distance was taxed. Since the development of the mass movement in the southern part of the county, in areas like Liuche and Niudouguang, the Sales Tax Bureau was unable to open a branch there to collect the tax. Anyway, the three branches collected more than 2,000 yuan each month. The branch in Jitan itself once collected more than 2,000 yuan in a month, and the branch outside the North Gate once collected more than 800 yuan in a month. There used to be no branch in Pangu'ai, but a new branch was opened there recently by Xie Jiayou. Although the tax was called the "business protection tax," the merchants in fact hated it very much.

Ox Tax

This was collected only in Xunwu City. A total of 1,700 yuan was collected each year by a handful of people who contracted to collect this tax. No bureau [was associated with it]. One person emerged as spokesman. For four years he has been He Xuecai, the father of He Zizhen of the New Xunwu faction. Although the tax farmers paid 1,700 yuan to the government, they actually collected about 2,300 yuan. The ox tax was a local tax and was administered by the county Tax Collection Bureau.

Gambling Tax

The gambling tax was called the "public interest tax" and was collected from gambling houses and brothels. It was a local tax. The gambling tax collector was appointed by the Tax Collection Bureau. (He Zishao did the job for two years.) The income from the gambling tax was 1,100 yuan each month from Xunwu City, although on one occasion 1,800 yuan was collected there. The gambling tax was also collected from other places in the county. The year before last over 3,000 yuan was collected from the entire county. At that time Liu Shiyi[41] sent more than ten soldiers to collect the gambling tax. But Liu Shiyi received 2,000 yuan each month from this money, calling it a "protection tax." He did the same thing in every county in southern Jiangxi. Later on, the Southern Jiangxi Native-place Association censured Liu Shiyi before the Jiangxi [provincial] government. Liu was forced to stop doing this. But the other powerful gentry kept doing the same thing as Liu had. This was but one act in the struggle between the powerful gentry and Liu. Many other counties had this kind of struggle.

General Income of the Tax Collection Bureau

The annual income was:

Ox tax	1,700 yuan
Business protection tax	24,000
Examination hall land rents	2,000
Sojourning Stipend Shrine land rents	3,000
Confucian Temple land rents	300

The total was around 30,000 yuan per year. This sum funded the KMT, the Pacification and Defense Corps, Tax Collection Bureau, Reconstruction Bureau, Education Bureau, the Rural Reform Bureau, Public Security Bureau, the New Xunwu School (established by He Zizhen and He Tingba), and the Puhua School (in Chengjiang, established by Xie Jiayou and Lan Yuqing). Generally speaking, this bankrolled the eating, gambling, whoring, and drug habits of the gentry and their lackeys.

Contributions and Loans

The [Jiangxi] provincial government forced this county to buy 3,000 yuan of government bonds, 2,000 yuan of the 2.5 percent Surtax Treasury Bonds,[42] and 1,000 yuan of central government bonds, and to lend 4,000 yuan for other kinds of loans. In addition, more than 40,000 yuan was collected by the warlords who passed through the county, such as Lin Hu, Liu Zhilu, Li Yibiao, Huang Renhuan,[43] Xu Chongzhi, and Lai Shihuang. The county government made assessments on every district, village, and market [xu] in the county. Every person in the county who had either a one-dan field or business capital in excess of 100 yuan shared the responsibility. But the powerful gentry, landlords, and large merchants with political influence, and officials at every level of government did not have to pay. Those who were exempt from collection also tried every method to reduce their relatives' and friends' obligations. Therefore, all the money was collected from the upright small landlords, rich peasants, and other merchants. Furthermore, a service fee, transportation fee, and tea fee were added to the assessments. In addition, for every 1,000 yuan originally required, the Tax Collection Bureau would collect 1,200 yuan and the district and township governments would add a percentage. They all cashed in on this method. In the rare case when bonds or debts were redeemed by the county from either the provincial government or the warlords, the commanders of the local militia in the towns as well as in every district would gobble it up, and the money never got back to the people. When Wang Ziyuan was general commander of the local militia, for example, he took 1,000 yuan that had been intended to repay a debt incurred by the army. The result was that all the lenders in Huangxiang sued him, but in the end they did not get a copper.

CULTURE IN XUNWU

We can say that essentially no women can read, for no more than 300 women in the whole county are literate. The cultural level of men is certainly not low—the southern half of the county is more advanced than the northern half because of more developed transportation facilities and because of the influence of Guangdong. Based on the population of the whole county, the figures are as follows:

illiterate	60%
literate	40%
can read 200 characters	20%
can keep accounts	15%
can read the *Romance of the Three Kingdoms*	5%
can write a letter	3.5%
can write an essay	1%
lower primary students	5% (5,000 people)
upper primary students	8% (8,000 people)
middle school students	500 people
college students	30 people
returned students	6 people
xiucai	400 people
juren	1 person

(The above percentages are in terms of total population.)

There are more upper primary students than lower primary students because most upper primary students enter directly after studying at private schools. In the whole county there are not more than ten lower primary schools in each district. With 70 schools in seven districts, taking a figure of 50 students in each, there is a total of 3,500 students. In addition there are 80 hybrid [44] lower primary schools that either exist on paper but not in reality or have not even put up a sign. Students in such schools number about 1,500. Together these two categories total about 5,000 people.

There is at least one upper primary school in each district. Shuangqiao District normally has two, although at one time (before the 25 March uprising) it had four. Nanba District has two, but at one time (before the 25 March uprising) it had three. Xunwu City District has two schools (the East School in the city and the Cao Lineage School in Tianbei). At one time Huangxiang District had three schools (before the 25 March uprising). Xunwu City has three (excluding the East School). The whole county normally has thirteen upper primary schools and at the height, that is, around the time of the high tide of the cultural movement [*wenhua yundong*] (before the 25 March uprising but after China's great revolution), there were eighteen. Normally every school has a hundred students. The oldest have a history of twenty-odd years, from the end of the Guangxu period in the Qing to the present, with a total of about 10,000 students. Of these 10,000, 2,000 have already died. Upper primary school students, for the most part, are children of small landlords, with the children of large landlords and rich peasants each constituting a small part.

This county has had four middle schools, but all have had a short life. The large landlord Uncle Shitcrock of Xiangshan established the Zhichi Middle School in Xiaohang in Xiangshan, which lasted a year. The Shangzhi Middle School (in Qiufang), which lasted half a year, was established by a group of Shuangqiao landlords. In Chengjiang [District] the publicly established Puhua Middle School (in Chengjiang) lasted two years. The Sun Yatsen [Zhongshan] Middle School established by the Revolutionary Faction (in Xunwu City) lasted two months. Together these schools had more than a hundred students, but there were no graduates. Most [current] middle school students attend schools in three places: Mei County, Pingyuan County, and Ganzhou City (each place has around 100 students). All of them are children of landlords; most of them are from small-landlord families.

College students come mostly from the large- and middle-landlord class. Only five students are from the small-landlord class. Liu Weilu studied one term at Sun Yatsen University in Canton, Liu Weie studied two years at Beijing University, and Kuang Caicheng studied over a year at Beijing Normal University. These three were all Communist party members. The two Liu were killed during the 25 March uprising. Kuang was a chief of staff of the Fiftieth Regiment of the Red Army and was tortured to death by Xie Jiayou in Chengjiang. Kuang Shifang, who studied for four years at Chaoyang University in Beijing, became ill and died—his thought was revolutionary. Ling Delu studied at Culture University in Beijing for a year and then went to Russia to study, but he did not have enough to live on so he tutored the children of the [Chinese] ambassador to Finland. His thought is revolutionary. These five were able to go to college only because their tuition was provided by their ancestral halls.

The 25 college and vocational students from large-landlord families are all reactionaries. The most important are:

He Zizhen: two years of study at a Henan mining school; head of the Xunwu Pacification and Defense Corps.

Lai Shiyuan: two years of study at Beijing Normal Preparatory School; participated in counterrevolutionary activities in Huangxiang.

Liu Hongxiang: two years of study in Beijing at Culture University; a leader of counterrevolutionary forces in Nanba District.

These three people are in Xunwu; the rest are elsewhere and are members of Chiang Kai-shek's faction. Of the 30 people who have been to college, 80 percent studied law.

Six people have gone overseas to study:

Pan Zuoqin: a graduate of an English medical school; practices medicine in Shantou.

Qiu Lingyun: although he has been to England and back, he really cannot be considered a returned student; an engineer with a Tianjin mining company.

Qiu Weiwu: a graduate of Imperial University in Japan and a core member of the New Xunwu faction; he fled with He Zizhen.

Gu Ziping: returned to China from Japan after purchasing

a diploma; a person who whores and gambles; from Huang-xiang; has served as president of the Education Society; he was attacked at a stronghold in Huangxiang by the Red Army and fled.

These four all have large- and middle-landlord back-grounds.

Zeng Youlan: the first to go overseas to study; during the Guangxu period, he went to Japan and graduated from a law course; he served as a judicial official in Fengtian, Beijing, and Hubei; the Sun Yatsen Middle School faction has treated him as their nominal leader; after the defeat of the 25 March upris-ing, his home was burned; now he is a member of the Reor-ganization faction.

Kuang Mohan: studied in Japan; refers to himself as a Marx-ist; is dean at Culture University in Beijing; formed a trans-portation company in Nanjing along with the large Xunwu landlord Xie Jie.

The background of these two people is neither that of large or middle landlord. Zeng is a small landlord who studied in Japan on government money; Kuang is a poor peasant, a grad-uate of an upper primary school who entered the Nanchang Military School, where someone saw his promise, sponsored him, and gave him money to go to Japan.

There are still 400 xiucai scattered throughout the county. Of the 600 Gu in the single-surname village of Tangbei in Huang-xiang, eleven are xiucai. This is the place where xiucai are most concentrated. When Gu Bo's great-great grandfather died at 70 sui, an imperially sanctioned memorial arch was con-structed. Over the arch is inscribed: "He personally saw seven generations." On each side is inscribed: "His eyes saw five who held the *lingong* degree" and "Twelve *shengyuan* gathered at his knees."[45] This means that at that time there were twelve xiucai among his descendants. In the whole county, the old culture was richest among the Tangbei Gu. They occupied a central position in administration in the past. Among the 2,000 people of Chetou Township in Nanba District are nine xiucai, which is a lot. Among the 1,400 people of Longtu Township in Nanba District are two xiucai, which is few.

Recently most xiucai have not had anything to do, and in the countryside they are called *laotai*. (Within a lineage peasants call the most respected person a *laotai*; he is called *xiansheng* by the local people.) These people are mostly rent-receiving small landlords; a small number teach (both old and new curricula). And another small number make their livelihood by practicing medicine. Xiucai are essentially products of the landlord class, but an extremely small number have a poor peasant background. They were nurtured by landlords, studied, and entered school.

Xunwu only has one juren now: Gu Luping. His father was a hired hand, and the family had nothing to eat. When he was young, Gu Luping carried small baskets of snacks (sweets, water chestnuts, and salted turnips) for sale. Later, while studying, a teacher saw he was bright and would not accept tuition. Thus, he really advanced in his studies. He served as a [Qing] magistrate twice and twice as a provincial assembly representative. In the countryside he is extremely smooth and everyone likes him. On the surface he supported the New Xunwu faction, but at the same time he prohibited his daughter from cutting her hair and he restricted her freedom of marriage. When the land struggle began in the southern half of the county, he opposed it. This time when the Red Army entered and attacked the Gu family stronghold, he advocated surrender.

After the victory of the land struggle in the southern half of the county, every township soviet has built at least one Lenin primary school. Each township usually has two, and in exceptional places (Longtu, Niudouguang) four have been built. Every school has 40 to 50 students, which is more than double the number of schools and students during the old days of KMT schools. The children say: "If it hadn't been for the land revolution, we wouldn't be able to study." As for upper primary schools, because of a lack of money and teachers (revolutionary intellectuals are busy participating in the struggle), schools have not been opened.

·5·

The Land Struggle in Xunwu

THE QUESTION OF LAND REDISTRIBUTION

There are a few methods for distributing land. The major one is equal redistribution per capita. Only 20 percent of the land in the county was not redistributed. Of the land already redistributed, 80 percent of the land was reallotted on the basis of equal redistribution per capita, regardless of age or gender. At the beginning of the land struggle, no law existed that could be applied to this situation. The Xunwu County Revolutionary Committee (the county government) suggested the following four methods, asking that the district and township soviets summon mass meetings to discuss and choose one method.

1. Equal redistribution per capita.
2. Redistribution according to productivity. Those who have greater productivity receive more land and those who have less productivity receive less land. In other words, anyone over 4 years old and under 55 is regarded as one labor unit and receives one share; those who are under 4 or over 55 receive only one-half share.[1]
3. Redistribution according to financial resources. Artisans

get less land, and those who do not have an occupation get more.

4. Redistribution according to soil fertility. Those who receive poorer lands receive more; those who get fertile lands get less.

In the event, most places chose the first method. Later on, the Xunwu County Communist Party applied the first method to all districts and was supported by the majority of the poor peasants and the masses. At present about 80 percent of the areas that redistributed land used this method. Within these areas, regardless of age, gender, or productivity, the total amount of land was divided by the number of persons. Some villages did not redistribute the land to people under four. Among those over four years old, regardless of their productivity, some got a 50 percent share or a 70 percent share, the rest received a full share. This was the method practiced in Liuche, Fengshan, Shangqi, and Datong townships, which have a population of about 10,000.

Some areas redistributed the land equally by the number of persons and then had those who were incapable of farming return part of their share to the soviet; this land was then added to the share of those with greater productivity. (The amount of shares returned were unequal; each person decided individually.) In the end, persons capable of greater physical labor got more land and those not as capable got less. This method is similar to the second method suggested by the county government. The difference is that peasants returned some part of the land of their own accord after the land was redistributed instead of redistributing the land according to productivity from the beginning. Longtu Township followed this method. In another township, Huangsha, a similar situation occurred, except this time the land was not returned by the peasants on their own accord. When the government saw that some people could not farm the land they had received, it ordered them to return part of the land to the government.

The peasants did not complain when asked to return part of the land unless the government forced them to return the fertile part and would not let them return the poor part; then they got upset. The combined population of Longtu and Huangsha is 2,500.

In addition, there is the free-farming method practiced in Datian Township. Whoever wants to farm can farm, and there is no limit on how much land these people should get. This is because Datian Township experienced a White terror in which nearly a hundred able-bodied men and dozens of elderly people and children were killed. In some cases, entire families were slaughtered. Some thirty people became Red Guards or went to other counties to participate in revolutionary work. The population of the township was reduced from 800 to 600, and much land was left uncultivated. Meanwhile, all the oxen in the township were taken away by the reactionaries. Thus, the land is open, without restriction, to anyone who wants to farm. Farming oxen were [then] fetched from rich households in other townships.

THE QUESTION OF REDISTRIBUTION OF HILLS AND FORESTS

The hills in the county, except for those in Niudouguang Township, still have not been redistributed and are being farmed by the original cultivators. In name, the soviet owns these hills and forests, and the cultivators pay land taxes to the soviet. Why were hills and forests redistributed only in Niudouguang? Because there are many people and little land in that township, and the peasants urgently asked that hill land be redistributed. Many peasants in other villages are also eager for the hills to be redistributed. For example, because the hills are owned by the ancestral trusts in some big lineages, the peasants in the areas outside Xunwu City's North Gate and South Gate and peasants from small lineages have no hill land to farm and are thus pushing to redistribute the hills.

THE QUESTION OF REDISTRIBUTING PONDS

The owner is the soviet, but the right of usage goes to the peasants. Pond management rotates annually among families that live around the pond. This method applies to the whole county.

THE QUESTION OF REDISTRIBUTING HOUSES

There was no redistribution of houses. However, people who had fewer houses or whose houses were burned down by the reactionaries were allowed to move into the houses owned by those who have more houses. Many houses in Shuangqiao and Nanba districts were burned down by the enemy, and those who were burnt out moved into the landlords' and rich peasants' houses; some also moved into middle and poor peasants' houses too.

This created a problem. The owners of the houses disliked these newcomers giving birth to male infants in their houses. It is believed in Xunwu that if an outsider gives birth to a son in a house, the spirit of the family will be taken away by the newborn and the family's prosperity will decline. There was once a *jinshi* named Zeng Xingsong in Fangtian Township, Shuangqiao District. He was born in his maternal grandfather's house and later became a jinshi and an official. People believe that he thus took the good fortunes of his grandfather's family. This is a well-known story throughout the county. After the failure of the 25 March uprising, the wife of the commander of the rebellion in Liuche, Zhong Xiqiu,[2] took refuge at her maternal grandfather's house. Her grandfather worried that she might be in labor soon and told her to leave right away. She finally escaped to a village in Longchuan County, built a hut in the hills, and gave birth to a son there.

Although at present most people whose houses are occupied by poor peasants and workers do not openly oppose the latter giving birth to male infants in their houses, they still are resentful of this. The only solution is to change the status of "temporary residence" to "permanent residence"; in other words, to redistribute landlords' houses based on the land redistribution method. This is also a strategy to gain the support of poor peasants and thus shake the foundations of the feudal system.

THE AREA STANDARD FOR LAND REDISTRIBUTION

For two reasons, peasants like to take a small district as a unit and object to taking a large district as the unit within which land redistribution takes place. First, they are concerned that the land in their area will be redistributed to other areas. Because of this, not only will they not agree to take the district as a unit for redistributing land, but they also are not inclined to take the township as a unit. What they wholeheartedly want is to take the village as a unit so that village land is redistributed to local villagers. Thus, although 85 percent of the land in Xunwu was redistributed within townships, the majority of the peasants did not support this method even though they did not strongly object.

They did not actively disagree because the difference in the quantity of land owned by villages was not so great; hence the peasants suffered only a small economic loss with the application of this redistribution method. In those villages where the differences in the quantities of the land are large, or in villages that cover a large area almost equal to that of a township, the peasants strongly oppose taking the township as a unit. Xunwu City Suburban Township (which is divided into four villages) and Xinzhai Township (divided into two villages) of the Xunwu City District, and Zhucun Township (which is divided into six villages) of Nanba District, all took the village as a unit for redistribution. This type of area was not very common, constituting only about 15 percent of the county.

The other reason is that the peasants disliked moving. They did not want to move from district to district, or from township to township. "Whenever you move, you need a basket of grain" means that in moving one suffers great losses. In addition, the peasants have a blind faith in geomancy and consider it unlucky to abandon their ancestors' tombs. The peasants believe that geomancy is good for production. Peasants value familiarity with their fields and accustomed living arrangements. In leaving all this and moving to another township, they suffer a sense of loss without knowing why. Also, for geographical reasons some people are not willing to move. For example, owing to Chetou's convenient location, commerce flourishes there. People do not want to move to out-of-the-way places (even though these places are still in the same district and only a dozen or so li away). This can be regarded as an economic factor too. It is wrong to think that these peasants' localism is simply old-fashioned thinking, and it is also a mistake to regard this type of thinking in psychological terms instead of economic terms.

LOAFERS WHO LIVE IN THE OUTSKIRTS ASK TO SHARE IN LAND REDISTRIBUTION

The peasants in Xunwu City received the least land during redistribution. Every person got land yielding 1 dan 8 dou [of grain]. This is the smallest amount of all the districts in the county. There were fewer peasants than in other districts, yet many loafers and prostitutes who did not farm also asked to share in land redistribution, thus reducing the amount of each share. Those prostitutes who had lovers ran away with them; those who did not have lovers asked to share in the land redistribution. They said, "There's no business; we will starve to death if we don't get our share of redistributed land." People criticized them for not being able to farm. They replied, "We can learn how to farm." In fact, they are farming in the fields already.

Most of the loafers and prostitutes have received some land. Among the loafers, some have the ability to farm, whereas others have sons or a small bit of capital. Some prostitutes have husbands or sons. Those with a number of family members are even more earnest in asking for redistributed land. Without it, they might have created a disturbance. Under these circumstances, the government distributed some land to them. Those inveterate loafers and prostitutes who absolutely had no ability to farm still have not been given any land. In the suburban district, 60 percent of the loafers received land; the remaining 40 percent had no knowledge of farming.

THE QUANTITY OF LAND PER PERSON AND THE SUPPLEMENT FOR LIVING

The peasants in the suburban area got the least land. Each person got only 1 dan 8 dou per *dang*. (There are two crops a year; each crop is called a *dang*.) Peasants in the four wards of the Xunwu City District got a little more. Each person got over 3 dan. Shuangqiao District had the highest allotments. Each person got over 7 dan per dang. In Longtu and Hejiao, each person got 7 dan. In most places each person got 5 dan per dang. Daily rice consumption is 1 jin, or 360 jin a year. One hundred eighty jin equals 1 dan, and 2 dan of [hulled] rice equal 4 dan of [unhulled] grain. When redistributing the land, wet grain (that is, *maogu*) is always taken as a unit. Each dang produces 5 dan of wet grain, two dang a year equals 10 dan. Ten dan of wet grain yield 8 dan of dry grain. Four dan are consumed, leaving 4 dan, of which 3 dan of grain are made into rice cakes and rice wine. The rest is insufficient for daily expenses, such as clothes, oil, and salt, and for social intercourse (e.g., weddings, funerals, and festivals).

In this case, how do people manage to make up the difference? Raising pigs, chickens, and ducks; growing some vegetables (in the suburbs of Xunwu City), sugarcane, bamboo, and miscellaneous crops (like sweet potatoes, taro, chestnuts, soybeans); and also making handicraft products (all kinds of articles made with rounded wood and with bamboo, such as wok lids, buckets, rice containers, foot basins, urine buckets, water dippers, bamboo chairs, straw rainhats, winnowing fans, rice sieves, bamboo scoops, fire grates, bamboo baskets, and other items. Most of the peasants do this as sideline work, very few of them do it as an occupation. Some peasants even make desks, benches, chairs, and tables). Some work as porters (carrying rice, salt, soybeans, oil, and miscellaneous crops; they all are hired by other people to carry these things, mostly rice and salt; the rest of those things being less common); run small businesses (like selling oil, salt, rice, soybeans, pigs, chickens, and even rice cakes, etc.); and also working for the capitalists (picking mushrooms and tea, making paper). Everyone does one or two of the above as sideline occupations in order to supplement his income. In general, income from land constitutes two-thirds of a family's income, and the miscellaneous income makes up the remaining third.

THE QUESTION OF WHETHER TO HAVE CORPORATE LAND

There is no corporate land. During the meetings, the peasants were very eager to redistribute all the land; no one ever suggested keeping some of the land as corporate land. Because of the high population density and the scarcity of land, there is barely enough land for the peasants to feed themselves, not to mention that some of the peasants still do not have enough land. Who would agree that the government should still allow corporate land?

THE SPEED OF REDISTRIBUTION

After the uprising, land in the northern part of the county was redistributed very quickly. For instance, from the insurrection and taking of Xunwu City, redistribution took the Xunwu City District only twenty days to complete. Chetou and Longtu in Nanba District and Shangping in Sanshui District accomplished the redistribution at an even faster rate. They finished the investigation within one day, completed calculations within two days, promulgated the results for a day, and then spent the rest of the time determining the division of each share of redistributed land according to the principle of "drawing on the plentiful to make up for the scarce" [i.e., taking land away from those with more than the average share and giving it to those with less than the average share]. In such cases, it takes at least one week because the real struggle is in using the principle of drawing on the plentiful to make up for the scarce. This type of struggle is the peasants' struggle against landlords and rich peasants. Those who have plenty of land and need to have land taken away do not want to give away the fertile part. Those who lack land do not want to accept the poor part. Thus, it takes time to mix them well.

Most of the southern part of the county (except Chetou and Longtu) experienced a rather slow redistribution. Since last February [1929], there has been an armed struggle in the Shuangqiao area. However, it was not until the end of November that the County Revolutionary Committee was established and the statistical forms for the land investigation were distributed. After a month the investigation was still incomplete because of improper methods.

The investigation forms contained innumerable items (population, class status, cultural level, ethnicity, age, landownership, land boundary, land area, yearly harvest), including some that did not need to be investigated. On top of that, the procedure was quite inconvenient. (The County Revolutionary Committee first distributed the investigation forms to each township, and then each township returned the completed forms to the County Revolutionary Committee for review.) This slowed the speed of redistribution. In January of this year the method was changed. The investigation forms contained only a few simple items: the name of the household head, total number of family members, how many family members can farm, how many make a living in commerce or industry, the quantity of land, and the quantity the household should get. The investigation procedure was as follows: the township government convened a "conference on the redistribution of land." Each household sent one delegate to discuss the method of redistributing land. Then the conference investigations began. (Many tables were set up at the conferences, and representatives from each village sat at tables and took down the information that people reported.) The forms were turned in to the township governments, which checked and ratified this information and then figured out the amount for each person by dividing the total quantity of land by the total number of persons. The results were then announced. Thus, it took only four days from the investigation to the announcement (one day for investigation, two days for checking, and one day for announcing).

It remained, then, to redistribute the land. This was started on the fifth day. Each township government sent out a dozen or so political instructors [*zhidaoyuan*], who fanned out to all the villages to investigate whether the land was fertile or infertile and to confirm whether the reports made by the peasants on the first day of the investigation were true or false. Based on the investigation, redistribution was then carried out. The most troublesome work was applying the principle of drawing on the plentiful to make up for the scarce and in determining the boundaries of the land. This is where the struggles occurred. This aspect of redistribution takes about a week to complete. Nevertheless, with the application of this method, the whole procedure of investigation and redistribution takes only two weeks. The northern part of the county later applied this method.

FAIRNESS

Frequently discussed issues at many land redistribution conferences included whether the township or the village should be taken as a unit, whether the standard of redistribution should be the person or productivity, and how fish-ponds, gardens, and embankments should be redistributed. (There was no discussion of the redistribution of hills, forests, and houses.) Making a false report was strictly forbidden, but how should those who make a false report be punished? There was no need to discuss confiscation standards at all, because, without any written orders, whenever people see the red flag, they know that confiscation has been announced.

The simple question is how to redistribute this massive amount of land. Apparently, dividing the total quantity of land by the total number of persons was the most direct and equitable land redistribution. It also was supported by the majority of the masses. The minority who did not approve of this method (landlords and rich peasants) was frightened by the power of the masses and did not dare say a word. In other words, the word "fairness" contains the meanings of confiscation and redistribution.

THOSE PEOPLE WHO RESIST THE FAIR REDISTRIBUTION OF LAND

A small landlord named Liu in Fengshan Township, Shuangqiao District, hoarded his own fertile land and turned only poor land over to the government. When the masses tried to force him to turn over his fertile lands, he replied with indignation, "Over my dead body!" The township government could not solve the problem. The county government sent someone to Fengshan to bear down on him, and then he turned over the land.

There were other small landlords and rich peasants in Niu-douguang, Nanba District, who failed to turn over their land. The township government was afraid of them and did not take any action. It was not until the county government sent someone to summon a mass meeting that these small landlords and rich peasants were forced to give in.

In Datian Township, Shuangqiao District, the house of a

small landlord, Mei Yuankun, was burned down by the reactionaries. Mei considered this to be his contribution to the revolution. When the masses wanted him to distribute his land, he replied with vicious abuse, "Redistribute my land, but chop my head off first!" The masses informed the county government, which had the district government arrest him. The person in charge in the district government, Mei Lisan, is a Communist who also is a member of Mei Yuankun's lineage. He covered up this mistake for him. Mei Yuankun later denied having said such a thing, and his land was redistributed.

Another case involved the person in charge of the government of Huangtangdu Township, Shuangqiao District, a certain Lin, and the person in charge of the Xuxi Township government, also named Lin (he is also a Communist); both received fertile lands in the land redistribution. The masses cried, "The persons in charge got fertile lands, and we got poor lands." Being upset with this, the masses became apathetic in the land struggle. The county therefore took the fertile land from those two people and redistributed it to the masses, to their satisfaction.

Except for Mei Yuankun, who opposed the confiscation of his land, the others mentioned above argued over the redistribution of fertile and poor land rather than the confiscation of land. The masses did not consider confiscation of rich peasants' land an issue. It was the issue of who got fertile land and who got poor land that concerned them. And that is the heart of the land struggle, as is the struggle between the rich peasant and the poor peasant.

TOTAL REDISTRIBUTION OF THE
ORIGINAL FARMING LAND

The principle of "the township as a unit" was applied to the population and not to the land. The land cannot be divided by district. People from Township A farm land in Township B; Township B's people farm land in Township A; people from one township might farm land belonging to a neighboring district. The boundaries between districts, counties, and provinces are all crisscrossed by peasants when farming. So that when the people of one township totaled up the land they farmed in their township and in neighboring areas and then redistributed it equally, this was considered a reasonable act. The land redistribution was carried out this way too.

HOW TO TAKE CARE OF THE LAND IF THE INSURRECTION OCCURRED AFTER THE RICE SEEDLINGS HAD BEEN TRANSPLANTED

There are three ways of dealing with this issue. The first one is the method being carried out in the northern part of Xunwu County (the land redistribution in the southern part of Xunwu occurred before the rice seedlings had been transplanted. Therefore, this problem did not exist). The first crop (also called early rice) goes to the original cultivator, and the second crop (also called late rice) goes to the new cultivator. In this way, the rich peasant does not suffer a loss. However, the poor peasants with less land and those who do not farm, such as landlords and loafers, were not satisfied, especially because they felt that they had no financial resources. If the landlords cannot collect land rents, they have no grain. Loafers no longer had a means of livelihood since gambling had been abolished, and there was no one to borrow money from.

The second way is to have the new cultivator reimburse the original cultivator for the first crop. This method also offers two standards for reimbursement, one of which is less than the other. The original cultivators were naturally not contented if they thought the subsidy was too little and were happy with a greater subsidy. This situation provoked general criticism among the poor peasants and loafers. Some even said, "There are so many big landlords who are flat broke nowadays, and you are still trying to hold onto that tiny bit of property!" No written law in Xunwu recognizes this method;

the peasants adopted it themselves. In the Xunwu City District, poor peasants who did not have enough to eat offered a small sum of money to the rich peasants, requesting them to let them have a part of the first crop. This was actually quite common.

The third method is that no matter what the state of the crop, whoever got the land gets the harvest. Some parts of Pingyuan County, Guangdong, adopted this method.

SHOULD NON-PEASANTS GET REDISTRIBUTED LAND?

In Xunwu City loafers with the ability to farm were allowed to receive redistributed land, and those who did not possess any farming ability did not get a share of land. In districts with few loafers, all of them were allowed to get redistributed land. Artisans, merchants, and students without a stable income got redistributed land. In Xunwu City and in large townships, people who had a stable income did not get a share; those who did not have enough income got some part of the land as a supplementary source for their livelihood. Red Army soldiers and revolutionaries not only got land, the soviet also mobilized peasants to farm the land for them. Landlords shared in the redistribution if they lived in the township. Buddhist monks, Daoist priests, and Christian pastors were required to change their occupation. If they were no longer monks, priests, or pastors, they could share in the land redistribution. Otherwise, they could not. Because of the small number of fortune-tellers and geomancers, there are no regulations about them; they were generally allowed to share in the land redistribution. There are no monks, priests, pastors, fortune-tellers, or geomancers in the southern part of the county anymore; all changed their occupation. When the father of the chairman of the Huangsha Township government died, the peasants opposed having the monks offer a Buddhist ceremony. There are very few geomancers in Xunwu County; most of them are from Xingguo.

There are about a hundred Buddhist monks in the county. Xunwu City has one Protestant church with over 200 members, and one Catholic church with over 100 members. Huangxiang has one Protestant church with 100 members or so; Niudouguang has one Protestant church with 70–80 members; Jitan has one Protestant church with about 100 members; Chengjiang has one Protestant church with about 70–80 members. In the county there are five Protestant churches with about 700 members and one Catholic church with over 100 members. Altogether there are over 800 members. The Protestant churches belong to the Americans. There was an American minister in Xunwu City; Chinese ministers were in charge of the other four churches. The Catholic church belongs to the Germans, with one Chinese priest in charge of it. Members include widows (including poor peasants) and elderly women (landlords' wives) (30 percent); sly and capricious gentry and their families (30 percent); peasants of small and powerless lineages (20 percent—peasants belonging to big and powerful lineages do not convert); and young intellectuals of landlord origins without prospects (10 percent); the remaining 10 percent of members are of all types. These converts can be divided into two groups: the very bad and the very weak. The bad ones are not loafers, but they are wicked and crafty local people who want to be strongmen—the church is a means by which to accomplish this. The other group of people are the weak; their purpose is to seek shelter in the church.

THE QUESTION OF ABOLISHING DEBTS

This question is divided into loans and bills of credit. The purpose in abolishing loans was to wipe out highly exploitative loans with interest rates of 20 percent or more. A bill of credit from a merchant was paid if it was made after January 1928. Since no debt carried less than a 20 percent interest rate, all debts were wiped out. Money that was lent without interest and as a favor from relatives and friends was still returned by the masses, but this happened rarely. The merchants had not extended the poor peasants credit; most of the credit was for the rich peasants and some for the middle peasants.

LAND TAX

Last year, every dan [of yield] was taxed 2 dou in land taxes. This was practiced in both Shuangqiao and Nanba districts. In February of this year, the County Revolutionary Committee held an expanded meeting that drew up tax regulations. The land tax was set at 10 percent regardless of the quality of the land. The tax rate is the same as the tax on land rent. This type of taxation makes no distinction about the quality of the land (it is not a progressive tax). In May, the county soviet congress adopted the progressive taxation announced by the West Jiangxi [Ganxi] Soviet.

WOMEN IN THE LAND STRUGGLE

Women and men are equal partners in production in Xunwu. Strictly speaking, in terms of farming, women's duties are much heavier than those of men. Because certain tasks require physical strength, men are more likely to take charge of plowing and raking the fields and carrying the muck and grain. However, women assist men in carrying the muck and grain, transplanting rice seedlings, weeding fields, uprooting the weeds in the paths between the fields and on the edges of the fields, turning over the soil, and cutting the grain. But although men help out, women are chiefly responsible for hulling grain, polishing grain, watering gardens, transplanting vegetables, cutting wood, mowing grass, making tea, cooking meals, raising pigs and other domestic animals [*tousheng*] (the six domestic animals are called *tousheng*), washing and ironing clothes, mending clothes, making shoes, sweeping floors, and doing dishes. Besides these tasks, raising children is also a woman's duty; thus, the toil of women is harder than that of men. Women's tasks come one after another, and their work never ends.

They are appendages of the male economy (that is, the economy from the feudal economy to the first stage of a capitalist economy). Although men are no longer serfs, a woman is still a man's serf or semi-serf, without political rights and personal freedom. No one suffers more than women.

As the land struggle developed, many local women bravely participated in it. When the Second Column of the Fourth Army attacked the reactionaries holed up in their stronghold, groups of women from Huangxiang carried wood to burn it. They also seized grain from reactionary landlords. With the victory of their struggle, these women attained self-consciousness.

Soon after the establishment of township governments in every township, a number of divorce cases were received. Most of these cases were initiated by women (about 90 percent); very few were started by men (only 10 percent or so). Men were firmly opposed to divorce. A small group of men, on the other hand, became passive. "The revolution wants to get rid of everything, wives included." This is a sigh of resignation, for they cannot stop divorces from happening. This group of men was made up of mostly poor peasants.

The majority of men are very opinionated. In Fangtian, the captain of the Red Guards, Zeng Jiaxun, who was married, got involved with another woman. His wife asked for a divorce. He would not agree and told her: "Never can a wife leave this family while she is alive. If you want to get a divorce, then I will kill you first." In Longtu, a rich peasant named Liu Xuesheng refused his wife's request for divorce. He told the chairman of the Revolutionary Committee: "If she wants to divorce me, I will exterminate her. After I exterminate her, I will then die without complaining." This category of men is mostly made up of rich peasants.

The policy adopted by the political organs on this issue has been changed four times. The first was based on a resolution of the congress of peasants in November of last year. The resolution did not take a clear stand against a husband's having more than one wife; it allowed a married man to have a lover as long as his wife did not object; the proposed conditions for divorce were not rigid. If one spouse had a disease, if the woman was oppressed, if the husband and wife had a falling out and had not lived together for half a year, or if the man went to another area and had not been heard from for a year—these people were allowed to get divorced. The landlord class could divorce without any conditions.

In addition to the legal provisions, it was explicated that no one should try to catch a person in the act of adultery. However, after this was made clear throughout the county, much turmoil occurred between men and women in the southern part of the county, especially in Longtu and Hejiao (in Nanba District). Armed fights almost broke out between groups of men and women. The reason was that groups of young men from both townships frequently assailed young women of the other township with obscenities. So the women themselves organized women's associations, and with this unity they became more liberal in their behavior when engaging in hard work. (They went to the hills in groups to cut firewood and tended to return home later than usual.) Meanwhile, love affairs between them and their young male friends (from other townships) increased, and couples had dates freely in the hills. People from these two townships are from the same lineage but from different branches. Because the masses, who were against the rule of trying to catch people in the act of adultery, intervened with the people who were involved in doing so, this almost led to an armed fight this January. In addition to this type of incident, there were married people in almost every township and village who had new lovers. The wives rallied together to oppose such affairs.

Under these circumstances, the government made another law quite different from the preceding one. This February, the enlarged meeting of the County Revolutionary Committee came to a resolution on the "issue of fidelity": "Married men and women are prohibited from having sexual intercourse with a third party; whoever engages in illicit intercourse will be punished with severity." At the same time another law was passed to regulate the "lover" issue: "Oppose polygamy and polyandry. [Estranged] husbands and wives who have yet to be divorced cannot have lovers. Those who have made mistakes in the past must separate immediately and unite with only one person." The resolution did not change the policy for divorce cases. Ever since this was promulgated, disputes have stopped. Peasants united together to face the crisis at that time and managed to break the enemy's attack.

On 2 May we took over Xunwu City. At the same time, the Fourth Red Army had taken over the reactionary northern part of the county and aroused the masses in Huichang, Anyuan, and Pingyuan to action. In this situation, on 6 May, the first soviet congress of the whole county withdrew the fidelity resolution. And even though the congress did not clearly forbid people to catch others in adultery, it no longer talked about "whoever engages in illicit intercourse will be punished with severity." With regard to the "lover" issue, this congress adopted the resolution of the meeting in February and continued the policy on divorce of the previous two meetings.

However, within one month, a soviet congress in a third area adopted a totally different resolution on the "lover" and divorce issues. Its slogan was "Absolute freedom in divorce and marriage." Naturally, the result is to forbid efforts to catch people in adultery and to ensure the freedom to have lovers. The district that approved this is the district that has had the longest period of struggle in all of Xunwu County (from 1928 to the present) and is also the district that first had capitalism. Its struggle began with the arrival of the Fourth Army and with the development of the struggle in Huichang, Anyuan, Xunwu, and Pingyuan counties. When this proposal was mentioned, the person who made the proposal spoke out: "The people from the Fourth Army said that conditional divorce implies feudal thought." After this speech, the proposal was approved immediately.

This [i.e., the marriage policy] is a new issue in Xunwu City District. Although the new government is less than a month old, the question of relations between the sexes has become very turbulent. One of the townships rejected the propagandist [*xuanchuanyuan*] sent by the government by saying: "Comrade, please do not give us any propaganda. With more propaganda, the women in our township will all run away." In fact, the propagandist had come to propagandize about "overthrowing the feudal forces" and "bringing down the village bosses and redistributing land." The divorce and marriage policy was explained according to the regulations. Nevertheless, once the masses are aroused, just as water flows from high hills to low plains, they cannot be reversed. In one township in Xunwu City District, over ten women ran away. Their husbands went to the township soviet and complained tearfully. Heeding their desperate pleas, the township soviet was forced to put up a notice that read: "Young people have misinterpreted the meaning of freedom and hence have run away in the dark of night in pursuit of their lovers and are finding new lovers before divorcing their mates. These are absurd, inappropriate, furtive doings . . . ." This official notice clearly expressed the voice of the older husbands. However, this "incongruous" trend—the trend of a democratic system taking the place of a feudal system—could not be halted.

Women have expressed their appreciation for the land struggle, because it can help dissolve the restrictions on their personal freedom. Regardless of their class, all unmarried young people support the slogan of freedom in marriage. However, married men in the poor-peasant class generally oppose the right to divorce. But their opposition differs from the obstinacy of the counterrevolutionaries. They worry that they will lose their wife's labor and will not be able to farm if their wife runs away. They sigh, "The revolution wants to get rid of everything, wives included." They go to the township government and ask for help. Meanwhile, although they feel annoyed with their wives, they do not dare hit them. The attitude of adult males from the rich-peasant and small-landlord classes is completely different. Their expressed desire to kill their wives if the latter ask for a divorce shows their tendency toward counterrevolutionary attitudes. And why do these adult peasants oppose the freedom to get a divorce? (They have no objection against marriage freedom.) Apparently, it is because of labor resources.[3]

Do male peasants oppose liberating women? No, they do not. Once the whole class is liberated, poor peasants and farmhands will soon free their women. The reason why they are afraid that their wives will run away is that before the land struggle develops in depth, they cannot fully foresee the outcome of overthrowing the feudal system and exploitation, and they develop such thoughts. As long as the land struggle is developed in depth, their attitudes toward marriage will change greatly.

Appendixes

APPENDIX A

Currency and Prices
in Xunwu

The currency situation in China in 1930 was extremely complex. Although Mao does not specifically discuss all aspects of this question, we can safely assume that daily transactions were carried out in coppers (minted copper one-cent coins) and silver coins (20-cent and possibly 10-cent pieces). It is possible, also, that bank notes in 10-cent (silver) and 20-cent (silver) denominations were used. These were the currencies of commerce, both within Xunwu and with its nearby trading partners. Colloquially these currencies were called "small foreign-style money" (*xiaoyang*) to distinguish them from the silver dollars, minted by various central authorities, or the silver-dollar bank notes that were used for government business and large commercial transactions. These currencies were called "large foreign-style money" (*dayang*). The National Currency Regulations issued in 1914 had envisioned a uniform standard, with one Yuan Shikai silver dollar equal to, for example, five 20-cent silver coins or 100 copper cents (coppers). In reality, however, the currencies of daily commerce and of government and large commercial transactions were separate. The so-called subsidiary silver currency (*xiaoyang*), mostly 20-cent pieces or bank notes (called fractional currency notes), were discounted slightly relative to the standard Yuan Shikai and, later, Sun Yatsen dollars (*dayang*). In similar fashion, the 1914 regulations specified that 100 copper cents equaled one silver dollar. This exchange rate also existed only on paper. In the 1910's and 1920's, the exchange rates between copper cents and silver coins fluctuated significantly. In Shanghai, for example, one silver dollar could buy 132 coppers in December 1912, 206 coppers in December 1924, and 278 coppers in

December 1929. This last figure represented a recovery from summer 1928, when it took 290 copper cents to buy one silver dollar. Because of the volatility of the value of copper relative to silver, figures given in the text in the form of so many *mao* and so many *fen* must be interpreted as a reference to silver alone, with 10 fen equal to 1 mao. There were, however, no silver coins denominated in fen. Figures expressed in fen, then, represent the silver equivalent of a certain number of copper cents. Since Mao gives a local exchange rate of 21 coppers for 1 mao, we can assume that a figure of 5 fen, for example, represents the equivalent in silver of about 10 coppers.

This note and the following list are based on Eduard Kann, *The Currencies of China: An Investigation of Gold & Silver Transactions Affecting China, with a Section on Copper* (Shanghai: Kelly & Walsh, 1926), pp. 295–351; and *The China Year Book, 1931*, ed. H. G. W. Woodhead (Shanghai: North-China Daily News and Herald, 1931), pp. 392–403. Kann, a member of the Shanghai Exchange Brokers' Association, was the author of the section on money in the *China Year Book*. Useful information on the currency situation in the major cities, Shantou, Ganzhou, and Jiujiang, near Xunwu can be found in *Decennial Reports, 1922–31* (Shanghai: Inspectorate General of Customs, Statistical Department,1933), 1.587 [Jiujiang] and 2.157 [Shantou]; and *Shina shōbetsu zenshi*, vol. 11 [Jiangxi] (Tokyo: Tōa Dōbunkai, 1918), p. 976 [Ganzhou].

silver dollar In 1930 this could refer to actual silver dollars, which bore the likeness of either Yuan Shikai or Sun Yatsen, or dollar notes issued by various banks. Taxes, the cost of brokerage licenses, and the accounts of government agencies were expressed in silver dollars. For example, Xunwu's annual land tax was about 4,300 silver dollars. Colloquially, this was called "big foreign-style money" (*dayang*). Mao's hypothetical exchange rate, given in the text, put one silver dollar as equivalent in value to 1.2 yuan (which would consist of six 20-cent pieces). In 1928 one Chinese silver dollar was worth about U.S. $0.90. By early May 1930, the Chinese silver dollar had declined in value relative to the U.S. dollar by 30 percent.

yuan The national unit of currency, equivalent in value to 24 grams of silver, introduced in 1914. In this book, when yuan refers to "small foreign-style money" (*xiaoyang*), it is a unit of account only, equal to 10 mao. In 1930 this was equivalent to 210 coppers. The top assistants in Xunwu's shops earned an annual salary of 40–60 yuan. During normal market conditions, a subsistence diet of rice cost about 15 yuan a year. Whenever possible, amounts given in mao or fen in the original were expressed in yuan in the translation.

mao A unit of account and an actual silver coin. In the 1914 currency reforms, a mao was defined as one-tenth of a yuan. Most commonly issued in the form of a 20-cent coin, although some 10-cent coins were produced. In Xunwu in 1930 a 10-cent silver coin was worth 21 coppers (minted copper cents). A pound of chicken in Xunwu City's market might cost about 4.5 mao.

fen A unit of account only. In the 1914 currency reforms, it was defined as one-tenth of a mao or one–one hundredth of a yuan. Although the term was originally intended to refer as well to the copper cent, the depreciation of the value of copper relative to silver eliminated this correspondence.

copper A minted copper coin used in daily transactions. Twenty-one coppers equaled one silver 10-cent piece in Xunwu. A minted copper cent piece could be referred to as a 10-cash coin. First minted in 1890, copper cents were intended to replace the traditional copper "cash," small coins with square holes in the middle that could be strung together in "strings" of 1,000 "cash" coins. In Xunwu in 1930 a wineshop might charge 2 coppers for a cup of wine and a shop might charge 3 coppers for a large piece of bean curd.

ounce of silver A translation of *liang*, traditionally a unit of weight and a unit of currency. One ounce of silver was equal, in value, to one tael. In late Qing times a Treasury (Kuping) tael was equal to 0.72 Chinese silver dollars, a ratio that remained constant with subsequent silver dollars, such as the imperial "dragon," Yuan Shikai, and Sun Yatsen dollars. Although the central government had announced, in summer 1928, its intention to eliminate the tael, this was still unrealized in 1930. In Xunwu in 1930 the land tax, though still expressed in taels, or ounces of silver, was calculated in silver dollars, with one tael set equal to three silver dollars. Since the market rate at the time was one (Kuping) tael for 1.4 silver dollars, the local official conversion rate represented a de facto doubling of the tax rate.

Weights and Measures
in Xunwu

The following list is based on figures given in Mao's text. It is fortunate that Mao tried to collect these data, because in 1930 there were
many variations across China. For example, a jin could range in
weight from 12 to 42.5 ounces, and the number of jin in a dan from
90 to 280 (*China Year Book, 1929/30*, ed. H. G. W. Woodhead, Tientsin:
Tientsin Press, 1929, p. 342). This variation is evident in Xunwu,
where a dan consisted of a different number of jin according to the
product. For example, a dan of tea weighed 70 jin, of firewood 70 jin,
of chicken 60 jin, and of iron about 40 jin. The variation in the number
of ounces in a jin requires some deductions to be made, since Mao
did not specify this relationship in the text. A jin is assumed to equal
about a pound because of Mao's statement that an annual minimum
subsistence diet in rice required 360 jin of hulled rice. Dwight H. Per-
kins, in *Agricultural Development in China, 1368–1968* (Chicago: Al-
dine, 1969), p. 14, gives a comparable figure of 400 jin and specifies
a jin to be equal to 1.1 pounds.

Two characters are used for dan in the text. One is sometimes romanized as *shi* and refers to a unit of dry measure for grain. This character is used in the text mostly for reckoning land rents, which were
expressed in amounts of unhulled rice. For example, a small landlord
was defined as one receiving less than 200 dan. The other character
romanized *dan* can be translated either as a unit of weight equal, in
standard trade terms, to about 133 pounds or as a carrying pole and
the loads on it. It is this second meaning that makes most sense in
Mao's text, if we assume that a jin is a measure of weight equal to
about a pound. Since most goods were moved in Xunwu by porters,

a reference to a quantity of goods in terms of the standard load makes sense. Different weights for a standard load of any given product were also found by Japanese investigators in nearby Ganzhou, where a standard dan of unhulled rice weighed 92 jin and a standard dan of soybeans weighed 120 jin (see *Shina shōbetsu zenshi,* vol. 11 [Jiangxi], Tokyo: Tōa dōbunkai, 1918, p. 977 [Ganzhou]). Likewise, Mao found great variety in Xunwu, where, for example, he stated that one dan of soybeans could contain from three to five dou.

The English equivalents associated below with the various Chinese measures are included only to show the relationship between various measures. They do not represent the standard volumes and weights associated with these terms.

dan 180 jin of rice (a bushel). The ratio of the weight of unhulled to hulled rice is 2:1.

jin about one pound

dou (a peck) one-fifth of a dan of rice

sheng (quart) one-fiftieth of a dan of rice

ge (a cup) one five-hundredth of a dan of rice. A subsistence diet consisted of almost 3 ge (about a pound) of hulled rice a day.

shao (scoop) one five-thousandth of a dan of rice

liang a Chinese ounce equal, for purposes of foreign trade, to 1.31561 ounces avoirdupois. Sixteen liang equaled one jin in foreign-trade transactions.

li a measure of distance commonly taken to equal one-third of an English mile. In reality, a li was a function of both distance and the difficulty of traversing that distance.

Qing Examination Degrees Held by Xunwu Men

This table is based on information in Chang Chung-li, *The Chinese Gentry: Studies on Their Role in Nineteenth-century Chinese Society* (Seattle: University of Washington Press, 1955), pp. 3–32, 94–111; and Chapter 4 of Mao Zedong's *Report from Xunwu*.

jinshi A person holding the highest examination degree, won after successful competition in the triennial series of tests (*huishi*) conducted in Beijing. Only several hundred men passed each time.

juren A person holding the second-highest examination degree, awarded to successful candidates in the triennial provincial exams (*xiangshi*). These men could take the examination for the jinshi degree and were qualified to hold official posts. According to Mao, there was one juren, Gu Luping, in Xunwu in 1930.

gongsheng A person holding a degree comparable in prestige to a juren degree. A gongsheng degree could be gained by virtue of accomplishments, success in an examination held by provincial authorities, or by purchase.

bagong A person holding a type of gongsheng degree awarded to a select group of individuals on the basis of competitive exams. Holders of this degree could serve as county-level officials.

shengyuan A person holding one of three degrees (linsheng, zengsheng, or fusheng) awarded to candidates after examinations conducted at the prefectural level by provincial officials. These degrees were awarded on the basis of strict quotas established by the central government, and only one or two men out of a hundred were successful.

linsheng The most talented, privileged, and powerful of the sheng-yuan. These men could be granted a stipend by the county government and were allowed to compete for the gongsheng degree.

fusheng A person holding the lowest degree within the various sub-divisions of shengyuan.

jiansheng A person with a degree, usually purchased, that could be obtained by men who had registered to compete in the entrance examination conducted by county officials.

xiucai A "flourishing talent," colloquial term for a shengyuan. Mao reported that about 400 xiucai were still alive in Xunwu in 1930.

tongsheng A honorific given to men who had passed a noncompetitive entrance examination—the first of three steps leading to the lowest degree—conducted by county officials.

Reference Matter

Notes

Unless otherwise indicated by "Trans.," the notes to the translation of the *Report from Xunwu* were written by the editor of the *Mao Zedong nongcun diaocha wenji*. For complete authors' names, titles, and publication data, see the Bibliography, pp. 259–64.

INTRODUCTION

1. Schram, *Mao Tse-tung*, p. 89.
2. See Isaacs, *Tragedy*. See also Harrison, pp. 42–117.
3. McDonald, pp. 296–316.
4. Brandt et al., pp. 89–93.
5. Schram, "Mao Tse-tung's Thought," pp. 826–27.
6. Wen, pp. 85–87.
7. Xia, pp. 279–80.
8. Wen, p. 58; *Mao Zedong nongcun diaocha wenji*, p. 359; Everett S. Burket, letter of 2 Feb. 1929, American Baptist Foreign Mission Society Records (hereafter ABFMS Records), Reel FM233.
9. For a general history of this period, see Harrison, pp. 118–88; and Schram, *Mao Tse-tung*, pp. 118–43. For a bibliographic essay on source materials and the secondary literature, see *Cambridge History of China*, 13: 885–87.
10. In Mao Zedong's own narrative of this period, he mentions the "brilliant successes" in early 1930 when "nearly the whole of southern [Jiangxi] fell to the Red Army" (Snow, p. 155). But it is hard to determine what Mao was doing and where he was. Edgar Snow, Mao's first biographer, observed that at this precise moment "Mao Tse-tung's account had begun to pass out of the category of 'personal history,' and to sublimate itself somehow intangibly in the career of a great movement in which, though he retained a dominant role, you could not see him clearly as a personality. . . . As his story drew to

a close it became more and more necessary for me to interrogate him about himself. What was *he* doing at that time? What office did *he* hold then? What was *his* attitude in this or that situation?" (Snow, p. 157.) For examples of how various scholars have been forced, because of the lack of source material, to slight this period in Mao's life, see Rice, pp. 62–64; Terrill, pp. 109–10; and Schram, *Mao Tse-tung*, pp. 141–43.

A chronology of events in Jiangxi for 1927–35, published in China in 1986, adds some details to this period in the lives of Communist leaders like Mao. In mid-December 1929, Mao was in Shanghang County, Fujian Province, for the famous Gutian meeting. The chronology then puts Mao in the following counties in central and southern Jiangxi in early 1930: Ningdu (late January), Ji'an (6 February), Xingguo (mid-March), Dayu (27 March), Xinfeng (11 April), and Huichang (17 April). Although this chronology fills in some missing details, it is worth noting that the day of neither Mao's arrival nor his departure from Xunwu is given. Apart from stating that Mao was in Xunwu in May 1930, when he wrote the *Report from Xunwu*, and that he presided over a gathering in Xunwu City on 4 June 1930 celebrating the Communist victory, this chronology gives little specific information on Mao's activities after 17 April and before 25 June. See Wen, pp. 104–13. I thank Stephen Averill for bringing this chronology to my attention.

11. This congress, originally scheduled to begin 1 May 1930, was finally convened on 31 May. See Harrison, p. 173.

12. Zhang and Zhang, pp. 106–84. This important book, published in August 1987, was written by Zhang Weiping and his collaborator, Zhang Liejun. In a postscript written after Zhang Weiping's death, Zhang Liejun noted that various units of the CCP's Central Committee had provided assistance.

13. Data on Gu Bo's early years, the obscure history of the 25 March 1928 uprising in Xunwu County, and the events leading up to the arrival of the Red Army in May 1930 are recounted in the 1980 memoir of Gu Bo's widow, Zeng Biyi (Zeng, pp. 88–98). This memoir was used by Xia Daohan in his recent biographical sketch of Gu Bo. Xia also relied on two works available in Jiangxi: *Xunwu xian renmin geming douzheng shi* (A history of the people's revolutionary struggle in Xunwu County) and *Gu Bo lieshi dang'an* (Documents relating to the martyr Gu Bo). Zeng Biyi subordinated her own revolutionary story to that of Gu Bo. She was part of a group of CCP members, including Qu Qiubai, that left the Ruijin area in January 1935 in hopes of reaching the coast. Few in this group survived very long. Zeng Biyi

was pregnant at the time and would deliver a baby boy while avoiding KMT patrols in Fujian. (Salisbury, pp. 208, 214; Salisbury's informants, interviewed in 1984 and 1985, appear not to have told him about Zeng Biyi's memoir.) For a socioeconomic analysis of Xunwu in the late nineteenth and early twentieth centuries based in part on the *Report from Xunwu*, see Averill, "Local Elites."

14. Xia, p. 276. The history of these schools is unclear. The first of the schools established by men who were members of the Cooperative Society faction may have been founded in 1926. According to Lillie Bousfield, an anti-Christian school was established in that year. See Lillie Bousfield, Circular, 19 Apr. 1927, ABFMS Records, Reel FM232. On 11 March 1927, writing from Shantou, Cyril Bousfield mentioned a letter from Xunwu that claimed the anti-Christian school had "become so unpopular that they had to change their name. . . . The new Principal of the school, for they had to get another, is a man very favorably disposed toward Christianity." Cyril E. Bousfield, Circular, 11 Mar. 1927, ABFMS Records, Reel FM232. These schools may have been the institutional predecessors of the Sun Yatsen schools.

15. Zeng, p. 91.

16. Ibid., p. 90.

17. Local revolutionaries were reportedly acting in accordance with the decisions made on 7 August 1927 at an emergency conference held in Hankou. See Zeng, p. 91. The conference called for systematic peasant insurrections in which political power would be transferred to and organized in forms of government called "soviets." See Brandt et al., pp. 97–123.

18. *North China Herald* 166 (Jan.–Mar. 1928): 515. Nearby in Guangdong, Peng Pai established a soviet in Haifeng County that lasted from November 1927 through February 1928. See Marks, pp. 249–77.

19. For reports on "Communist bandits," see *North China Herald* 167 (Apr.–June 1928): 54, 96, 276, 277.

20. L. S. Bousfield, p. 109. This book is a compilation of vignettes of events in the 1910's and 1920's. Dr. and Mrs. Bousfield were missionaries sent by the South China Mission of the American Baptist Foreign Mission Society. Lillie Bousfield, Dr. Bousfield's wife, was not in Xunwu at the time of the uprising. Her account of these events is based on Dr. Bousfield's correspondence (ABFMS Records, Reel FM232), but she or her editors occasionally repunctuated or reworded the texts of Dr. Bousfield's letters; in the process some errors of fact were introduced. In cases of discrepancies between Mrs. Bousfield's book and Dr. Bousfield's letters and reports, the latter are con-

sidered authoritative. Professor Stephen Averill kindly brought Lillie Bousfield's book to my attention.

21. According to Xia (p. 277), the uprising had been scheduled to take place at a later date, but the capture of local CCP member Kuang Shifen in Liuche on the evening of 23 March presented the possibility that the plans for the uprising might be revealed.

22. In a 29 March report, Bousfield wrote: "They had a central committee, with a boy named Koo at the head of it." In a letter written on 3 April, Bousfield stated: "I think I told you of Koo Pih, he is the very worst of them all. His father has offered a large sum of money for his capture" (this statement is contained in a circular letter of 13 April 1928, with quotes from Dr. Bousfield's letters, sent by Mrs. Lillie Bousfield; ABFMS Records, Reel FM232). Bousfield, who was inconsistent in his romanization of Chinese names, must be referring to Gu Bo in both cases. We know that Gu and his associates divided the county into six regions, with Gu Bo responsible for Xunwu City and the nearby countryside. Gu was also responsible for leading the students of the Sun Yatsen Middle School in the attack on Xunwu City (Xia, p. 277).

23. Those executed included the general commander of the uprising, Liu Weilu, and an assistant commander, Liu Weie. The *Report from Xunwu* (Chapter 4) mentions that these sons of small landlords had some college training. Liu Weilu had studied at Sun Yatsen University in Canton and Liu Weie at Beijing University. This information is corroborated in Bousfield's report of 1 April (L. S. Bousfield, p. 118), which mentions that the "criminals" included "students . . . of schools as high up as Peking University."

24. See Xia, p. 279. Kuang Caicheng, who had studied for more than a year at Beijing Normal College, would not survive to see the CCP's triumph in Xunwu. According to the *Report from Xunwu* (Chapter 4), he was tortured to death by Xie Jiayou. Xie, a middle landlord receiving rents of 300 dan, was a regimental commander under Xie Jie in the Fourteenth Army and the head captain of the Xunwu militia. Xie Jiayou was also responsible for wiping out the First Battalion of the Fiftieth Regiment of the Red Army.

25. Xia, p. 281; and Wen, p. 101. The CCP used these various committees to establish administrative and political control in local areas. Party county committees administered a county through subordinate special district committees and party branches and cells. Actual administrative affairs were handled by "people's committees" or "soviets" controlled by the party. Mao attempted to ensure the party's control of the army by establishing military committees at various lev-

els in the military hierarchy. The military committees were short-lived, evident only in 1928–30. Ideally a company of 150 men selected a military committee of five to nine men. See Harrison, p. 144.

26. See Xia, p. 282; and Zeng, pp. 95–97. This summary of events in Xunwu from 1928 to 1930 is based in part on the memoir by Gu Bo's widow, Zeng Biyi, published in 1980. Her account may exaggerate the degree to which events in Xunwu were orchestrated by national and regional leaders of the CCP. A key issue in the study of the Jiangxi period is the relationship between national leaders like Mao Zedong, Zhu De, or Li Lisan and local activists like Gu Bo. Scholarly emphasis on the struggle between Mao and Li for control of the rural soviets in Jiangxi, Hunan, and Fujian overlooks the relationship between local insurrections and the broader revolutionary movement. Mao's stay in Xunwu, with the knowledge he gained and the ties he established, contributed to his ability to defy the instructions of Party Central. Mao was interested in *what worked*; hence, his collaboration with men like Gu Bo. The history of Jiangxi's local revolutions is just beginning to be written, because documents like the *Report from Xunwu*, which show so clearly the important and sometimes autonomous contributions of local revolutions, are finally emerging. For an excellent discussion of the local contexts of the so-called Jiangxi Soviet, see Averill, "Party." For two recent efforts at understanding similar themes in nearby eastern Guangdong, see Galbiati; and Marks.

27. Wen, pp. 109–11.

28. Xia, p. 283. The Chinese name of the hospital was Timin yiyuan (lit. "peaceful people's hospital").

29. Ibid. Names had been collected since the 25 March 1928 uprising. Dr. Cyril E. Bousfield wrote in a letter of 9 April 1928 to James Franklin: "On Saturday I learned that a book had been found prepared by those students [who had led the uprising] containing the names of those whom they wanted to murder and would have murdered if they had had the chance. As it was they got a few of them. My name was on the list, and Pastor Liao's, and the names of practically all of the very best people in the place." In this typed letter, in the phrase "containing the names," the word "the" was struck out and replaced with a handwritten "600." See ABFMS Records, Reel FM232. The compilation of name lists, though not necessarily for the same purpose, had a long history in China. An example, described in the classic *The Story of the Stone* (also known as *The Dream of the Red Chamber*), is the "Mandarin's Life-Preserver" in which "every provincial official carries a private handlist with the names of all the richest, most influential people in his area" (see Cao Xueqin, *The Story of the*

Stone, trans. David Hawkes, New York, Penguin Books, 1973, 1: 111). My thanks to Melissa Thompson for bringing this reference to my attention.

30. For a discussion of the events in June 1916, see note 15 to Chapter 3. These events affected commerce and education in Xunwu City for months. Dr. Cyril E. Bousfield, writing in January 1917, said: "The uprising of last June wrought as bad havoc with the schools of Changning [Xunwu] as it did with the trade. Until recently every school in the City was closed, and now not more than one sixth of the normal number are in school. . . . For a while it seemed as tho every merchant in the City would be ruined after the outbreak and we feared our Chinese contributions for this year would be way below what they have averaged." See the Annual Report for 1916, ABFMS Records, Reel FM180. One of the main targets of Mao's wrath in the *Report from Xunwu* was Pan Mingzheng. That the struggle for supremacy in Xunwu went back at least a decade is clear, for we can cite evidence of the link between the faction in Xunwu led by the Pan family and Yuan Shikai, which may have contributed to Guo's loss in 1916. According to Lillie Bousfield, a "Pan Kwat-Chin," the "richest man in the whole section of southern Kiang-Si [Jiangxi]," who lived in Xiangshan bao in Jiansan District, received a complimentary four-character inscription from Yuan Shikai in 1916. See her second circular of 3 March 1917 in ABFMS Records, Reel FM180.

31. Schram, *Mao Tse-tung*, pp. 38–40.

32. Xia, p. 276.

33. For Gu Youyao's degree, see *Changning xianzhi* (1901 ed.), 11: 9a. Gu Youhui, possibly a relation of Gu Bo and his grandfather Gu Youyao, was also an editor of the 1899, 1901, and 1907 editions of the Xunwu gazetteer. See the preface to the 1901 edition of *Changning xianzhi*. Local gazetteers for Xunwu County, known as Changning County until 1914, were published in 1579, 1673, 1749, 1855, 1876, 1881, 1899, 1901, and 1907. See *Zhongguo difang zhi lianhe mulu* (Union list of local gazetteers in China) (Beijing: Zhonghua shuju, 1985), p. 512.

34. L. S. Bousfield, pp. 67–68.

35. Zeng, pp. 88–89; Xia, p. 274.

36. Xia, p. 274.

37. See Snow, pp. 129–30; and Li, pp. 84–85. Mao's traveling companion, Xiao Yu, described this journey in his memoirs; see Siao-yu, pp. 76–160.

38. Li, p. 90.

39. Terrill, p. 47; Li, p. 159.

40. See Li, pp. 200, 205, 211. A chronological listing of Mao's writings in the final volume of Takeuchi Minoru's supplementary collection of Mao's writings gives no indication that Mao compiled a formal report on these investigations; see pp. 37–43.

41. Terrill, p. 74; Li, p. 281; Schram, *Mao Tse-tung*, p. 78.

42. Brandt et al., pp. 77–89; Schram, *Mao Tse-tung*, pp. 94–95; Schram, *Political Thought*, pp. 250–59; Mao Zedong, *Selected Works*, 1: 23–59. For the polemical context of this report, see McDonald, pp. 290–96; and Li, pp. 298–310.

43. *Mao Zedong nongcun diaocha wenji*, pp. 9–11. The essay "The Work of Investigation" ("Diaocha gongzuo") is better known under the title "Oppose Bookism" ("Fandui benben zhuyi"). According to a recently published book on Mao's role in the early history of the CCP, Mao first used the term "bookism" (*benben zhuyi*) in a letter of June 1929. In recalling the development of this idea, Mao said: "I first wrote a short essay entitled "Oppose Bookism" when I was in Xunwu County in Jiangxi Province." Thinking this essay too short to be of use, Mao expanded it and entitled the longer version "The Work of Investigation." This, too, appears to have been written in Xunwu in May 1930. See Zhang and Zhang, pp. 168–69. Unfortunately, this passage is not entirely clear. Zhang Weiping says that in the spring of 1930 Mao wrote "Oppose Bookism" and that in May 1930 he wrote the longer "Work of Investigation." I have found no evidence suggesting that Mao's 1930 visit to Xunwu took place before May. Thus, it appears that both essays were written in Xunwu. The long version of this essay was lost, not to be rediscovered until January 1961. Printed in 1961 for distribution within the party only, the essay was finally published in 1964 under the title "Oppose Bookism." See *Selected Readings from the Works of Mao Tsetung* (Beijing: Foreign Languages Press,, 1971), pp. 40–50; *Mao Zedong nongcun diaocha wenji*, p. 355n1; and Zhonggong, Zhongyang, Wenxian Yanjiushi, pp. 562–63. Here I distinguish between the original version ("Oppose Bookism") and the reworked, longer version ("The Work of Investigation"). For a discussion and translation of the longer essay, see Rue, pp. 209–11 and 305–12. For a recent discussion of Mao's "revolutionary fact-finding," see Womack, pp. 114–23.

44. Young.

45. See Myers, pp. 256–69. See also the bibliographic essay in *Cambridge History of China*, 13: 887–89.

46. *Mao Zedong nongcun diaocha wenji*, pp. 3–4.

47. Ibid., pp. 5–6.

48. Ibid., p. 6.

49. Chen. One of the first uses Mao would make of his investigations was to influence policy debates at the Second National Soviet Congress. On 27 January 1934 Mao distributed copies of his investigations of two subcounty districts: Changgang in Xingguo County in Jiangxi and Caixi in Shanghang County in Fujian. See Wen, p. 184; and Waller, pp. 90–93. The importance of the "work of investigation" can also be seen in documents from the rectification campaign begun in February 1942. This campaign, which sought to ensure a semblance of ideological orthodoxy among the thousands of new members of the CCP who had come to Shaanxi with the patriotic determination to resist the Japanese invasion, emphasized the importance for cadres of communicating with peasants and encouraging mass participation. For a discussion and three key documents of this campaign, see Brandt et al., pp. 372–419. The publication in 1941 of Mao's Jiangxi investigations in *Rural Investigations* provided cadres with concrete examples of how the work of investigation should proceed. (The *Report from Xunwu* was to have been included in this collection.) The data from these investigations were injected into policy debates. Mao's *Economic and Financial Problems*, a report written for a high-level meeting held from October 1942 to January 1943, mentions many investigations and contains repeated exhortations to careful research. See Watson, pp. 1, 29, 74–75, 77–85, 144.

50. Xia, pp. 284–85.

51. Wen, p. 150.

52. Ibid., p. 155.

53. Ibid., p. 157.

54. Zhang and Zhang, p. 187; Rue, pp. 257–64.

55. Wen, p. 168.

56. Xia, pp. 287–88. Gu's transfer came in the context of increasing attacks on the Luo Ming line. Deng Xiaoping was explicitly criticized for abandoning his post in Huichang in the face of Chiang Kai-shek's fourth suppression campaign. See Isaacs, p. 348.

57. Wen, p. 189.

58. Ibid., pp. 194–97.

59. See Zeng, pp. 104–5; and Xia, pp. 290–91. The March 1935 date of Gu Bo's death is given in Salisbury, p. 378n25.

60. Even this sentence, which Jerome Ch'en (*Mao Papers*, pp. xviii–xix) feels reflects Mao's use of Lu Xun's device of beginning an essay with a casual remark, was itself omitted from all editions of Mao's selected works published after 1949). The editors of *Mao Zedong nongcun diaocha wenji* (p. 356n8) also note that the 1953 edition of *Mao Zedong's Selected Works* (*Mao Zedong xuanji*) does not contain this sen-

tence. The 1941 preface to *Rural Investigations,* as reprinted in *Mao Zedong nongcun diaocha wenji,* follows the precedent established in the *Selected Works.*

61. Gong, "Ruogan wenti," p. 5. The *Report from Xunwu* was identified as a "lost" text written in 1933 in Jerome Ch'en's exhaustive 1970 bibliography of Mao's works (*Mao Papers,* p. 169), and the text was not included in the definitive edition of Mao's writings, and a later supplement, compiled by Takeuchi Minoru.

62. Schram, *Ideology,* pp. 3–4. According to Ross Terrill (p. 28), the phrase "Seek Truth from Facts" was displayed prominently at the Hunan First Normal School, which Mao attended. For Mao's own discussion of "seeking truth from facts," see his important May 1941 essay "Reform Our Study" in *Selected Works,* 3: 22–23. This passage was also included in the so-called Little Red Book published at the beginning of the Cultural Revolution. See *Quotations from Chairman Mao Tsetung,* 2d ed. (Beijing: Foreign Languages Press, 1967), pp. 231–32.

63. Harding, p. 60.

64. Mao, *Selected Works,* 3: 12.

65. Harding, pp. 64–65.

66. Zhonggong, Zhongyang, Wenxian Yanjiushi, pp. 556–63. "The Work of Investigation" discussed in this Introduction is the work called "Oppose Bookism" in the annotated "Resolution."

67. *Mao Zedong nongcun diaocha wenji,* p. 355n1.

68. *Guangming ribao,* 12 Feb. 1983, p. 3.

69. The useful indexes published bimonthly by the People's University in Beijing cite about a dozen journal or newspaper articles that deal specifically with *Mao Zedong nongcun diaocha wenji.* See Zhongguo Renmin Daxue.

70. For a discussion of the transformation of the lead sentence of "The Work of Investigation" into the pithy phrase of the April 1931 directive, see Zhang and Zhang, pp. 169–70. This directive was previously published in Japan. See Takeuchi (1970–72), 2: 255–57.

71. Qian, p. 7.

72. The new orthodoxy in this chapter of CCP history can be seen in several recently published books. See Wen; Zhang and Zhang; Salisbury; and Franz.

73. Harding, pp. 101–8.

74. *Guangming ribao,* 12 Feb. 1983, p. 3.

75. Xia, pp. 283–84.

76. *Guangming ribao,* 12 Feb. 1983, p. 3.

77. Ibid.

78. Ibid.

79. The Xingguo report was the focus of Womack's research and is summarized in his 1977 dissertation. In his 1982 revision of this work, Womack said that the Xingguo report was "probably the most important of Mao's untranslated works from the pre-1935 period" (p. 222n59). Womack wrote this unaware of the existence of the *Report from Xunwu*, for otherwise he surely would have revised his assessment of the Xingguo report. The *Report from Xingguo* is only half as long as the *Report from Xunwu* and deals with one small subunit of the county as described to Mao in discussions with eight peasants sent to join the Red Army. See Hsiao, *Land Revolution*, p. 29. Although the *Report from Xingguo* contains biographical data on the eight peasants, analysis of social structure, an assessment of land redistribution, taxation, administration, and military affairs, its coverage is not as broad as that of the *Report from Xunwu*. Indeed, in Mao's preface, written in January 1931, to the *Report from Xingguo*, he criticized his inattention to the status of women and children, commerce, agricultural production after the land revolution, and cultural affairs. See *Mao Zedong nongcun diaocha wenji*, pp. 182–83. Most of these categories were covered in the *Report from Xunwu*.

80. For the 1930 Xingguo report and the 1933 reports, see *Mao Zedong nongcun diaocha wenji*, pp. 182–251, 286–332, 333–54. Mao's rural investigations in Jiangxi have been studied by several scholars. Philip C. C. Huang, Lynda Schaefer Bell, and Kathy Lemons Walker each wrote essays in a volume published in 1978 under the title *Chinese Communists and Rural Society, 1927–1934* (see Huang et al.). Huang focused on the Xingguo report in his contribution, "Intellectuals, Lumpenproletarians, Workers and Peasants in the Communist Movement: The Case of Xingguo County, 1927–1934."

81. Xia, p. 283.

PREFACE

1. In early 1929, Chiang Kai-shek sent Nationalist troops based in Hunan and Jiangxi to attack the revolutionary base in Jinggangshan during the third suppression campaign. At that time, the Jiangxi troops were the First Army under the command of Chiang Kai-shek; the Hunan troops were the Fourth Army under Li Zongren and Bai Chongxi of the Guangxi clique.

2. The Pitou Conference, also called the 7 February Conference, refers to the joint conference that was held in Pitou, Ji'an County, Jiangxi Province, in the first ten-day period of February. The participants were the Front Committee of the Fourth Red Army, delegates

from the Fifth and Sixth Red armies, and delegates from the West Jiangxi Special Committee. Mao Zedong, delegate of the Front Committee of the Fourth Red Army, chaired this conference. The most important organizing responsibility of the southwestern Jiangxi party organization was to expand soviet areas, accomplish a far-reaching land revolution, and expand the armed force of the workers and peasants. In regard to the land issue, the inappropriate proposal of redistributing the land according to productivity was refuted. The method of redistributing the land on a per capita basis was confirmed. [See also Hsiao, *Land Revolution*, p. 148.—Trans.]

3. The Tingzhou Conference, also called the Nanyang Conference, refers to the joint conference of the front committee of the Fourth Red Army and the special committee of the western Fujian area. It was summoned and chaired by Mao Zedong in June 1930. It began in Nanyang, Changting County, Fujian (Nanyang is now in Shanghang County) and was later moved to Tingzhou. The conference discussed political, military, and economic issues. In regard to the issue of land redistribution, the conference not only confirmed the principle of "draw on the plentiful to make up for the scarce" but also added the principle of "draw on the fat to make up for the lean" as well. [See Chapter 5 for an explanation of these terms; for a discussion of various CCP documents and of the rich-peasant question during the period, see Hsiao, *Land Revolution*, pp. 3–45, 148.—Trans.]

4. Mao's interest in business affairs was not new. In March 1921 he edited a report on the Cultural Book Society, which ran a network of bookstores in Hunan and elsewhere, beginning in 1920–21, which stated: "Those of us who manage the business have an obligation to report on the sale of our publications. . . . Chinese businesses are always secretive. Except for the inner circle, no one can get any information. This secrecy is really wrong." See Li, p. 156.—Trans.

5. Throughout Mao gives ages in terms of *sui*, the Chinese system that reckons age in terms of the number of calendar years in which a person has lived.—Trans.

6. "County soviet" [*xiansu*] is an abbreviation for "county soviet government" [*xian suweiai zhengfu*]. During the second civil revolutionary war, all democratic governments for the workers and peasants in the revolutionary bases were called soviet governments. In this book the terms *qusu*, *xiangsu*, and *shisu* are abbreviations for the district, township, and city soviet governments, respectively.

7. Chen Jiongming was a warlord in Guangdong Province. He also was a former governor of Guangdong Province and the general commander of the Guangdong troops.

8. Mao's inattention to the question of loafers (*youmin, liumang*) presents some problems for the translator, not to mention the cadre attempting land redistribution. *Youmin* and *liumang*, used synonymously by Mao, are terms long in use, often translated as "vagrant" or "vagabond," but neither seems appropriate in the *Report from Xunwu*. Mao defines *youmin*, in a rural context, as people without an occupation and states that they constitute 1 percent of the population. In Xunwu City, however, 10 percent of the population was defined as *youmin*. Mao lists the activities of *liumang* as gambling, extortion, and serving as the "running dogs" of the ruling class.

A document issued on Mao's authority in October 1933, which defined these terms, shows their ambiguity: "Workers, peasants, and other people who shortly before the uprising lost their occupations and land as a result of the oppression and exploitation by the landlord and capitalist class, and who have resorted to improper methods as their principal means of livelihood for three consecutive years, are called idler-proletarians (customarily they are called vagabonds)." Among the improper means of earning a livelihood were theft, robbery, swindling, begging, gambling, and prostitution. But the terms were applied loosely and improperly: sometimes they were used to characterize persons who went to brothels, gambled, or smoked opium (see Hsiao, *Land Revolution*, p. 274). Mao's negative definition of *liumang* in the *Report from Xunwu* as someone who did not farm, produce handicrafts, or sell goods is perhaps more useful.

Although these may have been "marginal" people, Mao noted their relationship to the ruling class and, in an earlier work, thought about their political utility. In 1926 Mao identified landless peasants and unemployed artisans, the lumpenproletariat, as brave, but unruly, fighters who could be a revolutionary force (see Mao, *Selected Works*, 1: 19). But Mao also saw the problematic nature of these elements, noting in 1933 that loafers could oppose the revolution (see Hsiao, *Land Revolution*, pp. 274–75). It is the dual nature of the class of loafers that perhaps explains the more recent connotation of *liumang*, more accurately translated as "hoodlum," "rogue," or "gangster." For a discussion of this class in nearby Xingguo County in 1927–34, see Philip C. C. Huang's essay in Huang et al., pp. 5–28.—Trans.

CHAPTER 1

1. According to a map in the 1881 edition of the gazetteer for Xunwu County, the area beyond Xunwu City was divided into 12 *bao* (lit. fortress) and four wards (*xiang*). Except for Renfeng (Huangxiang) District and Shuangqiao District, the subcounty districts in Re-

publican Xunwu County took their names from a consolidation of the Qing jurisdictions: Nanqiao bao and Bafu bao became Nanba District; Xiangshan bao, Yaogu bao, and Zixi bao became Jiansan (lit. unites three) District; Xunwu bao, Dadun bao, and Guiling bao became Chengjiang District (taking the name of the major market); and San-biao bao and Shuiyuan bao became Sanshui District. See *Changning xianzhi*, 1: 2b–3a. Until January 1914, Xunwu County was known as Changning County.—Trans.

2. Renfeng District was renamed Huangxiang District after the Xunwu County soviet government was established in May 1930.

CHAPTER 2

1. The 30-day lunar month is divided into three 10-day periods. In addition to postal deliveries, periodic markets were also scheduled in terms of the lunar calendar. For example, a market town might host a regularly scheduled market on the first, fourth, and seventh days of the ten-day cycle.—Trans.

2. The 25 March uprising was the county-wide uprising that was organized by the Xunwu Communist party, which led the peasants and young students on 25 March 1928.

3. According to Dr. Cyril E. Bousfield, the postmaster had been ordered, during the uprising, not to dispatch any mail. For refusing to obey, he was given a death sentence. Bousfield continues: "Some of his friends interceded and saved his life by paying $500." See L. S. Bousfield, pp. 119–20.—Trans.

4. Dr. Cyril E. Bousfield reported that a telegraph operator and his assistant were arrested and executed by the Communists leading the insurrection. The telegraph operator, who was shot at point-blank range, had sent a telegram to officials in Ganzhou asking for help. Bousfield thought this telegram, transmitted on 24 March, was in-strumental in prompting government authorities to dispatch troops to Xunwu. The arrival of these troops on 29 March effectively ended the uprising. See L. S. Bousfield, pp. 111–12, 116–17.—Trans.

CHAPTER 3

1. *Chayou* and *muyou* refer to the oil pressed from the seeds of the tea-oil plant. They are used mainly as a foodstuff. ["Tea-oil" (*chayou*) refers to oil pressed from the camellia plant; see S. Wright, pp. 69–71.—Trans.]

2. *Dan* in this book means both the measure of capacity and the measure of weight. The capacity of these units varied from place to place. The typesetting and printing of this edition were based com-

pletely on the original text. [This note was added to an essay preceding the *Report from Xunwu* in *Mao Zedong nongcun diaocha wenji*. See also Appendix B.—Trans.]

3. The exchange rate among the three currencies mentioned in this book—*dayang* (*guangyang, zayang*), *xiaoyang* (*haoyang, maoyang*), *tongyuan*—varied according to time and place. The typesetting and printing of this edition were based completely on the original text. [This note was added to an essay preceding the *Report from Xunwu* in *Mao Zedong nongcun diaocha wenji*. See also Appendix A.—Trans.]

4. The text reads *guyu*, one of the 24 solar periods of the Chinese solar year. This corresponds approximately to the period from 20 April to 4 May.—Trans.

5. *Dongjiang* refers to the catchment of the East River, which is fed in part by the Xunwu River. The East River passes through Long-chuan and Huizhou in eastern Guangdong before entering the Pearl River estuary near Canton.—Trans.

6. Mao's research coup in Xunwu contrasts with his experience a dozen years later in Shaanxi. In his *Economic and Financial Problems*, written in 1942, Mao says: "We have not discussed commerce in the private sector since we still lack the necessary information. For the moment we have to ignore it." See Watson, p. 227.—Trans.

7. Mao is probably referring to his Fourth Army comrade Liu An-gong, who, among others, was the target of a June 1929 letter in which Mao coined the phrase "bookism" (*benben zhuyi*)" See Zhang and Zhang, p. 168. See also Snow, p. 155.—Trans.

8. The New Policies (*xinzheng*) were promulgated beginning in 1901. Among the reforms under this rubric were reorganizations of government administration and the military; educational reforms, including the abolition of the examination system in 1905; and attempts to establish electoral bodies at the local, provincial, and national levels. See M. C. Wright, pp. 24–30.—Trans.

9. For a discussion of the practice of minor marriages referred to in the text, see Wolf and Huang, pp. 1–15; see p. 7 for a report on this custom as practiced in southern Jiangxi at the turn of the century.—Trans.

10. Liquid distilled from honeysuckle flowers or lotus leaves.—Trans.

11. Leather was among the types of material, which also included bamboo, porcelain, and wood, used for making pillows. According to Hommel (p. 313), leather pillows are "lacquered and stuffed with chaff or bamboo shavings. They are about two feet long, with a square cross section."—Trans.

12. The text has "more than a string of capital," which is glossed parenthetically as "over a thousand yuan of capital."—Trans.

13. *Mingqian* is copper cash [*tongqian*].

14. *Tongpian, tongban,* and *tongkezi* are all copper coins [*tongyuan*].

15. This episode is almost certainly the one witnessed by Mrs. Lillie Bousfield—no other event in the Bousfield correspondence of 1916 matches the scale of the event described by Mao. From 12 June until the morning of 20 June, Xunwu City was under the control of a "Rebel Committee" that had declared independence, marked by a bomb burst, at 8:30 in the evening of 12 June. According to Mrs. Bousfield, men had streamed into the city from all directions earlier in the day. After the bombs went off, mobs from within and without the city began demolishing the county yamen and filled the newly emptied prisons with the magistrate and other yamen personnel. On 14 June, according to Mrs. Bousfield, a "general panic prevailed, and the whole place was filled with armed mobs, with revolvers, guns, and long knives and spears. One of our neighbors lay in a pool of blood by the South Gate of the city, and no one's life was safe." That same day, upon hearing news that soldiers were arriving from the north, the mob killed fourteen people, including the magistrate's brother, a yamen secretary, and the chief of police. On 20 June, "soldiers from the north" arrived, ending the episode. See American Baptist Foreign Mission Society (ABFMS) Records, Reel FM180, Lillie S. Bousfield, 28 June 1916, circular letter. Dr. Cyril Bousfield, who had not been in Xunwu at the time (he returned on 25 June), wrote that the "cause of the trouble was a few young men who have had a smattering of western education at the Capital and else where, and they persuaded a few with money to help them." See ABFMS Records, Reel FM180, Dr. Cyril E. Bousfield to Dr. James Franklin, 28 June 1916. Given Mao's description, probably based on information provided by Guo Youmei, the owner, of the fate of Guo Yihe Shop in 1916, it is possible the shop was implicated in the uprising; this would explain the reprisals suffered.

It is unclear what "Guangfu faction" refers to. There had been units of a Guangfu Army (*jun*), associated with Zhang Binglin's revolutionary faction, active in Shantou during the 1911 Revolution. The episode mentioned in the text and reported by Mrs. Bousfield was part of a larger political struggle in April–June 1916 in which military and civilian leaders in southern China were leading the battle against Yuan Shikai, in an attempt to force him to give up the presidency. Many provinces and counties declared their independence of Beijing. Yuan's death on 6 June 1916 ended this campaign in much of China, but not in Guangdong or in Xunwu. The troops "from the north" were associated with the Beiyang military clique, then in control of Jiangxi. The "Beiyang Army" or "Beiyang clique" was associated with the northern treaty port of Tianjin, which, in imperial times, was under the jurisdiction of the "Northern Ocean," or Beiyang, commissioner of trade. Under the control of Yuan Shikai from 1895 until his death, the Beiyang Army was then riven into cliques identified with warlords in three provinces—Zhili (Hebei), Anhui, and Fengtian (Liaoning).—Trans.

16. A more specific translation might be "articled clerk," to borrow a coinage from early-nineteenth-century England. This type of clerk agreed to certain articles of apprenticeship, much as the "gentleman" in a Xunwu shop might have. This Chinese term for "gentleman" can also be used for "teacher," "sir," or "mister." In the past it could be appended to various occupations, like that of bookkeeper (*zhangfang xiansheng*) or fortune-teller (*suanming xiansheng*). As the text makes clear, in Xunwu a "gentleman" was considered capable enough to take over the business eventually.—Trans.

17. A parenthetical comment in the text glosses *da futou* and *da leigong* as meaning, literally, "to eat fried doughcakes" (*chi youbing*), which the editors of *Mao Zedong nongcun diaocha wenji* explain as behavior in which one secretly gains petty advantages.—Trans.

18. For a discussion of brokering in this period, see Mann, pp. 174-78.—Trans.

19. The contest between the Communists and their enemies was bound up in part in the KMT's varying approaches to law and order in Jiangxi. The KMT wavered between advocating Western-style police forces and resigning itself to relying on more traditional local militias. The former approach was typified by the establishment of county-level public security bureaus (*gongan ju*), called for in regulations issued in September 1928. In some cases these bureaus attempted to co-opt local militias, renaming them *jingcha dui* (police). For example, existing pacification and defense militia (*jingwei tuan*) were incorporated into police forces (*jingcha dui*). The checkered record of these efforts, which caused a proliferation of various local militias organized to combat the Communist insurgency, led the Nanjing government to sanction local militias. To that end, the Nationalist government promulgated the County Militia Law, which called for the incorporation of local militia into official militias known as *baowei tuan*, which were to be under the management of the county magistrate and provincial authorities. This reorganization was to have been completed by August 1930. See Wei, pp. 83-96.—Trans.

20. Rock sugar [*bingtang*] is a crystallized sugar formed into lumps.—Trans.

21. This kind of sugar is white and looks like rice ground into small grains.—Trans.

22. For a description of sugar production, see Couling, pp. 529–30.—Trans.

23. The text has *Min*, the classical way of writing Fujian.—Trans.

24. Melon seeds, almonds, and walnuts are among the types of seeds and nuts used to make this cake.—Trans.

25. According to the 1881 gazetteer for Xunwu County, the Dragon Boat festival was held on the sixth day of the sixth lunar month, instead of the usual fifth day of the fifth month. *Changning xianzhi*," Fengsu," 1b.—Trans.

26. The character *xiang* (stuffed) is written with the food radical in the text; a wine radical should have been used.—Trans.

27. Cloud ears are a type of white fungus that grows on trees.—Trans.

28. *Gongtang* land refers to land owned by all types of ancestral halls, religious associations, and village associations. These lands were controlled mostly by the landlords and rich peasants. [This note was added to the 1941 preface to *Nongcun diaocha*, reprinted in *Mao Zedong nongcun diaocha wenji*; see pp. 26, 357n17.—Trans.]

29. *Nugu* means "male servant" in Hakka.

30. The Catholic mission in Xunwu was under the direction of the Lazarist Order. In the 1929 edition of J.-M. Planchet's *Les Missions de Chine*, p. 232, the Catholic father in the Xunwu mission was identified as "Louis Tschèn." Since the Chinese character for the surname of Planchet's Louis Tschèn and Mao's Father Chen is the same, both names probably refer to the same person.—Trans.

31. Lai Shihuang was the division commander of the First Division of the Guangdong Seventh Army, the division commander of the Fourth Division of the Jiangxi troops, and the commander of the Fourteenth Nationalist Army.

32. Center-cut (*poxiong*, lit. split-the-chest) refers to shirts and jackets that buttoned down the middle rather than being fastened on the side as traditional Chinese jackets were.—Trans.

33. This term of opprobrium was used by CCP opponents in the Jiangxi countryside. Western observers noted in April 1928 that Communists were allying with so-called local bandits (*tufei*). In fact, a new compound—*gongfei*—was coined to refer to the alliance of Communists (*gongchan*) and local bandits (*tufei*). See *North China Herald* 167 (Apr.–June 1928): 54. This double meaning could often

be obscured, with *gongfei* meaning simply Communist bandits. —Trans.

34. *Biane*, a horizontal inscribed board.—Trans.

35. "Pastor Bao" refers to Dr. Cyril E. Bousfield.—Trans.

36. The grinding disks for hand-operated rice-hulling mills could be made with stone, clay, or wood. The rice huller (*longpan*) mentioned in the text was made of wood. For a description, with three photographs, of this type of huller, see Hommel, pp. 91–95. Mao's text glosses *longpan* as *tuizi* (lit. pusher). This refers to a rice huller whose grinding wheel is turned by a push-pull type of motion. A turning pole, attached to the outer edge of the top grinding disk, turns the wheel by being pushed and then pulled.—Trans.

37. For photographs and descriptions of rice buckets, flails, a chopping board, a wooden bowl cover, and water dippers, see Hommel, pp. 49, 73, 74, 136, 152, 157.—Trans.

38. *Doujin* is glossed as "times of emergencies."—Trans.

39. The Pacification and Defense Corps, also called the Pacification and Defense Militia, was a type of local counterrevolutionary armed force.

40. For another description of bean curd production, see Hommel, pp. 105–9.—Trans.

41. The text reads *xianluo you*; the first two characters are a classical reference to Thailand, and the last character refers to a grapefruit-type citrus known as pomelo or shaddock.—Trans.

42. *Huaqi*, or checkered flag, refers to the U.S. flag, hence, "American." Other colloquialisms include "sun flag" for Japan and "rice flag" for Great Britain. The "rice flag" designation derived from the similarity of the design of the Union Jack to the character for "rice" (*mi*). See Li, p. 79.—Trans.

43. In this book, *kanyu* is the same as *dili xiansheng* and *kan didi* [geomancers]. This refers to those who, through the use of superstitious practices, helped people select the location of a house or tomb. Usually they were called *fengshui xiansheng* or *yinyang xiansheng*.

44. *Dan* and *qing* are two pigments commonly used in Chinese painting. *Danqing* usually means painting, but refers to painters here.

45. Mao uses the compound *guotou*. *Guo*, the Mandarin pronunciation for the character for cooking bowl, is pronounced *wok* in Cantonese. This refers to the round-bottomed cooking vessel associated in the West with Chinese-style stir-fry cooking.—Trans.

46. Pictures of a harrow, hoe, iron rake, sickle, kitchen cleaver, charcoal tongs, firewood cleaver, cooking ladles, tailor's flat iron, axe,

and door hinges can be found in Hommel, pp. 60, 63, 67, 68, 135, 149, 151, 196, 220, 292. —Trans.

47. Pig iron ingots cast in sand molds from smelted iron ore, when resmelted in a cupola furnace and poured into molds, become cast iron. Wrought iron refers to an even more purified iron. See *New Columbia Encyclopedia*, p. 1366. For a description of iron casting as observed in China in the 1920's, see Hommel, pp. 28–31.—Trans.

48. In the text "small tin lamps" is glossed *budeng*, which, on p. 61 of the Chinese text, is itself glossed "rush-wick lamp" (*caodeng*, lit. grass lamp). These are lamps in which light is produced by the slow burning of two or three piths of rush extending from a raised dish filled with oil. Oils pressed from soybeans or rapeseeds were frequently used as fuel. This traditional type of lighting was replaced by kerosene lamps. See Hommel, pp. 313–14.—Trans.

49. *Chazi*, *muzi*, *tao*, and *taozi* all mean seeds from the tea-oil plant.

50. Mao is paraphrasing a passage in the "Waiwu" chapter of the *Zhuangzi*.—Trans.

51. For pictures of a grain sieve, a bamboo scoop, a threshing sieve, a mill handle, a broom, and a bamboo chair, see Hommel, pp. 77–78, 95, 303, 309.—Trans.

52. Impressed-character (lit. seal) cakes are fried cakes impressed with decorative designs such as flowers or Chinese characters. A hinged mold, which could be made of camphor wood, might impress, for example, the auspicious characters for "double happiness." See Hommel, p. 155.—Trans.

53. The United Welfare Society was a secret society [*huidao men*] that was an offshoot of the Xiantian dao. It originated in Yongchuan County, Sichuan Province, at the end of the Qing dynasty. With the aid of the reactionary government, it gradually spread into many other provinces.

Within this society, there are sixteen levels of wisdom. Those at the first three levels of wisdom are called *daotu* [follower of the Way], those at the fourth level are called *tianen* [heavenly blessing], those at the fifth level are called *zheng'en* [demonstrated blessing], those at the ninth level are called *shidi* [completed situation]. Those beyond the fourth level are called *daoshou* [leader of the Way]. On pp. 115–16 of this book, it says: "The United Welfare Society had secret practices if you reached the fifth level. Then the Heavenly Blessing Master told you some secrets." And "Sichuan had a ninth-level Heavenly Blessing Master who came to Ganzhou." These two passages are not quite accurate.

[The United Welfare Society may have been related to the "Fellow-ship of Goodness" (Tongshan she) discussed by Chan (pp. 164–65). Chan argues that its origins can be traced to 1914. According to Paul deWitt Twinem, the Tongshan she, which he translates as "United Goodness Society," was the "oldest, most conservative, most prosperous, and most secret" (p. 464) of the modern syncretic religious societies he studied. Twinem, writing in 1925, said that "in all China there are at least 10,000 members. The members are for the most part well-to-do business men and officials." Based on the testimony of a "religious fanatic of the sect" and a former member, Twinem described the society's ethics, philosophy, and politics. Twinem, like Mao, found that the society had stages or degrees of membership that were reached by a combination of monetary contributions and the performance of acts influenced by Daoism and Buddhism. Twinem ends his account with a description of the society's Nanjing complex, a place "shrouded in silence and secrecy" (p. 467). See Paul deWitt Twinem, "Modern Syncretic Relgious Societies in China, I," *Journal of Religion*, no. 5 (1925): 464–67. Xunwu's United Welfare Society borrowed the nomenclature, but not necessarily the goals, of the benevolent societies discussed by Joanna Handlin Smith in her "Benevolent Societies."—Trans.]

54. Bodhidharma, the founder of the Chan School of Buddhism in China, is referred to in the text as *Dama zushi*. *Dama* is a Chinese transliteration of the Sanskrit dharma, which refers to the teachings of Buddha. *Zushi* refers to a founder of a sect. See Werner, pp. 359–61; and K. Ch'en, pp. 351–53.—Trans.

55. Lin Hu was the brigade commander of the Jiangxi Independent Brigade.

56. Xu Chongzhi was the army commander and general commander of the Second Army of the Guangdong troops. In 1922, Sun Yatsen established his headquarters in Shaoguan, Guangdong Province, to direct the Northern Expedition. Xu Chongzhi led the Second Army of the Guangdong troops into Jiangxi.

57. Tang Shengzhi was a brigade commander in charge of the Second Brigade of the First Division of Hunan troops, the division commander of the Fourth Division, and the governor of Hunan Province from 1920 to 1924. The text should read "to 1927."—Trans.

58. The text uses the abbreviation *pusa*, derived from the Chinese transliteration for the Sanskrit bodhisattva: *putisaduo*. A bodhisattva is a person destined for enlightenment who delays leaving the world so that he or she may help others attain enlightenment. See K. Ch'en, p. 13.—Trans.

59. Fang Benren was the commander of the southern Jiangxi garrison for the Beiyang warlords, director of frontier defenses in Jiangxi and Guangdong, and the military affairs director of the Jiangxi Army from 1922 to 1924.

CHAPTER 4

1. Throughout this chapter, "old distribution of land" refers to the situation before the land redistribution.—Trans.

2. This discussion of ancestral land trusts provides an entrée into the important world of South China lineages. For a general overview, see Baker, pp. 49–70. David Faure's recent work, based on research in Hong Kong's New Territories, provides additional detail. One of the topics in the anthropological debate on this subject concerns the distinction between lineages and clans. Clans are seen as defining large numbers of people with a common surname claiming descent from a common ancestor. Lineages have these elements, but are smaller, defining a corporate body with clearly recognized rights and claims. Faure emphasizes the importance of lineage membership in a village context in terms of defining rights of settlement and land use. See Faure, pp. 45–69. Mao discusses the inner workings of certain parts of a lineage. Over time a process of segmentation of a lineage creates a ramified network of branches and stems. Although claiming ritual inclusion in a large lineage, a branch or stem of a lineage could establish its own ancestral hall and corporate trust. It is the control of the assets of ancestral trusts that is the focus of Mao's analysis. For the policy implications of this analysis, see the section on corporate land in Chapter 5 below.—Trans.

3. The phrase used is *chi youbing*. See note 17 to Chapter 3.—Trans.

4. Various types of deities are represented in this list, including Buddhist (Guanyin, Potai), extra-local deified mortals (Duke of Zhao, Guandi [Guanye], Wenchang), and apparently local deified mortals (Laiye). For a discussion of these categories, see Arthur Wolf, "Gods, Ghosts, and Ancestors," in *Religion and Ritual in Chinese Society*, ed. Arthur P. Wolf (Stanford, Calif.: Stanford University Press, 1974), pp. 131–82. For descriptions of Guanyin, Guandi, and Wenchang, see Werner, pp. 225–30, 554–58.

Several of the gods of these god associations are mentioned in the 1881 Xunwu County gazetteer, in a section on shrines and temples (*cimiao*) (see *Changning xianzhi*). There appear to have been temples for Laigong (Laiye), Wenchang, the Duke of Zhao, and Zhenjun. Since Mao specifically mentions that god associations lacked temples, we must assume that temple associations, becoming divorced from their buildings, perhaps because of state-mandated secularization efforts, had become "god associations" that still controlled land resources.—Trans.

5. It seems that similar goals for different socioeconomic classes were met by different organizations. Those god associations whose antecedents can be found in the Xunwu County gazetteer are all located within or just outside the Xunwu City walls. The village associations are discussed by Mao in a decidedly agricultural context. Mao suggests that the political and social functions of each are similar, despite differences in terms of class, economic functions, and location.—Trans.

6. This temple for Guandi and Yue Fei may have been established after President Yuan Shikai's 1916 order directing the establishment of temples to both deified mortals. See Werner, p. 229.—Trans.

7. For the Ming dynasty origins of this temple, dedicated to a local official, see p. 183.—Trans.

8. The text puts in quotes a phrase found in local gazetteers that defines certain kinds of temples. For a discussion of these "ethico-political cults" of deified mortals, see Yang, pp. 158–64.—Trans.

9. The character for *dong*, a composite of the characters for "mountain" and "east," is probably a misprint for the character for "cave," which is also pronounced *dong*.—Trans.

10. It is not certain that by 1930 the monasteries (*si, shan, ge,* and *guan*) and nunneries (*an*), both Buddhist and Daoist, necessarily had either the numbers of adherents or specific purpose implied by the language used. In some cases these so-called Buddhist and Daoist monasteries and nunneries "had become common temples for public worship." See Yang, p. 310.—Trans.

11. See note 9 to this chapter.—Trans.

12. The text uses the compound "examination hall" (*kaopeng*). Although the funds generated from this type of public land seem to have been used in part for educational purposes, the text is not clear.—Trans.

13. According to the title page of the 1881 edition of the Xunwu gazetteer, the woodblocks used for that edition were kept at the Bureau of the Shrine for Esteeming Righteousness.—Trans.

14. The term *binxing*, borrowed from the *Zhouli* (Rites of Zhou), means to "raise the virtuous and entertain them as guests at banquets." *Shengyuan* who had been selected to participate in the provincial exams might be invited to attend ceremonies in their honor, feted at a banquet, or given traveling expenses. See Chang, p. 41 and

41*n*166. Mao uses the term in the last sense, and hence *binxing* is translated as "sojourning stipend."—Trans.

15. This refers to "branches" in the traditional 60-year cycle designated by 60 unique combinations of characters taken from the ten "stems" and twelve "branches." The first, fourth, seventh, and tenth branches in the text would appear, for example, in the combinations corresponding to 1900, 1903, 1906, and 1909.—Trans.

16. Deng Ruzhuo was the brigade commander of the Ninth Mixed Brigade for the Beiyang warlord army and the division commander of the First Division between 1924 and 1925.

17. The Reorganization faction was a Nationalist faction. At the end of 1928, Wang Jingwei, Chen Gongbo, and Gu Mengyu, resentful that Chiang Kai-shek had arrogated all power to himself, set up the Reorganization Comrade Association of the Chinese Nationalists in Shanghai. It was called the Reorganization faction.

18. *Laoshuihu* means those whose fathers or grandfathers were landlords.

19. *Shanlaoshu* means landlords who live in the mountains, rarely leave their house, and do not care about matters in the outside world.

20. Mao may have misunderstood his informants. If we assume "Imperial University in Japan" is a reference to the Imperial University of Tokyo, which was the proper nomenclature beginning in 1897, there was no course corresponding to the "Leather Course." Of the university's six colleges (Law, Medicine, Engineering, Literature, Science, and Agriculture) in the 1910's, the most likely place for Qiu's course of study would have been the College of Agriculture. This college had five courses (Chinese: *ke*) of study: Agriculture, Agricultural Chemistry, Forestry, Veterinary Medicine, and Fisheries. See the *Calendar* (1917–18) of the Imperial University of Tokyo, pp. 202–3.—Trans.

21. Here the text refers to all the lands that Zeng Chaoqun received after the family property was split up. Before this, Zeng Chaoqun and his brother had over 200 dan.

22. Militias from Anyuan, Huichang, Pingyuan, Xingning.—Trans.

23. The editors of *Mao Zedong nongcun diaocha wenji* mentioned Zhong "Damian" Liu as an example of the types of puzzles presented by the text that they were able to solve during their investigations in Jiangxi. In this case, a man surnamed "Zhong" had a large face (*damian*). "Liu," the editors found out, referred to his place in the family tree. See *Guangming ribao*, 12 Feb. 1983, p. 3.—Trans.

24. There are some discrepancies. The final definite statement that

there are 113 middle landlords in Xunwu County contradicts Mao's earlier statement that it is "difficult to name" all of the middle landlords in Sanshui District. Also, 116 middle landlords are named in the preceding list. Of that number, Pan Guanlan, Pan Mingdian, and Pan Guoqing (Jiansan); Yan Guoxing (Huangxiang), and Zeng Chaoqun (Shuangqiao) had less than 200 dan, the minimum amount required for the middle-landlord classification. Furthermore, the only way there could be "several small landlords" in Huangxiang, besides the clear case of Yan Guoxing, would be to assume that Luo Fushou became a small landlord after his land was redistributed and that the joint ownership of 300 dan by Gu Lesan and his brother meant that both men, separately, were classified as small landlords.

This survey of Xunwu's middle landlords was skewed toward areas that had already been subject to land redistribution earlier in the year. There are 93 names given for landlords in the three southern districts in Xunwu: Huangxiang (20), Shuangqiao (36), and Nanba (37). There are 23 landlords listed for the four northern districts, which fell to Red Army troops in the spring of 1930: Chengjiang (3), Xunwu City District (5), Sanshui (5), and Jiansan (10).—Trans.

25. *Zhengchang* monies covered the expenses of memorial ceremonies. In ancient times, people offered sacrifices to gods and ancestors. The type of ceremony that was held in the winter was called *zheng*, the one held in the autumn *chang*.

26. The text reads *yinzi hui*. *Yinzi* can refer to the mark made by a "chop," a stone carved with the characters for a person's name and used to make ink impressions on paper. However, *yinzi* can also refer, as it does in the text, to a small loan made for a short period at a high interest rate.—Trans.

27. In this book *cha shan, chazi shan, you shan, youcha shan, muzi shan,* and *muzi lin* all refer to hillsides planted with tea-oil plants.

28. *Zaozi* and *fanzi* refer, respectively, to the first and last crops of grain during the year.

29. *Luo*: a square-bottomed bamboo basket.—Trans.

30. In a note to this song Mao Zedong added the following glossary for passages in the lyrics in the Xunwu dialect:

ai	me
mao	do not have
xiang qi zuo	continue
an qing nüzi	pretty women
yang de lao	how to make a living
an hao xuetang	good school
ge ye jiu	just after harvesting

zuo zei tou	very bad, like a thief
daizi yi da kun	sacks for land rent
guo jie liu	umbrella
ma ge dou wu wen	nothing to ask
fang chu xia ma tou	like an official
shui hu tou	major landlord
a he	all gone
ai tong xin	be of one heart

Mao makes no special note of it, but there are numerous phrases scattered throughout the text that are Hakka in origin. Leong (pp. 297, 318, 324) argues that Xunwu County was a "pure Hakka" county in the core of the Hakka-dominated region of south Jiangxi. We do know that Mao sometimes needed help from investigation meeting participants like Gu Bo, Guo Youmei, and Fan Daming in translating the information being conveyed by the people of Xunwu. See Xia, p. 283.—Trans.

31. For an excellent short story published in 1933 concerning the issues of tenancy, tensions at harvesttime, and the often harsh plight of the peasantry, see Zheng Nong's "On the Threshing Field," in Isaacs, *Straw Sandals*, pp. 371–93. Zheng Nong, born in 1904, was the pen name for Xia Zhengnong, a native of Nanchang County in Jiangxi (ibid., pp. lxix–lxx).—Trans.

32. This refers to the third or fourth year of the first term or the seventh or eighth year of the second term of a small lease.—Trans.

33. *Qiu*, the word for "mound," also means "grave."—Trans.

34. Lit. waiting for the rice to cook.—Trans.

35. The Chinese *guoshou* [lit. pass from one's hand], as described in the text, is similar to the type of transfer of ownership referred to in Roman law as *fiducia cum creditore*. The debtor is allowed to keep legal title and can be a tenant at will, but ownership is transferred de facto to the creditor. The Chinese *buguoshou* [lit. not to pass from one's hand] is similar to the Roman legal term *antichresis*, in which the possession of the land goes to the creditor but the debtor retains ownership. See *New Encyclopedia Britannica*, 15th ed., 26: 188.—Trans.

36. Liu Zhilu was the commander of the garrison in Chaozhou and Meixian, Guangdong Province, and the army commander of the Second Army of the Guangdong troops before 1925.

37. *Chazi shu* is the tea-oil plant.

38. These savings and loan associations, also known as "rotating credit societies" or "cooperative credit clubs" provided money for unexpected large capital outlays. Each member had one chance, or turn, during the life of the association, to receive money from the others.

The longer one waited, the lower the interest rate on funds received. In Mao's example, the association organizer received 50 yuan at the beginning of the association's existence. At the next meeting, a year later, another member would receive a sum of money provided by the others. The organizer would pay 15 yuan, and the others would pay the regular 10 yuan. Thus, the second recipient would receive 55 yuan. The first six-year cycle would proceed as follows (italicized figures indicate amount received):

Member	Start	Year 1	Year 2	Year 3	Year 4	Year 5	Year 6
Organizer	*50*	15	15	15	15	15	15
Member 2	10	*55*	15	15	15	15	15
Member 3	10	10	*60*	15	15	15	15
Member 4	10	10	10	*65*	12.5	12.5	12.5
Member 5	10	10	10	10	*67.5*	12.5	12.5
Member 6	10	10	10	10	10	*70*	10
							80

At the end of the first six-year cycle, the organizer, who received 50 yuan at the outset, had paid out 90 yuan. Therefore, he paid interest of 40 yuan, spread over six years. The last member paid only 60 yuan, but received 70, thus implicitly receiving interest of 10 yuan. The second cycle would begin with an initial fund of 80 yuan, which, as Mao points out, represents the total of all reinvested interest payments for the first cycle. Interest payments totaled 92.5 yuan, of which 2.5 yuan and 10 yuan were paid to members 5 and 6, respectively, and the remaining 80 yuan formed the initial fund for the beginning of the second cycle. See also Ball, pp. 596–605. The associations were often identified by the periods of payment: fortnightly, monthly, quarterly, or annually (p. 597). Ball makes the illuminating remark that these associations were at once a borrowing club and a lending club (p. 601).—Trans.

39. The story was part of the oral and written tradition in Xunwu. A record of shrines dedicated to Yang (Yanggong ci) can be found in the 1881 edition of *Changning xianzhi*, "Yiwen," 4: 19a–21a.—Trans.

40. This festival is listed in the Customs ("Fengsu") section of the local gazetteer. See *Changning xianzhi*, 1b.—Trans.

41. Liu Shiyi was the division commander of the Jiangxi Seventh Independent Division and the brigade commander of the Fifteenth Independent Brigade in 1928.

42. The 2.5 Percent Surtax National Treasury Bonds were floated by Chiang Kai-shek's regime in May and October 1927 in order to

raise funds for military expenditures. These bonds were secured by a 2.5 percent surtax on custom duties that was being collected, by the end of 1927, in all treaty ports in China. This surtax on imports had been authorized, in the view of Chinese officials, by the Chinese Customs Tariff signed in Washington on 6 February 1922. See Stanley F. Wright, *China's Customs Revenue Since the Revolution of 1911*, 3d ed., revised and enlarged with the assistance of John H. Cubbon (Shanghai: Inspectorate General of Customs, Statistical Department, 1935), pp. 345–52.—Trans.

43. Li Yibiao was military commissioner for Guangzhou and Huizhou under the Beiyang warlords and the army commander of the Fourth Army of the Guangdong Army before 1925. Huang Renhuan was the commander of the First Division of the First Army of the Guangdong Army before 1925.

44. Mao uses the phrase "half-old not-new" in reference to schools combining the traditional Confucian curriculum and the Western-influenced curriculum.—Trans.

45. These inscriptions refer to various Qing civil service examination degrees. Shengyuan are represented by the word "collar" (*jin*), which refers to the so-called Confucian gown worn by scholars in late imperial China. The other inscriptions quoted in the text refer to five men who held either the linsheng or gongsheng degrees. These degrees were just below the juren degree in prestige. Holders of the linsheng degree were given stipends and could become powerful and privileged members in their communities. They could compete for a gongsheng degree, the receipt of which, in the opinion of Chang Chung-li, marked one's arrival into the ranks of the upper gentry. They could be named to educational or administrative posts. See Chang, pp. 17–18, 27–29; and Appendix C.—Trans.

CHAPTER 5

1. Although the editors of *Mao Zedong nongcun diaocha wenji* think that the text should actually read "over 14 and under 55," based on their analysis of the March 1930 "Xingguo Soviet Government Land Law," they decided to leave the text as it appears in the manuscript. See *Guangming ribao*, 12 Feb. 1983, p. 3.—Trans.

2. The organization of the 25 March 1928 uprising included a general command post led by Liu Weilu, with Zhong Xiqiu, Gu Bo, Liu Weie, and He Jiachang serving as assistant commanders. Six command posts were established in the county. See Xia, p. 277.—Trans.

3. For a formalistic and rather sanguine presentation of issues concerning the rights of women in soviet areas like that of Xunwu, see

Hu Yepin's "Living Together," in Isaacs, *Straw Sandals,* pp. 207–14. In this 1930 short story, Hu, who had never been in Jiangxi, conveys none of the pain and turmoil presented in the *Report from Xunwu*. Hu, the companion of the eminent writer Ding Ling, was executed by the KMT in 1931.—Trans.

Bibliography

Averill, Stephen C. "Local Elites and Communist Revolution in the Jiangxi Hill Country." In *Chinese Local Elites and Patterns of Dominance*, ed. Mary Backus Rankin and Joseph W. Esherick. Berkeley: University of California Press, forthcoming.

———. "Party, Society, and Local Elite in the Jiangxi Communist Movement." *Journal of Asian Studies* 46 (1987): 279–303.

———. "Revolution in the Highlands: The Rise of the Communist Movement in Jiangxi Province." Ph.D. dissertation, Cornell University, 1982.

Baker, Hugh D. R. *Chinese Family and Kinship*. New York: Columbia University Press, 1979.

Ball, James Dyer. *Things Chinese; or, Notes Connected with China*. 5th ed. Rev. E. Chalmers Werner. Shanghai: Kelly & Walsh, 1925.

Bousfield, Cyril E. Correspondence, 1901–1929. Valley Forge, Pennsylvania. American Baptist Historical Society, American Baptist Foreign Mission Society Records, Reels FM180 and FM232.

Bousfield, Lillie Snowden. *Sun-wu Stories*. Shanghai: Kelly & Walsh, 1932.

Brandt, Conrad, Benjamin Schwartz, and John K. Fairbank. *A Documentary History of Chinese Communism*. Cambridge, Mass.: Harvard University Press, 1952. Reprint—New York: Atheneum, 1966.

Buck, John Lossing. *Land Utilization in China: A Study of 16,786 Farms in 168 Localities, and 38,256 Farm Families in Twenty-two Provinces in China, 1929–1933*. Shanghai: 1937. Reprint—New York: Council on Economic and Cultural Affairs, 1956.

Burket, Everett S. Correspondence, 1920–1929. Valley Forge, Pennsylvania. American Baptist Historical Society, American Baptist Foreign Mission Society Records, Reel FM233.

The Cambridge History of China, Vol. 13. Ed. John K. Fairbank and Albert Feuerwerker. Cambridge, Eng.: Cambridge University Press, 1986.

Chan, Wing-tsit. *Religious Trends in Modern China*. New York: Columbia University Press, 1953.

Chang, Chung-li. *The Chinese Gentry: Studies on Their Role in Nineteenth-century Chinese Society*. Seattle: University of Washington Press, 1955.

Changning xianzhi (Gazetteer for Changning [Xunwu] County). 1881.

Ch'en, Jerome. "The Communist Movement, 1927–1937." In *The Cambridge History of China*, 13: 168–229.

———. , ed. *Mao Papers: Anthology and Bibliography*. London: Oxford University Press, 1970.

Ch'en, Kenneth K. S. *Buddhism in China: A Historical Survey*. Princeton, N.J.: Princeton University Press, 1964.

Chen, Yung-fa. *Making Revolution: The Communist Movement in Eastern and Central China, 1937–1945*. Berkeley: University of California Press, 1986.

Chu Shih-chia. *A Catalog of Chinese Local Histories in the Library of Congress*. Washington, D.C.: U.S. Government Printing Office, 1942.

Couling, Samuel. *Encyclopaedia Sinica*. Shanghai: Kelly & Walsh, 1917.

Faure, David. *The Structure of Chinese Rural Society: Lineage and Village in the Eastern New Territories, Hong Kong*. Hong Kong: Oxford University Press, 1986.

Franz, Uli. *Deng Xiaoping*. Trans. Tom Artin. San Diego, Calif.: Harcourt Brace Jovanovich, 1988.

Galbiati, Fernando. *P'eng P'ai and the Hai-Lu-Feng Soviet*. Stanford, Calif.: Stanford University Press, 1985.

Gamble, Sidney D. *North China Villages: Social, Political and Economic Activities Before 1933*. Berkeley: University of California Press, 1963.

———. *Ting Hsien: A North China Rural Community*. New York: Institute of Pacific Relations, International Secretariat, 1954. Reprint— Stanford, Calif.: Stanford University Press, 1968.

Gong Yuzhi. "*Mao Zedong nongcun diaocha wenji* de zhexue yiyi" (The philosophical significance of *Mao Zedong's Collected Rural Investigations*). *Renmin ribao*, 30 December 1983, p. 5.

———. "Mao Zedong zhuzuo bianji chuban de ruogan wenti" (Some problems in publishing compilations of Mao Zedong's works). *Mao Zedong sixiang yanjiu* (Studies on the thought of Mao Zedong), 1984, no. 3, pp. 1–6.

Han Wei. "Jinggangshan hongse zhengquan de dafazhan" (The great development of Red political power in Jinggangshan). *Mao Zedong sixiang yanjiu* (Studies on the thought of Mao Zedong), 1984, no. 3, pp. 7–11.

Harding, Harry. *China's Second Revolution: Reform After Mao*. Washington, D.C.: Brookings Institution, 1987.

Harrison, James Pinckney. *The Long March to Power: A History of the Chinese Communist Party, 1921–72*. New York: Praeger, 1972.

Hommel, Rudolf P. *China at Work: An Illustrated Record of the Primitive Industries of China's Masses, Whose Life Is Toil, and Thus an Account of Chinese Civilization*. New York: John Day Company, 1937.

Hsiao, Tso-liang. *The Land Revolution in China, 1930–1934: A Study of Documents*. Seattle: University of Washington Press, 1969.

————. *Power Relations Within the Chinese Communist Movement, 1930–1934: A Study of Documents*. Seattle: University of Washington Press, 1961.

Hsu, King-yi. *Political Mobilization and Economic Extraction: Chinese Communist Agrarian Policies During the Kiangsi Period*. New York: Garland, 1980.

Hu Sheng. "Du *Mao Zedong nongcun diaocha wenji*" (On reading *Mao Zedong's Collected Rural Investigations*). *Renmin ribao*, 11 February 1983, p. 5.

Huang, Philip C. C., Lynda Schaefer Bell, and Kathy Lemons Walker. *Chinese Communists and Rural Society, 1927–1934*. Berkeley: University of California, Center for Chinese Studies, 1978.

Isaacs, Harold R. *The Tragedy of the Chinese Revolution*. 2d rev. ed. Stanford, Calif.: Stanford University Press, 1961.

————, ed. *Straw Sandals: Chinese Short Stories, 1918–1933*. Cambridge, Mass.: MIT Press, 1974.

Laves, Edward. "Rural Society and Modern Revolution: The Rise of the Jiangxi Soviet." Ph.D. dissertation, University of Chicago, 1980.

Leong, S. T. "The Hakka Chinese of Lingnan: Ethnicity and Social Change in Modern Times." In *Ideal and Reality: Social and Political Change in Modern China, 1860–1949*, ed. David Pong and Edmund S. K. Fung. Lanham, Md.: University Press of America, 1985, pp. 287–326.

Li Jui. *The Early Revolutionary Activities of Comrade Mao Tse-tung*. Trans. Anthony W. Sariti. White Plains, N.Y.: M. E. Sharpe, 1977.

Liu Wusheng and Zheng Shikeng. "Yibu zhengui de lishi wenxian—Xuexi *Xunwu diaocha*" (A valuable historical document: Studying the *Report from Xunwu*). *Dangshi yanjiu*, 1983, no. 4, pp. 17–21.

Mann, Susan. *Local Merchants and the Chinese Bureaucracy, 1750–1950*. Stanford, Calif.: Stanford University Press, 1986.

Mao Zedong. *Mao Zedong nongcun diaocha wenji* (Mao Zedong's collected rural investigations). Beijing: Renmin chubanshe, 1982.

———. *Quotations from Chairman Mao Tse-tung*. Beijing: Foreign Languages Press, 1976.

———. *Selected Works of Mao Tse-tung*, vols. 1, 3. Beijing: Foreign Languages Press, 1967, 1975.

Mao Zedong sixiang yanjiu (Studies on the thought of Mao Zedong). Chengdu. 1983– .

Marks, Robert. *Rural Revolution in South China: Peasants and the Making of History in Haifeng County, 1570–1930*. Madison: University of Wisconsin Press, 1984.

McDonald, Angus W., Jr. *The Urban Origins of Rural Revolution: Elites and the Masses in Hunan Province, China, 1911–1927*. Berkeley: University of California Press, 1978.

Myers, Ramon. "The Agrarian System." In *The Cambridge History of China*, 13: 230–69.

Planchet, J.-M. *Les Missions de Chine et du Japon, 1929*. Beijing, 1929.

Polachek, James M. "The Moral Economy of the Kiangsi Soviet (1928–1934)." *Journal of Asian Studies* 42 (1983): 805–29.

Qian Junrui. "Zhongguo nongcun jingji yanjiu hui chengli qianhou" (At the time when the Society for the Study of China's Rural Economy was established). In Xue and Feng, *"Zhongguo nongcun" lunwen xuan*, 1:6–12.

Rice, Edward E. *Mao's Way*. Berkeley: University of California, Center for Chinese Studies, 1972.

Rue, John E. *Mao Tse-tung in Opposition, 1927–1935*. Stanford, Calif.: Stanford University Press, 1966.

Salisbury, Harrison E. *The Long March: The Untold Story*. New York: Harper & Row, 1985.

Schram, Stuart R. *Ideology and Policy in China Since the Third Plenum, 1978–84*. London: University of London, School of Oriental and African Studies, Contemporary China Institute, 1984.

———. *Mao Tse-tung*. Baltimore: Penguin Books, 1967.

———. "Mao Tse-tung's Thought to 1949." In *The Cambridge History of China*, 13: 789–870.

———. *The Political Thought of Mao Tse-tung*. 2d ed., rev. and enl. New York: Praeger, 1969.

Schwartz, Benjamin I. *Chinese Communism and the Rise of Mao*. Cambridge, Mass.: Harvard University Press, 1951.

Siao-yu. *Mao Tse-tung and I Were Beggars*. Syracuse, N.Y.: Syracuse University Press, 1959.

Smith, Joanna F. Handlin. "Benevolent Societies: The Reshaping of Charity During the Late Ming and Early Ch'ing." *Journal of Asian Studies* 46 (1987): 309–37.

Snow, Edgar. *Red Star over China*. New York: Random House, 1938.

Takeuchi, Minoru, ed. *Mō Takutō shū* (Collected writings of Mao Zedong). Tokyo: Mō Takutō bunken shiryō kenkyūkai, 1970–72.

———. *Mō Takutō shū hokan* (Supplements to *Collected Writings of Mao Zedong*). Tokyo: Mō Takutō bunken shiryō kenkyūkai, 1984–86.

Tawney, R. H. *Land and Labor in China*. London: George Allen & Unwin, 1932. Reprint—Boston: Beacon Press, 1966.

Terrill, Ross. *Mao*. New York: Harper & Row, 1980. Reprint—New York: Harper Colophon, 1981.

Waller, Derek J. *The Kiangsi Soviet Republic: Mao and the National Congresses of 1931 and 1934*. Berkeley: University of California, Center for Chinese Studies, 1973.

Watson, Andrew, ed. and trans. *Mao Zedong and the Political Economy of the Border Region: A Translation of Mao's "Economic and Financial Problems."* Cambridge, Eng.: Cambridge University Press, 1980.

Wei, William. *Counterrevolution in China: The Nationalists in Jiangxi During the Soviet Period*. Ann Arbor: University of Michigan Press, 1985.

Wen Zengren. *Jiangxi suqu dashi jilue* (A brief chronology of important events in the Jiangxi Soviet). Nanchang: Jiangxi renmin chubanshe, 1986.

Werner, E. T. C. *A Dictionary of Chinese Mythology*. Shanghai: Kelly & Walsh, 1932. Reprint—New York: Julian Press, 1961.

Wolf, Arthur P., and Chieh-shan Huang. *Marriage and Adoption in China, 1845–1945*. Stanford, Calif.: Stanford University Press, 1980.

Womack, Brantly. *The Foundations of Mao Zedong's Political Thought, 1917–1935*. Honolulu: University Press of Hawaii, 1982.

Wright, Mary Clabaugh, ed. *China in Revolution: The First Phase, 1900–1913*. New Haven, Conn.: Yale University Press, 1968.

Wright, Stanley. *Kiangsi Native Trade and Its Taxation*. Shanghai, 1920. Reprint—New York: Garland, 1980.

Xia Daohan. "Gu Bo" (Gu Bo). In *Zhonggong dangshi renwu zhuan* (Biographies of eminent members of the Chinese Communist Party), vol. 12, ed. Hu Hua. Xi'an: Shaanxi renmin chubanshe, 1983, pp. 273–92.

Xue Muqiao and Feng Hefa, eds. *"Zhongguo nongcun" lunwen xuan* (Selected essays from *Rural China*). 2 vols. Beijing: Renmin chubanshe, 1983.

Young, John. *The Research Activities of the South Manchurian Railway Company, 1907–1945: A History and Bibliography*. New York: Columbia University, East Asian Institute, 1966.

Yang, C. K. *Religion in Chinese Society: A Study of Contemporary Social Functions of Religion and Some of Their Historical Factors*. Berkeley: University of California Press, 1967.

Zeng Biyi. "Yi Gu Bo tongzhi" (Remembering Comrade Gu Bo). *Hongqi piaopiao* (The Red flag waves),1980, no. 19, pp. 88–105.

Zhang Weiping and Zhang Liejun. *Mao Zedong jiandang xueshuo shi* (A history of Mao Zedong's theories on founding a party). Nanchang: Jiangxi renmin chubanshe, 1987.

Zhonggong. Zhongyang. Wenxian Yanjiushi (Chinese Communist Party. Central Committee. Research Center on Party Literature). *Guanyu jianguo yilai dang de ruogan lishi wenti de jueyi zhushi ben xiuding* (An annotated "Resolution on certain questions in the history of our party since the founding of the People's Republic," revised). Beijing: Renmin chubanshe, 1985.

———. ———. ———. Mao Zedong Zhuzuo he Shengping Yanjiuzu (Study Group on the Works and Life of Mao Zedong). "Wenxian bianji he diaocha yanjiu" (Editing documents and making investigations). *Guangming ribao*, 12 February 1983, p. 3.

Zhongguo Renmin Daxue Shubao Ziliao She (People's University Association for Materials in Books and Journals). *Mao Zedong zhuzuo, shengping, shiye yanjiu* (Studies on the works, life, and activities of Mao Zedong). Beijing, 1980– .

Character List

a he 阿呵
ai 埃
ai tong xin 愛同心
an 庵
an hao xuetang 暗好學堂
an qing nüzi 暗婧女子
bagong 拔貢
ban zigeng nong 半自耕農
bao 堡
baotu 暴徒
baowei tuan 保衛團
baozi 尬子
bayuejiao 八月角
benben zhuyi 本本主義
biane 匾額
bingbeiluoshishi 丼背羅食使
bingtang 冰糖
Binxing ci 賓興祠
binxing tian 賓興田
budeng 不燈
buguoshou 不過手
caitou 菜頭
caodeng 草燈
chairen 差人
Changning 長寧
changxi 唱戲
cha shan 茶山
chayou 茶油
chazi 茶子
chazi shan 茶子山

chazi shu 茶子樹
chengshi 城市
chezi 車子
chi youbing 吃油餅
chushi 出師
cimiao 祠廟
cuosuan 撮算
da 笪
da futou 打斧頭
daizi yi da kun 袋子一大捆
dajin 大襟
da leigong 打雷公
Dama zushi 達摩祖師
damian 大面
dan 擔，石
dang 檔
dangji 當機
dangwu 當烏
danjiu 單酒
danqing 丹青
daoshou 道首
daotu 道徒
dayang 大洋
diangui 點規
diannong 佃農
dianshi 典史
dianzhu (mortgagee) 典主
dianzhu (shopkeeper) 店主
diaocai 吊菜
diaocha gongzuo 調查工作

diaocha hui 調查會
dili xiansheng 地理先生
dingtui 頂退
dong 洞, 㟃
Dongjiang 東江
dou 斗
doufumei 豆腐霉
doujin 抖緊
doushi 豆豉
duan 段
duantian 墩田
duiwu 隊伍
duoerzi 掇耳子
fandui benben zhuyi 反對本本主義
fang chu xia ma tou 放出下馬頭
fanzi 番子
fen 分
fengshui xiansheng 風水先生
fengsu 風俗
fusheng 附生
Gaizu pai 改組派
ge (cup) 合
ge (monastery) 閣
gexin 革新
ge ye jiu 割也就
Gongan ju 公安局
gongchan 共產
gongfei 共匪
gonggong 公共
gonghui 公會
gongsheng 貢生
gongtang 公堂
gongtian 公田
gongtou 工頭
gongyu 貢魚
guan 觀
guangyang 光洋
guantian 官田
guantou 管頭
guanzu 官租
guo jie liu 過街溜
guoshou 過手
guotou 鍋頭

guyu 穀雨
hang 行
hao 豪
haoshen 豪紳
haoshi 蠔豉
haoyang 毫洋
haoyi ci 好義祠
heshang si 和尚寺
hongding gu 紅丁穀
huahong 花紅
huaqi 花旗
hui 會
huidao men 會道門
huishi 會試
huo 貨
huobanzi 火板子
jianchuan 尖串
jiangren 匠人
jiansheng 監生
jiao 繳
jiaohui 醮會
jiaoluo 角籮
jiaoyu 脚魚
jin (catty) 斤
jin (collar) 衿
jingcha duizhang 警察隊長
jingwei tuan 靖衛團
jinshi 進士
jinxianyu 金綫魚
jinzhang 禁長
juren 舉人
juzi 舉子
kan didi 看地的
kanyu 堪輿
kaopeng tian 考棚田
kazidao 卡子刀
ke 科
kengtian 坑田
kongxincai 空心菜
kuai 塊
lanjiao 欖角
lanshi 欖豉
lao 撈

laoji 撈箕
laoshuihu 老稅戶
laotai 老太
li 里
liang 兩
lianhualuo 蓮花落
libi 犂鎞
lieshen 劣紳
lingong 廩貢
linsheng 廩生
liumang 流氓
lizhi 荔枝
Longhua hui 龍華會
longpan 礱盤
longyan 龍眼
luo 籮
luoka 落卡
ma ge dou wu wen 嗎個都唔問
maizi 脉子
mao (do not have; currency unit) 毛
mao (year) 卯
maogu 毛榖
maoyang 毛洋
mi 米
mianhui 面灰
miao 廟
miaolao 廟老
Min 閩
mingqian 明錢
mutan 木炭
muyou 木油
muzi 木梓
muzi lin 木梓林
muzi shan 木梓山
naizi 奶子
nazi 那子
nuanfu 暖福
nuanjin 暖禁
nuanshen 暖神
nugu 奴古
pang 冇
panggu 冇谷

pengpidou 彭皮豆
poxiong 破胸
putisaduo 菩提薩埵
puzi 莆子
qi 棋
qiang 搶
qin 琴
qing 頃
qinghuang bujie 青黃不接
qiu 丘
qusu 區蘇
Sandian hui 三點會
shan 山
shangyi ci 尚義祠
shanlaoshu 山老鼠
shanzhang 善長
shao 勺
she 社
shen 神
sheng 升
shengyuan 生員
shenjianjiuzhang 身兼九長
shetan 社壇
shidi 十地
shifu 師父
shishi qiushi 實事求是
shisu 市蘇
shitouyu 石頭魚
shuangjiu 雙酒
shuihu tou 稅戶頭
shui jin niupi 水浸牛皮
shuijiu 水酒
shuitanzi 水炭子
si 寺
suanming xiansheng 算命先生
sui 歲
tan 壇
tao 桃
taozi 桃子
tianen 天恩
tianqing pu 天青鯆
tianzhu 田主
tiaohaozi 挑笔子

tielian 鐵練
tieshao 鐵勺
tong 桶
tongban 銅板
tongkezi 銅殼子
tongpian 銅片
tongqian 銅錢
Tongshan she 同善社
tongsheng 童生
tongyuan 銅元
tongzhi 統治
toubiao 投標
tousheng 頭牲
tuan fangdui 團防隊
tufei 土匪
tuizi 推子
wenhua yundong 文化運動
wu 午
xi 戲
xiang (sales tax stamp) 餉
xiang (stuffed beancurd) 釀,醸
xiang (township) 鄉
xiang (ward) 廂
xiang qi zuo 項起做
xiangshi 鄉試
xiangsu 鄉蘇
xiangtan 響炭
xianluo you 暹羅柚
xiansheng 先生
xian suweiai zhengfu 縣蘇維埃政府
Xiantian dao 先天道
xiaoba 小把
xiaofan 小販
xiao shougong 小手工
xiaoyang 小洋
xifen 西粉
xili 西利
xinde 新的
xin wenhua 新文化
xinxue 新學
xinzheng 新政
xiucai 秀才
xu 墟

xuanchuanyuan 宣傳員
xuegong 學宮
xunjian 巡檢
Xunwu 尋烏
yang de lao 樣得老
yi 醫
yinshui 銀水
yinyang xiansheng 陰陽先生
yinzi hui 印子會
yongcai 蕹菜
you 酉
youcha shan 油茶山
youcha shu 油茶樹
youguo 油果
youmin 游民
you shan 油山
yuan 元〔圓〕
yuanrou 元肉
yufen 玉粉
zaliang 雜糧
zaozi 早子
zayang 雜洋
zengsheng 增生
zhangfang xiansheng 帳房先生
zhengchang 蒸嘗
zheng'en 證恩
zhidaoyuan 指導員
zhuanyi 轉移
zhuren 主人
zi 子
zibenjia 資本家
zigeng nong 自耕農
Zijiu ribao 自救日報
zou 走
Zunyu tang 尊育堂
zuo zaozi 坐竈子
zuo zei tou 做賊頭

Index

In this index an "f" after a number indicates a separate reference on the next page, and an "ff" indicates separate references on the next two pages. A continuous discussion over two or more pages is indicated by a span of page numbers, e.g., "57–59." *Passim* is used for a cluster of references in close but not consecutive sequence. Place-names are listed under the name of the district in which they are located.

Library of Congress Cataloging-in-Publication Data

Mao, Tse-tung, 1893–1976.
  [Hsün-wu tiao ch'a. English]
  Report from Xunwu / Mao Zedong ; translated, and with an
introduction and notes, by Roger R. Thompson.
      p.   cm.
  Translation of: Hsün-wu tiao ch'a.
  Includes bibliographical references.
    ISBN 0-8047-1678-1 (cl):   ISBN 0-8047-2182-3 (pbk)
    1. Hsün-wu hsien (China)—Rural conditions.   I. Thompson, Roger
R.   II.   Title.
HN740.H78M3613   1990   89-21776
324.251'075'09—dc20   CIP

  ⊗ This book is printed on acid-free paper